Raymond Suttner was born in Durban in 1945. He became a leading activist in the African National Congress and the South African Communist Party. He spent over 10 years in prison and under house arrest for his anti-apartheid activities. He was elected to South Africa's first democratic parliament in 1994 and was South African ambassador to Sweden (1997-2001). He previously published *Thirty Years of the Freedom Charter* (1986) with Jeremy Cronin. Raymond Suttner is now a Visiting Research Fellow, at the Centre for Policy Studies, Johannesburg.

Inside Apartheid's Prison

Notes and letters of struggle

Raymond Suttner

OCEAN PRESS

Melbourne • NewYork

UNIVERSITY OF NATAL PRESS
Pietermaritzburg
South Africa

Cover design by David Spratt

Back cover photo: Giselle Wulfsohn

Ocean Press ISBN 1-876175-25-7
University of Natal Press ISBN 0-86980-997-0

First printed 2001

Printed in Australia

Library of Congress Control Number: 2001090025

Published by Ocean Press
Australia: GPO Box 3279, Melbourne, Victoria 3001, Australia
USA: PO Box 1186 Old Chelsea Station, New York, NY 10113-1186, USA

E-mail: info@oceanbooks.com.au
www.oceanbooks.com.au

Published in South Africa by University of Natal Press
Private Bag X01, Scottsville 3209, South Africa
E-mail: books@nu.ac.za
www.unpress.co.za

OCEAN PRESS DISTRIBUTORS
United States and Canada: LPC Group,
    1436 West Randolph St, Chicago, IL 60607, USA
Britain and Europe: Global Book Marketing,
    38 King Street, London, WC2E 8JT, UK
Australia and New Zealand: Astam Books,
    57-61 John Street, Leichhardt, NSW 2040, Australia
Cuba and Latin America: Ocean Press,
    Calle 21 #406, Vedado, Havana, Cuba

To Bram Fischer, who inspired me — though we never met.

To David Rabkin, who was in prison with me, who should have lived to make the great contribution of which he was capable. I miss you.

To Chris Hani, whom I knew too briefly. I remember your laughter and joy and irreverence. We need you now.

To Nomboniso Gasa, who has been with me through hard and good times, who puts up with some of the legacy of my imprisonment. She has opened me to things I would not have noticed, and helped me to voice emotions I would not have found.

CR

♥ CONTENTS ♥

ACKNOWLEDGMENTS

Any person who goes to prison depends on the support of others, who are outside. In the case of some prisoners, relatives lived so far away and were so poor they could not visit them often or at all. I was lucky to have consistent support from relatives and friends, too many to mention, who visited and wrote to me as often as the prison authorities permitted. My family was unwavering in their efforts to improve prison conditions on my behalf and others who were with me. I think of my mother Sheila Suttner, sister Sally Suttner, brothers John and Alan Suttner, sister Ann Gerson, in laws Myrna Suttner, Jenny Suttner and Eugene Gerson.

Various colleagues in the legal profession and academic life were particularly supportive: Professor John Dugard, the late Professor Etienne Mureinik, Professor Mervyn Shear, Judge Richard Goldstone, Professor Marinus Wiechers, (now Judge) Dennis Davis, Professor Hugh Corder, the firm of lawyers, Cheadle Thompson and Haysom, in particular Peter Harris and Clive Plasket, Raymond Tucker and George Bizos.

Friends who were particularly supportive included Barbara and Arline Creecy, Neil Coleman, Sue Albertyn, Erica Emdon, Jean de la Harpe, Jessica Sherman, Maurice Smithers, Ann Perry, Chris Ballantine, Wendy Thorpe, Peter Galt, Mike and Elfrieda Olmesdahl, David Fig, Belinda Bozzoli, Eddie Webster and Luli Callinicos.

In the writing of this book I have incurred important debts. In the first place, I am grateful to David Deutschmann and Deborah Shnookal of Ocean Press for their confidence in the project. It still took me some time to get going. Here I owe a great deal to Jean Middleton for her careful scrutiny and editing of early drafts when this hardly looked like a book. Her support was very reassuring. I am indebted to the noted Swedish author, now my friend, Per Wästberg, for his encouragement after reading an early draft. I am also indebted to Fiona Dove and my mother Sheila Suttner for reading and suggesting stylistic improvements to early drafts. Nomboniso Gasa suggested important changes that helped recast some of the chapters in a more interesting form.

I was fortunate that Ocean Press contracted John Jenkins to act as editor. He was a pleasure to work with and his careful scrutiny has made the text tighter and more readable.

FOR COMRADES IN SOLITARY CONFINEMENT

Every time they cage a bird
the sky shrinks. A little.

Where without appetite —
you commune
with the stale bread of yourself,
pacing to and fro, to shun,
one driven step on ahead
of the conversationist
who lurks in your head.
You are an eyeball
you are many eyes
hauled to high windows
to glimpse, dopplered by mesh
how — how — how long?
the visible, invisible, visible
across the sky
the question mark — one
sole ibis flies.

Jeremy Cronin, *Inside*

CHAPTER 1

In Police Hands

IT WAS what every political activist dreaded, and it happened to me at about 10 p.m. on June 17, 1975. The police had blocked the driveway of my home — and momentarily I did not realize who they were. I took out a cosh to protect myself, but after the police surrounded me and identified themselves, I threw it in the back of the car. They wanted my car in the garage, but would not let me switch on the ignition. I sat at the wheel as they pushed it into the garage.

There were about 30 of them, and they immediately set to work searching through my private belongings.

For some hours, I had been posting illegal political pamphlets in Durban and Pietermaritzburg. I was thoroughly exhausted. I just wanted to get to bed and rest — I had just been pleasantly anticipating a bath and the sleep I needed so badly.

The preceding months had been very stressful. I had been preparing a special edition of 10,000 copies of the underground pamphlet *Vukani!/Awake!*, including a translation of the Freedom Charter into Zulu. Each copy of the newspaper had to be painstakingly produced then inserted into an envelope. And each of these had to be stamped and secretly posted.

My routine had been to give my lectures at Natal University, Durban and then drive home to sit at the typewriter, operate my duplicating machine or prepare envelopes and put them in suitcases. I would get to sleep very late and repeat the same routine the next day.

Now, I was in police hands. This intrusion into my privacy was to become characteristic of my life as a political prisoner for the long years to follow. From the moment I was arrested, there was nothing about me that the state did not want to know or have access to. There was nothing I could shut away from the police and say this is "not your business." The law now gave them unfettered access to every corner of my life.

One of the police present was Major Stadtler, later to become a supposed expert on "terrorism." He seemed fairly affable and tried to engage me in discussion about my clandestine activities while the others searched. The police clearly savored their victory. They had spent many nights tracking down the irritant who had been issuing illegal pamphlets. Now they had me. I remember they made me ask permission to go to the toilet. Even there, I was constantly under their gaze.

South Africa had laws against assault, but they provided no protection for someone in my situation. I knew I could be held for long periods without scrutiny, without access to lawyers or other people from "outside." Numerous court cases, at every level of the judiciary, had confirmed exclusive access of the police to detainees, even where assaults were alleged. And, as I expected, and soon found out for myself, they did abuse their powers.

The events of that night marked a crucial turning point. From that moment on, I passed from being an independent person and fell under direct control of the South African apartheid state. In the years that followed, which saw me in and out of jail and detention, I would not be free of police intrusions. Even now — when this chapter in our history is over — I have habits that persist from this period of constant surveillance.

After they searched my house for some hours, the police took me to Security Police headquarters, then in Fisher Street, Durban. The offices and rooms were bare — because they were used almost exclusively for interrogation.

I had never been in these headquarters before — although I had seen similarly furnished offices at the so-called commissioners of the "Bantu administration" in Durban, where the desks were marked with government stamps.

The commissioners of the Bantu administration were presiding officers in courts that decided cases between Africans (then called "Bantu" by the government) concerning customary law. They also implemented the notorious pass laws that made the free movement of Africans subject to severe restrictions and criminal penalties.

Everything in these functional rooms was meant to move things along as quickly as possible — with a swift conversion of accused persons into convicted offenders. The furnishings were as bare as the summary justice dispensed here. No one spent much time in these rooms.

Long before my own arrest, I had read and heard about various people being tortured by South African police, particularly after the banning of the ANC in 1960. When I became involved in illegal activities, I knew I faced the prospect of being assaulted, or even killed, in detention. In preparing for my life as an underground activist, I had met several people who had been brutally tortured.

An array of legislation had been developed by the apartheid regime that shielded the police from public scrutiny, and it became routine practice to try to extract information and confessions through various forms of assault. Generally, courts accepted these confessions and refused to give credence to allegations of torture.

In the period before my own deployment, I tried to prepare myself as much as possible for coping with solitary confinement and physical torture. All of this was of some assistance when I found myself in the hands of the South African Security Police. Terrifying as it was, I was nevertheless on familiar ground. I had been warned, trained, prepared. It was terrible, but nothing my torturers said or did was surprising.

Perhaps I am underestimating the impact that torture has had on me; that in "coping" with it, I do not fully appreciate its damaging effects. But what concerned me back then, apart from getting by, was avoiding the betrayal of my comrades and the liberation movement. To be successful, I had to have some capacity to determine events – even in a situation that was so singularly weighted against me. Although I was a lone captive, having some idea of what to expect – and knowing something of my fate – gave me a fighting chance, however slight.

On the other hand, there was nothing in my own life experience to prepare me for the ordeal of falling into the hands of a group of single-minded sadists who, in the final analysis, felt no glimmer of sympathy for me as a fellow human being.

Indeed, I had grown up in a family where violence had no place. And I had never personally experienced violence. But I was now in an environment that was based on, and sustained by, violence.

In 1975 I was a young, very idealistic revolutionary, and I was prepared to die for my beliefs. I felt a strong connection with all those who had gone before me, and with all those who had faced similar tortures; and I felt a responsibility to the traditions of our liberation movement. That is what gave me strength. That is what made my resistance possible. And that is why I did not simply succumb to torture or lapse into despair.

Writing this now, 24 years after my arrest, I don't seem as single-minded as I was back then. I now tend to see myself as having been rather naïve. All the same, it remains true that single-mindedness was the weapon that got me through.

CHAPTER 2
Preparations

WHEN I arrived in England to study law at Oxford in 1969, I immediately began to "pester" Alan Brooks, a UK contact in the Anti-Apartheid Movement about the possibility of doing "something useful" on my return to South Africa. I was 23, and I wanted to meet those in the struggle who could give me a meaningful task to perform. I was aware that contact with the South African liberation movement — if one were serious — carried real risks.

People had been prosecuted or jailed for minor links with the African National Congress (ANC) and South African Communist Party (SACP).

The ANC had been declared illegal in 1960 and the SACP in 1950. Together, the two bodies made up the core of the South African liberation movement, under ANC leadership. The SACP, after allowing a few years to elapse, reconstituted itself as an underground organization in the 1950s. After the ANC was banned, it also operated underground. There had been little preparation for this change, which meant the core people of the underground were fairly well known as ANC members. This both limited their effectiveness and their "life span" as underground operatives.

The Sharpeville massacre of March 1960 demonstrated that engaging the apartheid regime on purely open, legal and peaceful grounds was no longer possible. Many had anticipated this repression. The ANC reasoned however, that it was first necessary for the mass of ordinary people to be convinced of the need for armed struggle before it could be embarked upon. And it was only on December 16, 1961 that the formation of the ANC's military wing, Umkhonto we Sizwe (The Spear of the Nation), later known as "MK," was announced.

At political meetings in Britain, students and activists did not hesitate to pass resolutions supporting armed struggle in South Africa. However, South Africans who supported these resolutions could be prosecuted if they returned home. Wide-ranging legislation allowed support for armed struggle to be penalized, with minimum jail sentences of five years. Sometimes I would have to leave meetings in the UK that veered in that direction. It was not easy to explain the legal implications that made this necessary, without also declaring that I did, in fact, support armed struggle. I also secretly read a lot of ANC and SACP literature. Other South Africans read the material quite openly, but they could claim they were merely curious or fulfilling their academic duty.

My political development can probably be traced back to my early life with my family. I was born in 1945, and grew up in the Western Cape in the aftermath of World War II. A white South African from a liberal Jewish family, I had imbibed certain core values, the most significant of which were the need for honesty and unselfishness. Translated into political terms, this meant concern for one's fellow human beings and trying to alleviate conditions that were degrading to others.

As a young boy, I encountered some anti-Semitism, both as an undercurrent and overtly stated. Unlike some other Jews who became politically active, anti-Semitism did not drive me towards Zionist organizations. I was never religious, nor even particularly conscious of being Jewish — except in the context of anti-Semitism. The experience of anti-Semitism, however, heightened my awareness of racism in general and my conviction that if racism towards Jews was objectionable, it was equally so in the case of black people.

My parents were members of the liberal Progressive Party. As a youngster at school and in my early years as an undergraduate student at the University of Capetown, I embraced liberalism, which then seemed the clearest alternative to apartheid racism. It was only later that I understood the baggage liberalism shared with capitalism. In the mid-to-late 1960s, the ANC and SACP were almost invisible in South Africa. There was little mention of them in newspapers. Membership was illegal and — from what I could see — there was nothing one could join. I did not know about the activities of the liberation movement outside the country; and what one did hear was filtered through South Africa's hostile, white-controlled media.

At the time, liberalism seemed to offer a way to combat apartheid and advance equality. In the 1960s, public protests were liberal protests. The ANC and SACP had been banned. And the liberals occupied the public space of the anti-apartheid struggle.

I became involved in student politics during my first year at university, but by the end of the 1960s — as a junior lecturer — I felt at a dead end. Liberalism, I concluded, was getting us nowhere. Protest politics were in my view morally correct, but seemed not to have a strategy for change. Until then, I had thought that liberalism represented what was right, against the values of the apartheid state and racism. It was when I began to think of how moral commitment translated into concrete goals that I doubted whether liberalism provided much guidance.

I did not agonize over the moral basis of liberalism — whether it had found an accommodation with apartheid relations of domination. I only knew it was getting us nowhere. Eager to do something that would make a difference, I concluded that it was necessary to join the forces employing armed struggle to bring down the apartheid government. My conceptions were rather vague and possibly romantic.

In late 1969, I also began reading Marxist literature. I obtained a book by Emile Burns, and the name hand-written inside the cover was "A. Fischer." The book had belonged to Bram Fischer, the famous Afrikaner communist, who was then serving a term of life imprisonment for his activities against the regime and who died a prisoner in 1975. The book's Marxist viewpoint shocked me. It reinterpreted aspects of history in a way that made me feel the wool had previously been pulled over my eyes. It also delivered a blow to my conceit. Until then, I had believed myself to be a well-educated and intelligent person who understood politics and the world. Obviously, I still had a lot to learn — with Marxism not the least of these things.

At this time, I was already a very successful young academic, very ambitious, publishing like mad and obviously "making it." But all this was suddenly interrupted — by my presentation of a thesis that contained extracts from the writings of the eminent banned author, Jack Simons. I was told to withdraw the quotations, as including them contravened the law.

In South Africa at the time, individuals were "banned" from political activities either because they were communists, or alleged communists, or deemed to be furthering the aims of communism. This entailed various restrictions on the freedom of movement and other activities of the banned individual. It also imposed restrictions on others. In my case, I was not permitted to quote a banned person such as Simons.

I refused to simply "lift" Simons's ideas without giving him credit for them, and withdrew the thesis instead. In a sense, this was one of my first adult decisions based on principle. It was also costly to me personally. (Simons, with whom I was in correspondence at the time, thought my decision was wrong and silly, and that I should simply have used his ideas without acknowledgment.)

Also around this time, I was looking after a flat owned by relatives. It was in Clifton, a suburb of Capetown, and my relatives' son arrived one night with dagga cookies. Dagga is the South African word for cannabis or marijuana. I had never tried dagga but found the cookies tasted pleasant and I ate a lot.

Long after the guests had left, I found my mind roving. I thought about my life, my reading of Marxism and the withdrawal of my thesis, and how I had considered myself such a "hot shot" academic. But, as I now understood from Marxism, my ambition was really not so exceptionally brilliant. It simply conformed to the norms and excessive competitiveness of bourgeois society. With the aid of Emile Burns on Marxism and dagga cookies, I started to look at my life afresh.

I was about to study overseas, and hoped to find ways of contacting activists in England. I was already ambivalent about undertaking a doctorate at Oxford. I really wanted to "slough off my bourgeois values." For the first time, I now had free access to revolutionary books. And I wanted to read them all.

At Oxford, my mind was torn in contradictory directions. On the one hand, I was reading revolutionary literature – Che Guevara on guerrilla warfare, Huberman and Sweezy on socialism, Franz Fanon, *The Wretched of the Earth,* Lenin and so on. I was also exposed to a fair amount of political activity – such as Marxist lectures and seminars, ANC and Anti-Apartheid Movement rallies, even meetings of the Black Panther Party of America. On the other hand, there were my law books, which were dull by comparison.

I chose a thesis topic that tied in with my political concerns – on civil disobedience. But I found it hard to find a supervisor who would allow me scope to explore the issues in the way I wanted. The supervisor allocated to me was very famous, but I felt his vision was too narrow and that I was unable to continue with my thesis.

The choices before me seemed stark: obtaining a doctorate that could not satisfy me; or continuing to study revolutionary writings – writings that Oxford seemed to treat as separate from and irrelevant to my thesis. I also wanted to break from the competitive Oxford environment – to reject the Oxford stamp of approval (that is, eschew a doctorate) and concentrate on what was necessary for my personal and political development.

I was very unhappy, but still grappling with what this new discovery, Marxism, meant for my life – and I applied it in a rather far-reaching, extreme and rigid manner.

Eventually, my abhorrence of Oxford elitism persuaded me to leave the university.

At the time, I spoke to an African comrade about my problems, the late Seretse Choabi, and he said he didn't like Oxford either but would stay and complete his studies.

Now, some 30 years later, I know Seretse was right but at the time I was agonizing over how best to "break with my past." So I set off on a new path, compatible with my newly embraced ideals.

I left Oxford and spent most of my 18 months overseas doing some independent research — mainly, reading revolutionary literature. In line with my extremist inclinations, I avoided all diversions and fun — neglecting most of the pleasures that London offered. And I took various jobs. At one point I was a late-night petrol pump attendant. There were few customers, and I used the spare time to read. I regarded this period as one of study and preparation for what lay ahead.

People gossiped at the time that young people studying overseas were seduced into joining the liberation movement then landed into trouble carrying out dangerous missions. In contrast to these stories, I nagged and pestered activists for months before they were prepared to take my wish to be involved seriously.

I was not satisfied with my own preparedness for the task — that is, to return home and help overthrow the apartheid regime. I was not yet sure of my capacity to withstand torture, to deal with solitary confinement and so on. I had followed very closely the arrest of some young university lecturers in the early 1960s, and the disgrace of one who became a traveling state witness, giving evidence that sent his former comrades to jail. I did not want to "break" in detention or do anything disgraceful.

I read a lot about other people's experiences and spoke to those who had been tortured. I tried to find out how they had been able to withstand the pressures. After a period of training, I developed more confidence and determination. I also came to embrace the concept of revolutionary conduct — which was to guide me in the years, and indeed decades, that lay ahead.

After much persuasion on my part, it was eventually arranged for me to meet someone to discuss my involvement in underground activities. I secretly hoped this would be Joe Slovo, whose writings I had come to admire and who seemed to be in the thick of preparations to dislodge the apartheid regime. Despite being a lawyer by training, Joe had become a key strategist on guerrilla warfare and was a full-time revolutionary, working for the SACP and the Revolutionary Council of the ANC. For years, Joe's writings would be discussed by small groups of revolutionaries all over South Africa and in the neighboring countries that hosted our cadres.

In fact, Joe turned out to be the very person I saw. We had a series of meetings. Joe certainly looked the part of the underground operator. And sometimes I had to "tail" him to our meeting places. We took no chances, suspecting (correctly, as we now know) that there were spies and other agents of the regime operating in London. Consequently, I could never be seen with someone like Joe. We might have to get to the same destination, but we would never go together. I would follow him, but that meant not appearing to have any connection with him.

For example, if we were in a shopping area, I would watch Joe's reflection in the shop windows — so I would seem to be window-shopping, while actually watching Joe. And he might be on the other side of the street. Sometimes I would follow him, and sometimes walk ahead and watch his reflection behind me.

Joe was also very funny — often teasing the young and serious aspiring revolutionary under his wing. I was filled with excitement. I had all the enthusiasm of the new convert and was anxious to know everything. Usually we would meet in a pub, and Joe would always have a beer and a packet of salted peanuts. Joe never patronized me. He always listened carefully to my ideas. He was always interested in reading and having articles passed on to him. Right until Joe's death in 1995, he would ask me to pass on whatever I was reading.

My questions were always answered in a matter-of-fact manner. Joe was warm but all of my questions were old hat to him. He had been in the liberation movement for decades. For me, it was all new and interesting, and I was eager to go on discussing everything.

It was not clear, at first, whether or not I would be recruited. There was no attempt to seduce me into joining the SACP or ANC. Rusty Bernstein guided me through the program of the Communist Party. Not all my questions were answered, but I was sufficiently satisfied to proceed with the work.

After a while, I was referred to the MK activist Ronnie Kasrils, now South Africa's minister of water affairs and forestry, who trained me in methods of propaganda work that were being used at the time. Everything would be done in a conspiratorial manner. We would have ways of recognizing one another at a particular venue and then follow to a particular place where we would have our meetings and then separate again, trying never to be spotted together.

I was taught how to attach timing devices to tape recorders and set off pamphlet/bucket bombs. These were harmless explosions that propelled pamphlets into the air, preferably coinciding with a simultaneous broadcast. As the pamphlets exploded into the crowded thoroughfares, people would suddenly be greeted by a booming voice announcing "This is the Voice of the ANC!" In those days, when the liberation movement appeared all but dead in South Africa, these messages were very stirring. I remember reading, after such an explosion, a quote from an internal underground bulletin: "All Africans went home with smiles on their faces that night."

Ronnie Kasrils also taught me how to conceal fingerprints, and some very basic methods for sending coded messages. Basic they may have been, but they worked quite adequately for four years. This training was meant to be fairly brief, but I enjoyed our discussions and plied Ronnie with questions on all manner of issues going well beyond the scope of the training.

While we walked around Hampstead Heath, I asked him about a whole range of contentious questions. My life was changing. A wide variety of things had to be reevaluated. I took my recruitment into the Communist Party very seriously, believing I should act in a manner befitting a member, adjusting my beliefs in order to embrace Marxist moral demands.

Between discussions, we simulated situations in which I was under surveillance or trying to shake off a "tail." We would do this in various parts of Hampstead. I would have to spot Ronnie, who would be concealed in an inconspicuous place, trying to observe me. The idea was that I should find him, but not necessarily let on that I had. Alternatively, I would have to shake off his "tail," if he were behind me. This might be through slipping briefly out of sight, changing aspects of one's clothing, then reappearing with a slightly different appearance.

For the remainder of my stay in London, I was to stay clear of any leftists other than Ronnie (whom I met under strictly conspiratorial conditions) and avoid known ANC people. As far as possible, I needed to establish a profile that ensured that I should return to South Africa without seeming a radical.

I have always accumulated vast quantities of books and other reading matter and did not want anything obviously subversive to be discovered when I returned by ship to South Africa. Ronnie and I went through the books. I wanted to take as much of what was useful as possible but exclude anything dangerous. A truck came to fetch my luggage to transport it to the ship. I expected huge packers to arrive and carry the trunks. But it was one scrawny driver and he and I had to laboriously push the trunks along the pavement and onto the truck.

I was on my way back. My life had changed, and I was ready to play a part in the struggle to liberate South Africa.

CHAPTER 3

Underground, 1970s

AFTER THE ANC underground structures were smashed in South Africa in the mid-1960s, the liberation movement had very little presence within the country. In the late 1960s and early 1970s, the ANC reestablished a limited underground presence, but its activities were few. The liberation movement inside the country mainly consisted of small groups or cells producing ANC or SACP literature.

Ronnie Kasrils told me of some people who had produced pamphlets in South Africa, but had then soon returned to London. Others returned without having produced anything. Underground publications were erratic, appearing occasionally in Johannesburg, Natal or the Cape.

Underground literature was illegal. It communicated ideas and news from organizations with zero access to the conventional, officially tolerated media. Without underground literature, there was no way South Africans could learn about the ANC and SACP. People usually had only second-hand, distorted knowledge of these organizations, which was filtered through the apartheid regime and the country's fairly compliant liberal media.

At this time, Umkhonto we Sizwe had not yet fired a shot within South Africa. People feared the power of the Security Police. There was a sense, in the 1970s, of the overwhelming power of the apartheid state and people feared to tell others of their sympathy for the ANC. It was hoped that underground literature would become a tool around which they could organize; that it would assist people to find one another, and to build, extend and strengthen the structures of the ANC.

A limited number of people received the *African Communist*, the official organ of the SACP; and *Sechaba*, the official organ of the ANC, which were both produced outside the country and posted into South Africa. Sometimes illicit publications had fake covers, or fake titles such as *Landscape Gardening – Flowers and Fruits of Fields and Hedgerows*. Useful though they were, many of these publications were intercepted by the police.

A limited number of underground pamphlets were produced inside South Africa. The most commonly seen in the 1970s were *Inkululeko*, organ of the Central Committee of the Communist Party; and *Sechaba-Isizwe*, from the ANC. Both were official publications, and the job of the underground cell was to prepare them on a duplicator and distribute them.

A publication like *Vukani!/Awake!* — for which I had responsibility — was, in contrast, written and produced within the country, but intended to reflect the broad approach of the ANC and its allies.

The work was planned in consultation with comrades overseas and carried out by activists returning to South Africa. I used invisible ink to communicate with the comrades who directed my activities. The actual message would be concealed and have to be developed with chemicals. An innocuous letter would then be typed above the invisible, concealed one.

I'm not sure how many underground operatives there were in South Africa at any one time. I know that others were operating at the same time that I was. I recall, for example, how Lawrence Schlemmer — then an academic at Natal University in Durban — brought a copy of *Inkululeko* to the table at lunch one day. I also remember how other academics had received pamphlets distributed in Capetown. They even consulted me, as a lawyer, about what they should do about having received them!

When I returned from England in June 1971, my parents met me at the docks in Durban. I was rather tense as I waited for my luggage to be cleared by customs. There was not much to worry about, apart from a wad of British pound notes stuffed in my back pocket — to buy a duplicator and other equipment. All went smoothly. My luggage was not searched.

I took over a holiday flat that my parents had rented in Durban. My instructions were just to set myself up and occasionally communicate with my contacts in exile. The main thing was to be sure I was not being watched or suspected of anything — other than having a broad liberal approach to politics. I was to familiarize myself with the local situation as I began work at the university.

So I began teaching at Natal University in Durban — first as a temporary lecturer in Comparative African Government and Customary Law; and then, six months later, as a Senior Lecturer in Law.

My brief as an underground activist was rather vague — there were no working groups or structures into which I could be integrated. This was an entirely new phase of the struggle. There was no example to follow, no one to offer advice. I had to survive on my own or not at all.

But it proved very hard to be apolitical in South Africa — and to appear detached from politics — especially when many terrible things were happening. And I was known to have been an active liberal in the past. Luckily for me, no one probed deeply into my lapse into apparent inactivity.

After I had been at my post a very short time, Ahmed Timol, an underground activist of the ANC/SACP, was arrested and killed in detention in 1971. Soon after this, I received a coded message — which must have been sent to all underground units — instructing me, among other things, to get rid of some equipment that I did not even have. For a while I suspected this was a police attempt to set me up; that a message had been intercepted and they were trying to prompt an incriminating response. I was silent for a time, to avoid any trap. But it was not an ambush — just one of those hitches that arise when you have to communicate in secret and under pressure.

This was the start of four very lonely years. Struggle is about comradeship, about sharing and cooperation with others. But I was alone. All I had were coded messages received every six weeks or so. The liberation movement was nonracial and fought for an equal society, but I never had the chance to work with black people.

Our anthem was *Nkosi sikelel' iAfrika* (God bless Africa), but I never sang it, until I was in jail with comrades who were on death row in the late 1970s, in Pretoria Maximum Security Prison. This moment is described in a poem called *Death Row*, written by Jeremy Cronin, who served seven years for ANC and SACP activities, and it is included in his collection titled *Inside and Out* (David Philip Publishers, 1999).

The main aim of the struggle was the liberation of the black majority, in particular the African people, led by the working class, but I had no political contact with Africans, nor much with working people. I was committed to the struggle but there was no nod of agreement from the oppressed majority around me in Durban.

I read Marxist texts, but could not admit to this secret acquaintance. I often had to listen to attacks on the ANC or SACP, unable to rebut them for fear of giving myself away.

There was no one with whom I could openly forge links. Known anti-apartheid supporters were banned or in jail. "Banned" meant being under constant surveillance and usually restricted to one's house after hours. It also meant a prohibition on your political activities, and on writing or preparing anything for publication or entering any educational institutions. There were people I would have loved to have contacted, people such as former ANC/SACP political prisoners Harold "Jock" Strachan, in Durban, or Ivan and Lesley Schermbrucker, in Johannesburg. Their experience and maturity could have assisted me. But approaching them would have led to immediate police attention.

I now know that there were other underground units in existence in the Pietermaritzburg area, involving people like Jacob Zuma, now Deputy President of South Africa, and the late Harry Gwala. But they did not know of me, and I knew nothing of them at the time.

There had been no network for me to contact on my return from England. I was "my own boss" and if I made mistakes there was no one to say, "Do something else." Or, if I hit on some good ideas, there was no one to say, "Yes, stick to that one."

UNDERGROUND WORK can take a variety of forms — all of which are very stressful and extract a toll on one's personal life. Everything essential — what one is, what one feels, and what is most significant in one's life — must be concealed. You reveal only the inessential, in order to safeguard the most meaningful aspects of your being. Working undercover makes it difficult to form or maintain intimate relations.

Mine was a very isolated existence. I longed for communications from my contacts in exile. Their brief coded messages, written in "invisible ink," were a lifeline, filling me with new resolve. Within the stringent limits of our situation, my contacts did what they could to support me. In the meantime, I did my best to maintain my morale and my cover.

Many of the people I saw in my work were smug liberals or complacent white South Africans, and I had to present my views on South African society and events to them in a sanitized form. I gave away nothing, tried to steer clear of political discussions and listened without offering opinions of my own.

I would never admit to any sympathy for Marxism or connection with the liberation movement, even to those who were sympathetic to the struggle or might even be recruited to join it. Instead, I would try to raise questions that would perhaps encourage them to read more or consider their own political role in a fresh way. It was only in the pamphlets I produced that I could say exactly what I believed.

This was the early 1970s, a period when the liberation movement was just starting to reconstitute itself in the aftermath of the Rivonia Trial, when Nelson Mandela and other leaders were sentenced to life imprisonment. It was also shortly after the Wankie campaign, when Umkhonto we Sizwe guerrillas fought side by side with Zimbabwean guerrillas against Ian Smith's regime of Zimbabwe (which was then called Rhodesia).

At that time, the ANC had no presence in Durban, where I was placed. Gatsha Buthelezi still had some credibility then, for having rejected the government's highly compromised "path to independence," even though he was a Bantustan head. Black Consciousness, a movement asserting black pride and dignity, appeared a real force at the time. And amongst its founders was Steve Biko, who was later killed in detention.

The Black Consciousness movement engaged in repeated intellectual attacks on apartheid, Bantustans and other targets. Through the National Union of South African Students (NUSAS) Wages Commission, white students were starting to make contact with the South African labor movement. Progressive lecturers like the late Rick Turner, who was subsequently assassinated, initiated some students into Marxism — but this was not connected with the liberation movement.

From 1971 to 1975, my underground activities forced me to lead a double life. (This was in contrast to 1985 and 1986, when I again went underground, during the state of emergency.) To all my friends I was an extraordinarily dedicated academic, a workaholic, who did not seem to have much else in his life besides academic scholarship.

Circumspect during the daytime, I worked secretly at night — laboriously preparing and duplicating pamphlets on a "roneo" machine in my home, then posting the pamphlets in postboxes in Durban and Pietermaritzburg.

I had to be careful about what I said in my university lectures — especially in more political courses such as Comparative African Government and Constitutional Law. But my cover seemed adequate. It was inconceivable at the time that someone in a law faculty should be an underground worker by night.

At that time, many people — especially white youth — were ignorant of any sense of history that included the ANC. I remember one discussion with a student in the early 1970s. The name of (Chief Albert) Luthuli came up — a Nobel Prize winner and President of the ANC until his death in a mysterious train collision in 1967. The student asked me if Luthuli was an Urban Bantu Councillor — that is, a member of an apartheid-collaborationist structure!

There was not simply hostile media attention towards the ANC and its allies, but an absence of any mention of the ANC. When newspapers did mention the ANC, they often confused it with the Pan Africanist Congress (PAC), a breakaway from the ANC.

While South Africans experienced this information void, a lot of work was going on outside the country. Just before my recruitment, the 1969 Morogoro conference (in Tanzania) reformulated ANC strategy and tactics.

What I read, convinced me that the ANC-led alliance had an overall long-term approach that would lead to substantial change. Being an underground propagandist was part of this strategy, empowering ordinary people to understand that apartheid oppression could be successfully challenged and ultimately ended.

When I returned to Durban I had no idea when or whether to expect any signs of success. I did not expect it to come soon. Nevertheless, I had no doubt that the course was correct. I had a general sense of a movement being built over a number of fronts, and that I was part of an attempt to rebuild structures within the country.

There is a degree of romanticism attached to working underground, but I did not experience it that way. Setting up an underground pamphlet production system raised a variety of practical problems. Every time I received a secret communication, I had to dispose of it. Simply throwing it down the toilet was not safe enough, in case I was suddenly raided or someone used the toilet and remnants of the message remained in the basin. I had to burn the message and there had to be no sign of the ashes.

At one time, I lived in a flat, and burning attracted attention because it was very unusual to light fires in the hot climate of Durban. Worried neighbors might then innocently knock on my door, drawing my attention to "the smell of burning"!

Publishing pamphlets does not evoke images of revolutionary daring. Rather, there were very irritating practical problems to be solved. In those days, there were no computers and no accessible photocopying machines that could be used in secrecy. Duplication entailed typing onto a stencil, which was reproduced on paper by turning the crank handle of a noisy machine. Many stencils were damaged and had to be retyped. Many pages did not come out clearly and had to be destroyed. How did one dispose of some thousands of pages of inciting literature in a white suburb of Durban? The quantity was always too great to burn. I could not leave my fingerprints on any pages I distributed or discarded. This was a laborious process.

I wore transparent gloves at night, or colorless nail varnish on my fingers. The varnish only protected the fingerprints for about 30 minutes, so I had to work quickly, or stop repeatedly to apply more coats.

After elaborately wrapping up the discarded pamphlets and putting them in plastic packets, I would dump them below a block of flats or underneath some rubbish in garbage bins, or some other place they would not be noticed.

The end product of all this work was not a very attractive publication. Each pamphlet was created entirely with a typewriter.

Sometimes headlines could be enlarged, but otherwise everything was in an unvarying typeface. Errors were corrected with correcting fluid and the paper could never have the clean look of computer-produced work. We hoped pamphlets would be read solely for their content, and their visual shortcomings overlooked.

Posting the pamphlets was a problem. At first, I would bundle them into suitcases at night and dump them all into a couple of large postboxes. But as Ronnie and Joe correctly pointed out when I saw them in 1974, if the postal authorities or police saw anything suspicious in one envelope, they could easily collect the lot. It was better to post the pamphlets in a number of separate boxes.

So, I gradually came to know the whereabouts of just about every postbox in Durban and Pietermaritzburg. I used a variety of envelopes, varied the typing of the addresses and staggered the times that I posted the envelopes, to make it harder for the pamphlets to be discovered.

I do not recall that this was a particularly stressful job, but it must have been. Recently, I had a dream in which I was trying to post something incriminating, and felt a great sense of anxiety. In the dream, all the postboxes were full, and I felt a great sense of suspense. I also wondered whether I was being followed, and saw a policeman coming after me, intent on identifying what I had put in the box.

I do not recall having these fears when I worked underground, but they must have been there, just below the surface. On one occasion, just as I was about to post some material, I locked my keys inside my Volkswagen beetle, forcing me to break into my own car. I now understand that this sort of thing happens when one is under pressure. At the time, however, I did not know enough about my own reaction to stress to be able to understand these symptoms of strain and fear.

I never actually set off a pamphlet bomb. Whenever I requested to do so, I was refused permission — because the risk was too great for someone operating alone. And I continued to operate alone until just before my arrest.

This may have been fortunate. I was not very technically skilled in such matters, however much I was interested in the *idea* of setting off explosions. I was later to meet Tim Jenkin, an expert on things technical, and I envied comrades who could work with someone like him, who would easily have sorted out anything to do with explosives.

In London, we had planned how my underground unit was to operate. We envisaged that I would find a garage — to store the incriminating duplicator and other items when they were not being used. But that was easier said than done. There were few garages for hire and not always funds available to pay for the extra rent. So, for some time, I kept the offending articles in a wardrobe in my bedroom.

This meant restricting visitors — including women — from my room, in case they opened the wardrobe. I was a young person with normal needs, and it made "dating" very difficult.

Another complication was the substance used for developing the secret messages I sent to London. The chemicals were applied to the paper and the message then appeared. This was probably very simple chemistry, but to me it was wondrous. One difficulty was that the chemicals left marks on my hands — marks that appeared gradually, much like those that emerge when "invisible ink" is developed. This meant I had to develop the chemical using gloves and avoid spilling any of the substance on my skin.

I've mentioned how my comrades overseas, through secret communications, provided what support they could. In addition, I was impressed when I met Joe Slovo and Ronnie Kasrils in London in 1974, on my return from an academic conference in the Netherlands. While we reviewed my work and I gave my report, Ronnie and Joe sat across the room taking very full notes. I had not thought my activities so important as to warrant this careful attention, and it validated my contribution, giving me a sense of its importance and encouraging me to return and do more.

One of the key things we discussed was the impact on our struggle of the Portuguese revolution of 1974 and impending independence of Angola, Mozambique and Guinea-Bissau. We concluded that these would be important steps forward, possibly giving impetus to various forms of resistance. We decided that my work should take on a more aggressive character, in keeping with more favorable conditions. In particular, I was to produce a new publication, in addition to official ANC or SACP ones sent to me. It would be called *Vukani!/Awake!*, and I would write it myself, in accordance with my interpretation of the perspectives of the alliance. The advantage of producing something on the spot was that we thought it would enable us to respond more quickly to developments on the ground and to give a sense of direction. Official publications, in contrast, took time to arrive, time to duplicate and distribute, and were often out of date when they appeared. *Vukani!* interpreted developments in the former Portuguese territories and encouraged people to organize and link up with the liberation movement.

An issue of *Vukani!* attacked Vorster's attempts to enter into dialogue with leaders of African states while South Africa still practiced repression internally. It was headlined: "Cocktails in Liberia — Fascism at home?" Comrades were very happy with this section of the issue and the ANC used it in their campaigning, through the Organization of African Unity and their objection to contact between

African states and the apartheid regime.

I remember referring to the trial of Black Consciousness activists under the Terrorism Act, concluding that their prosecution showed the time for legal activities was over and that we should all devote our efforts to setting up illegal organizations. My comrades criticized this view; correctly, I now believe. They encouraged the use of legal activities wherever possible, and not solely a one-sided emphasis on the illegal and underground pillar of the struggle.

We also discussed recruiting others, to form a unit with me. Previously, we had observed great caution, but now took a bolder approach. I described Lawrence Kuny to my comrades, a person I had known for a few years, both as a student and friend. I frequently socialized with Kuny and had come to know him quite well. I considered him an honest and compassionate person. Though Kuny had not raised the question of working for the liberation movement, I thought he would be willing to do so. I remember saying, however, that I did not believe his ideological understanding was adequate. Ronnie said I should remember that the way I came into the liberation movement was specific to my own background as an intellectual. If we required the same criteria of everyone, we would have very few members. In general, I was encouraged to go ahead, assess Kuny, and possibly recruit him.

Later, I raised the possibility of recruiting Jennifer Roxburgh. She was not a very political person at all. But I knew her well as a colleague and friend at the university. When I first arrived at Natal University, we were both in the School of African Studies. Although teaching separate courses, we interacted a lot. I knew she was a very reliable person. What she lacked in political understanding she appeared to make up for with steadiness and reliability. I was given the go-ahead.

When I raised the possibility of working illegally with them, both Roxburgh and Kuny expressed their willingness. I then set about teaching them what I already knew — about not leaving fingerprints, checking to see whether they were being followed, and so on. I worked with them quite separately, for security reasons. That way, they only knew what they did with me, and could provide no information about anything else. Obviously, the liberation movement did not have watertight methods of checking people. In recruiting Kuny and Roxburgh, I had simply to follow the broad guidance of my comrades, plus my own on-the-spot assessment. The role assigned to Kuny and Roxburgh was, broadly, to work for the liberation movement; and particularly, in support of the ANC. In general, Roxburgh proved equal to the task. She worked carefully and quietly, preparing material for distribution. She was valuable in another respect. Being a lecturer in

Zulu, she was able to translate documents for publication. We prepared a Zulu translation of the Freedom Charter for distribution in *Vukani!* This was to coincide with the 20th anniversary of the Congress of the People, which had adopted the Freedom Charter on June 26, 1955.

Kuny was different. He may not have understood what he had let himself in for. And when he did, he wanted to back out. After a relatively short time, he became very nervous. In some ways, Kuny expressed the same things that I also felt. But I suppressed my fears, by driving myself to get on with the job.

But Kuny's fears became overwhelming. He was unable to brush aside the thought of possible capture. He just wanted to get out. Around the time of my arrest, we were negotiating whether his leaving the organization might be possible. It was a difficult matter. After all, he knew about my illegal activities, and could easily end them.

I had recruited the pair in September or October of 1974, gradually taking them through a process of induction and training in clandestine work. But only seven or eight months later, our unit was smashed.

Circumstances did not permit Kuny and Roxburgh to have the advantage of time — to be able to settle very gradually into their roles. In contrast, I had some years to "acclimatize" to illegal work, so that when I was arrested, I was mentally prepared for it.

Not that working underground was something for which my life had prepared me. I had never broken the law in any way. I was also unaccustomed to secrecy. I was used to sharing what I valued, speaking about matters that pleased or upset me. I remember how frustrated I felt when Salvador Allende, the Chilean socialist president, was murdered. The *Natal Mercury* arrived under my door, with the headline that the Chilean president had "committed suicide." I knew this was a lie, but there was no one with whom I could share my pain.

I was also in no way prepared for *consistent* law-breaking, a program that must be carefully managed if it is to continue. Breaking the law means one sets oneself up against those who devote themselves to one's capture. Had I worked in a group, we would have regularly evaluated what we were doing, and assessed what the police might have been doing to combat us. I had no such reference group and consequently it was easy to make serious mistakes.

Throughout the years when I was involved in the struggle, we often heard the ubiquitous slogan or cliché: "victory is certain." Perhaps it was certain — but it didn't always look that way in the 1970s! In our underground units, we tried simply to maintain the flickering presence, and to continue the work, of the liberation movement.

CHAPTER 4

Torture and Silence

INCIDENT 7 (Assault — Raymond Suttner):

"The aforesaid was, I think, a lecturer at Natal University and was detained for the promotion of ANC activities through the distribution of pamphlets. He was assaulted with the open hand during interrogation by myself, although I do not remember exact details. Other members that I recall who were involved in this were a Captain Dreyer. These are the only members that I think were present and might have assaulted him, although similarly to what is stated above, I am unable to supply exact details as to who did what although I do admit that I did hit Suttner with the open hand. He was also tortured by electrical shock, which was applied through the dynamo of a telephone, which when wound, caused electrical shock to him."
[Extract from Amnesty Application of Colonel Andrew Russell Cavill Taylor (who died of cancer before the application could be heard), supplied by South Africa's Truth and Reconciliation Commission, Durban, April 1, 1997.]

AFTER MY arrest in 1975, the police may have thought they were onto something bigger than was actually the case. At Security Police headquarters an officer told me that some 12 to 15 cars had subsequently arrived on the scene — in addition to the 30 police who had searched my house.

I was caught red-handed and my own "guilt," in terms of the South African law of the time, was easy to establish. The question really was how to alert Roxburgh and Kuny, the two other people with whom I had been working, so they could escape. The rule in these situations was that if a member of an underground unit was arrested, anyone else working with that person should immediately leave the country. One's job, on being arrested, was not to hold out indefinitely but to try and find a way of alerting the others and hold out sufficiently long for them to escape.

The police knew their time was limited. Consequently, they would torture me fairly early in my detention.

I did not think of it then, but I held a certain power over them. I alone had the information they wanted. Nothing they had could substitute in value for that. There was nothing they could give me that could persuade me to part with the information. I had no kinship with the torturers. There were no bonds whatsoever. There was nothing they could persuade me to do of my own free will.

I tried to use what powers I had to avoid telling them anything. I also tried to determine the timing of my torture.

They did not offer me my freedom, or any concessions if I were to provide the information (which I would not have accepted in any case). They sometimes said, but without much conviction, that I would feel much better if I told the full truth. And they stressed how my career as a university lecturer was ruined, as if that might induce me to talk!

I had heard that some people had said nothing for days, only to become so exhausted that they collapsed or were surprised by an outbreak of police violence. I reasoned that I would definitely be tortured and it was best to provoke it sooner rather than later — while I had maximum strength to resist. If I waited, my judgment might be impaired and my resources sapped.

I did not try to remain completely silent, but to release information in a manner that avoided betraying my comrades and diverted attention away from them. One of the most important things was for Kuny and Roxburgh to know I had been arrested. I had no lectures the next day, so my absence from the university would not arouse concern. How was anyone to know of my arrest, before the police came upon them suddenly? So I volunteered some information about a hiding place on the university campus. By acting on this information, the police could no longer keep my arrest a secret.

They raided the university, trying to discover where I had hidden my pamphlets, and it quickly alerted everyone to my fate. Unfortunately, Kuny and Roxburgh did not use this opportunity to escape and were arrested just two days later. It is not strictly correct to say I "volunteered" this information. I told the police about what I had hidden at the university while I was under torture, in order to withhold the main information they wanted, which was the identity of Kuny and Roxburgh. I concocted an account of my activities, claiming I had acted alone, that there were no other comrades involved.

The police questioned me in teams, two or three at a time, with some police hanging around in the background, and sometimes butting in with obscenities. It was clear to me that I could not give them what they wanted. I continually said I did not wish to be rude but I would not answer any more questions. Captain van Zyl, one of the heads of the investigation, replied that I *was* being *very* rude. I suspected that at some point they would "burst," either losing patience or becoming, or pretending to be, enraged. The assaults would then begin.

I wanted, as far as possible, to remain master of the situation. I said I was not going to talk and they might just as well take me to be tortured. I hoped that I could provoke it *then* rather than be taken by surprise. Captain Wessels replied laughing: "You believe what you read in the newspapers?"

There was a break in the interrogation when they took me to point out the boxes where I had posted pamphlets, so they could retrieve them before they were delivered in the post. Kuny and Roxburgh had, at various times of the evening, posted pamphlets separately. I showed them the boxes I had used, as well as those I thought Roxburgh and Kuny had used, as if I had posted them all.

Then we returned to the police interrogation room and again reached a dead end. At one point, Colonel S. C. Steenkamp, then head of the Security Police in Durban and later General and Commissioner of Police, came into the room and all the SB (Security Branch) police stood up. I was already standing. Steenkamp's lip was quivering as he shouted: "This is serious, man." He twisted my nose and left a few seconds later. This may have been the signal for a change of approach.

It must have been in the early hours of the morning that Warrant Officer (later Colonel) A. Taylor, a very tall man, entered without his glasses, wearing a white butcher's apron, carrying handcuffs. He took off my glasses and put handcuffs on my hands, saying quietly that I would now be taught a lesson. He then blindfolded me and led me to a lift, which went up a floor or two.

I was stripped of all my clothes and made to lie down. One of my arms was put very painfully under my back. I am not sure how I was held down but there were bruises afterwards, possibly because handcuffs were still on. They held me at various points — by my legs and shoulders, and a cloth was put around my mouth.

Electric wires were attached to my penis. A voice, which I later came to believe was that of Captain Dreyer, said in a loud, whining tone that he was some or other rhyming name, perhaps "the monster of Main Street." I cannot remember exactly what he called himself. He said they now wanted to hear *everything*. "You are going to tell us who all your *comrades* are now!" "Comrades" was always sarcastically emphasized.

Dreyer, while making some or other obscene remark, pulled out some of my pubic hairs and hair from my head, beard and legs. The electric shocks started and they blocked my shouting with the gag.

They would stop periodically to see whether I would tell them what they wanted. Many obscene remarks were passed, for example: "I want to see him come *[ejaculate]* now."

They seemed aware of the danger of electric shocks. They wanted me to know that damage or death could result from such torture. Dreyer said: "This is bad for your heart, you know." They said that my mother and sister had been arrested in Johannesburg — while they continued to torture me, presumably so I would associate torture not only with myself but with my family, who were supposedly also being held. I knew these were tricks used to break a detainee's resolve and did not fall for them.

When the shocks stopped, I would try to burst into talking immediately before they could interrupt. They would respond by jeering and insisting I was lying (which was true) and that I had better "fucking well tell the truth."

Dreyer asked me whether Monty Suttner of Cradock was my father. I replied that my late father, who had come from Cradock, was Bertie Suttner, and Monty was my uncle. Dreyer claimed to know him from Cradock. As the shocks started up again, he said, mockingly: "What would Monty think, what would your father think?"

At one point they said: "We must put our kaffirs onto him. Tell him to speak!"

Then an African voice shouted: "Tell the truth man! Tell the truth!"

The torture continued until about seven or eight in the morning. At times, the cloth inhibited my breathing, though I think its purpose was to prevent my shouts being heard in the street.

When they stopped, Dreyer said: "Let's see if you can put on your socks." I could not. I felt very disoriented. He said: "I'll put them on for you." And he did this. I was led away, still blindfolded, down into the lift. As I came out of the lift, the blindfold was taken off and I was standing beside a quite short African man whose fist, displaying a ring on one finger, was clenched towards me. I never saw him or anyone I thought was this man, subsequently.

A white security policeman came and said "leave him alone" and unhitched me. I was taken into a reception room, where quite a few Security Police, wearing suits, sat with their feet on a coffee table. After a while, I was left alone sitting with my feet on the table, next to Warrant Officer Taylor, now wearing a suit. He commented on my "manners" in putting my feet on the coffee table and this led to an argument between us.

A little later, they resumed my interrogation. In the course of the morning, I was taken to Colonel Steenkamp's office. Behind his desk were bookshelves filled with confiscated books of Lenin and Marx. He sat, his lip quivering, as he studied my diary and the most recent issue of *Vukani!/Awake!*

"You know what this means!" he shouted, pointing to *Vukani!* After some discussion of the contents of *Vukani!,* he warned that I had better tell everything, otherwise he would order all the people listed in the address part of my diary to be arrested and this would be on my conscience. I said, as much as I would regret him doing that, I could not assist him, so he had better arrest them. I knew, of course, this was a bluff.

He lost his temper again and I responded with "you might as well arrange for me to be tortured with electric shocks again." Without saying anything, Steenkamp raised his eyebrows as if I was saying something incomprehensible or insane. I was to get this same reaction from Taylor and others. The police operated according to a fiction that if there were any irregularities, these occurred without the knowledge of the senior officers.

Interrogation continued, with teams of two men questioning me at a time, and two or three watching and shouting abuse. At times I would say "we decided" by mistake. There was then a chorus of: "Who's *we,* you fucking Jew?" I would explain that I used "we" interchangeably with "I," as I had noticed some French authors doing. This was greeted with derision.

Periodically, people would enter the room momentarily to shout things, such as: *"Hierdie Jood hy lieg. Ek sê vir jou, hierdie fokken Kommunis hy lieg!"* ["This Jew is lying. I am telling you, this fucking communist is lying."]

It must have been after 6 p.m. — at perhaps 8 p.m. of the second day — when interrogation with Warrant Officer Taylor and certain others ceased. Major I. Coetzee, a huge man, whose fearsome appearance was heightened by one half of his ear having been bitten off during a scuffle, said that he had to take me away. I was driven to Durban North police station, where I was booked in.

I was then taken to a urine-smelling, dusty, dirty cell in maximum security. I was exhorted to have a good night's sleep, so I could tell them "everything in the morning." Major Coetzee had said the same thing in the car on the way to the station.

I did not believe I would be allowed to sleep and within an hour heard a lot of shouting and banging and crashing. It was Taylor with another SB called "Hendrik" and two or three others (D. King, J. Stumpfer and another person). They took me out of the cell and into a waiting car. "Hendrik" drove, periodically turning to shout obscenities and threats at me. Taylor spent the entire journey in silence with his neck turned towards me, giving me an "icy stare."

We went up to the fourth floor of Security Police headquarters, to a room with two huge floodlights on the table and handcuffs on the floor. First I was asked some questions at the table and then made to face the lights, while "sitting" against the wall.

"Sitting" meant keeping my back straight against the wall, and sliding down to a sitting position without my calves touching the back of my thigh muscles. My arms were stretched out in front of me, and I had to balance what they called "my bibles" on each arm. They placed Marx's *Capital* on one of my arms, a work of Lenin's on the other. I was not very fit at the time, so that it did not take long to feel great pain and exhaustion.

When I dropped the books or fell to the floor, additional volumes were put on my arms. Drawing pins were put on the floor to force me not to fall. Occasionally, I was pulled up by my beard or by the hairs of my head. At one point, Taylor slapped me repeatedly on both sides of my head because I "sat" too low. They also stamped on my toes.

I was threatened with being "fucked up" properly. They also threatened to put the kaffirs onto me. When I protested that I couldn't think, crouched as I was, they swore at me. Eventually they allowed me to "rest," lying on the table, flat down, with my head uncomfortably raised, so that I could read from "my bible." Since my neck muscles were in great pain, I couldn't read clearly. I can still remember, however, what it was: Engels' introduction to *Capital*.

I still did not tell them what they wanted, which led to various threats. One SB said they would get a rat and put it on my stomach under a pot, so that it had no way of escaping other than eating into me. "Hendrik" said that when they put the kaffirs onto me I would really be "fucked up." He would sometimes hold a match in front of my eye while speaking. Remarks were repeatedly passed about my being Jewish, which predisposed one to criminality and communism in the eyes of the police. It was claimed that I had extensive relations with women, and even worse, in their eyes, with black women.

Some of those present did little more than hold my legs on the table or occasionally point a threatening finger when I dropped the books on the floor or read *Capital*. One would clap his hands next to my ears and keep on making inane remarks, such as: "He wasn't born. He happened."

At times, one or two of the police would fall asleep and it was left to the others to continue the barrage of obscenities and to pile further books on my arms.

As morning approached, I was exhausted. I was made to sweep up their cigarette ends with my hands, then ordered to remain on my knees and bark like a dog at the moon.

CHAPTER 5

"We'll give that Jew a hiding!"

THERE IS little that is comparable to finding oneself in the hands of the South African Security Police. You know they have already tortured and killed many people. You know this precludes any sense of human kinship between you and them. You are surrounded by these people, and have no access to family, friends or lawyers. The Security Police are a law unto themselves. They decide when and what you eat, whether you are allowed books to read, and how much exercise you get.

You look into the eyes of these people and sometimes there are glimmers of humor (perhaps, of sadistic humor) and other faint signs of humanity. In some cases — such as that of Colonel Taylor, who tortured me — all remnants of human feeling have been obliterated by years of abuse, systematically practiced upon fellow human beings.

These people guard you. They stand in front of you, at your side, and behind you. You never know what they are going to do next, if a blow is about to fall and from what direction it may come.

There is nothing you can do, nothing unobserved by them, nothing you can do without their permission. What limited washing is allowed is a luxury, and they will not permit you to wash until they have finished their intensive interrogation and torture. Sleep is out of the question — until they have completed their business.

There is much crudity, and violence is always in the air. Yet the police also try to maintain a contradictory self-image. They would like to appear to be civil servants who would serve under any government. They are just doing their job. That is why there is an elaborate pretense that torture and other violence is practiced without the knowledge of the senior officers, or while they are off-duty, since they would never approve of it.

Being a captive, and subjected to torture, robs you of the capacity to make all sorts of natural responses to situations. Normal pride in one's beliefs cannot be displayed unconditionally. One is in the belly of the beast. It will devour you if it so wishes. It is vital to preserve yourself from the worst of its ravages — not at any cost, but certainly at some cost. I had written revolutionary pamphlets. And they were meant to inspire the oppressed majority to rise up against apartheid. In detention, I was asked to explain just what I meant by all of this.

My interrogators were war criminals, people who practiced extreme human rights violations as part of their daily work. Our liberation movement had taken up arms against them in self-defense. How could I explain *this* to them? What value was there in arguing with these people?

I did not repudiate what I had written, but obviously was not in a situation in which I could proudly defend my views. I was prepared to be *klapped* [Afrikaans word, meaning to hit] but did not invite unnecessary blows. That is why I did not protest when ordered to "bark at the moon."

Anti-Semitism was an obsession with the police. For them, being Jewish was a crime in itself, predisposing a person to political "criminality" and particularly to communism. What then did their threat of putting the kaffirs onto me really mean?

Despite my perception that there was no kinship between the torturers and myself, the white torturers, in their reference to the kaffirs, may have assumed a kinship with me.

I may have been in jail for taking up the struggle of the black people, but they still claimed me as a fellow white who would fear, as they did, the thought of the kaffirs, the barbarians at the gate, the hordes waiting to be let loose on "us." With my white captors, reason allegedly had a place. What they wished to convey to me was that there was a threat that went beyond reason; and this was the kaffirs, a type of primeval force.

The kaffirs did not refer to sophisticated police, who turned the electricity on and off, usually stopping just short of mortal danger. Such behavior was supposedly rational. The violence of the kaffirs was, in contrast, a basic, unthinking violence.

In a sense, the police were responding to my polite refusal to talk, by saying that I should tell them what they wanted to know quickly — before the chance of rational communication became impossible.

So what we have, on the one hand, is a sense of *dissociation* from me as "a Jewish communist" — representing, to the police, the worst of the worst type of white treachery and betrayal. But on the other hand, we also have *association*. The police calculated that their racist associations between Africans and primeval violence would strike a chord with a fellow white.

I had prepared for detention. Yet, in detention, uncertainty is of the essence. There is a large unknown. One does not know what is going to happen. One knows it will be terrible, but there is great anxiety because of unawareness of what that entails. People say that every detention is different. It may be short. It may be long. It may result in a trial. It may not. It may entail torture. It may not. But it is always traumatic.

Even when one has been tortured, one does not know whether it is over, when the torturers will come back and what they will do next time.

I was tortured more than 20 years ago. I have not spoken much about this episode in my life. I did not have the opportunity to be debriefed by a psychologist. Instead, I continued in prison for another eight years.

I have written accounts of my abuse, once or twice, in what seems to some people to be a fairly detached style. I am beginning to wonder, now, whether I have ever come to terms with this episode in my life. I wonder whether I have sufficiently "worked it through," and now understand and acknowledge the character of the violation and the damage it has done.

My torture was widely known to have occurred in South Africa, but it was never publicly acknowledged until 1997, when former Security Police Colonel Andrew Taylor applied for amnesty for torturing me — though he provided a relatively shorthand account of what was actually done. Nevertheless, Taylor's statement, that certain unnamed people administered electric shocks, was the first public acknowledgment that this ever happened at all.

I did not publicly complain of torture at the time that it occurred, because the police might have simply intensified their abuse. And afterwards, it would have been difficult to prove.

When I was formally charged, after having spent six weeks in detention, I was ready to raise the matter in court. However, my legal team advised that this would be unwise, as I was not giving evidence under oath, but merely providing an unsworn statement from the dock. They reasoned that such a claim of torture could not be tested under cross-examination and would be treated as suspect. They said this had happened in a previous case — that of Sean Hosey.

Given the conditions of the time, this may well have been the case. As I have already mentioned, the tendency of the courts was to disbelieve most claims of torture, whether they were made in or out of the witness box. Besides, there was no way of proving that I had been tortured. I was blindfolded for much of the time, and I had no witnesses to call. So I did not raise the matter in court. Then I was forced to be silent for eight years while in jail. On being released, I could not speak a great deal about what had not been raised in court. It was as if this incident had not happened at all, and it remained almost totally unacknowledged. However, after his release, Kuny wrote an unpublished account of his prison experiences, which also notes how I was tortured for withholding information from the police. It was then, paradoxically, that the first official, public acknowledgment of my abuse came from one of the torturers.

On the second morning after my arrest, I was left for a short while with an Indian SB, Captain Naiger and an African SB whose name I do not know. Captain van Zyl came in and remarked that they should get me some breakfast (which never came). I had not eaten since lunch the previous day.

Interrogation resumed. By this time they had been through a lot of material found at the university. These papers, and ones from my house, were produced, with the police asking for explanations of abbreviations and codes.

They were still not satisfied. I was taken into Steenkamp again. More threats. Then questioning continued. At one point in the afternoon, both Captain Dreyer and Major Coetzee interrogated me. Dreyer shouted repeatedly, and at one stage kicked my shins, shouting, "You must speak, hey!"

Major Coetzee grabbed me tightly by my elbow, already swollen from the encounter with the electric shocks and I was made to "sit" again against the wall.

They must have already arrested Kuny and Roxburgh, perhaps that evening, judging from their questions and the atmosphere of jubilation. From then on, I was not tortured, although there was always the threat that it could start again.

Interrogation continued, though it was more in the nature of mopping up the case and trying to find out what I knew about underground activities in other parts of South Africa. Steenkamp again called me in, saying he knew that I was friendly with certain Capetown people, so I had better tell them who was producing illegal pamphlets there.

I think it was on the third or fourth night that they left me undisturbed in the police cell. I could not sleep. Police cells are very noisy. And when one has been tortured, some of what one hears is interpreted as a terrible fantasy. During my first night in the cells, I heard what I thought was the continuous beating of a prisoner against a wall, or against a basin, or something that sounded like a basin. In fact, there were no basins in the cells.

The longer I stayed in my cell, the more I came to discern what was actually going on in neighboring ones. What sounded like someone receiving a battering was, in reality, the antics of common-law prisoners awaiting trial. They were using their steel mugs as percussion instruments, while singing songs such as *Old MacDonald had a farm*.

My cell was made for about 12 prisoners. It had a dirty flush toilet and water from a tap above shoulder level. I slept on a dirty mat covered by a filthy blanket. One gets an idea of the longings of one's predecessors from looking at the walls of these cells. This one had obviously held no political prisoners before me (unlike what I saw in John Vorster Square, over a decade later). The only expressions of passion were such statements as "I love MacDuffy Myburgh."

I had an asthma attack and the next morning was taken to the District Surgeon, Dr. Buchan, for an examination. I had not expected to be seeing a doctor, but to go straight to Security Police headquarters for more "medicine." What sort of opportunity was this? I had read of the obsequiousness of district surgeons in relation to the SB and had little hope of my situation being remedied. In fact, I felt a sense of fear.

Steenkamp was waiting, grim-faced, at the surgery. I interpreted this as a warning. I feared to mention my torture. I had no idea how much longer I would be in police hands, or what they could still do to me. I did not want to provoke further assaults.

So I was silent.

I was alone with Dr. Buchan, however, while he examined me from top to toe, noting various injuries. I did not volunteer information or a true explanation of their cause, since I was not sure what consequences would follow. I thought I still had a long time to spend with my captors. I also had no reason to regard the doctor as independent.

Buchan noted a series of injuries, starting with bruises and cuts on my legs. When he asked how they had been caused, I usually answered that I had fallen or must have bumped myself.

I thought Buchan would realize what had happened, since my answers were similar to the glib police explanations of deaths in detention. For example, "slipping on soap" and the like caused my injuries.

There was a scratch on my penis from the electricity. I said I didn't know how it had happened. Buchan noted that the bruising on my elbow was very recent, since it was only starting to form.

Buchan gave the report of my injuries to Colonel Steenkamp. I do not know if he kept any record of it for himself. Nor do I know what Steenkamp did with the report. Throughout this interaction, Steenkamp adopted a threatening posture towards me.

Looking back on this visit to the doctor, I do not think I handled it correctly. I was wrong to adopt a stance of helplessness, to accept that there was no redress. I failed to fight for my rights as a human being. I concentrated on getting by, not giving away certain things, and in so doing, surrendered my right to be protected from assault. But I felt very intimidated at this time. It is a paradox that I was able to hold up under torture, refusing to provide vital information, but could not complain to a doctor — nor had I devised a strategy to deal with the situation.

Some years later, during my second term in detention, I did take certain steps to protect myself. By that time, I had spent time in prison with other prisoners and better understood how to defend what legal rights we had. I learned to use the strategies at my disposal better than I had the first time around.

After the visit to the doctor, I was returned to my cell. I think this was on a Saturday. At about 5 p.m. that night, I was fetched from the police cell. I had heard Colonel van Niekerk outside the gate of the security cell saying: *"Vanaand gaan ons daardie Jood 'n pak slae gee!"* ["Tonight, we are going to give that Jew a hiding!"] I was subsequently interrogated until 1 a.m. the next morning.

I was driven to Security Police headquarters, where I was taken to Colonel Steenkamp, who was sitting in front of his desk. He told me to sit on the floor at his feet, "because of the difference in our ages." He then assured me I would not succeed in my aims. He would "crush" me. I would die in front of him. He would hate to use "KGB methods" but would have to if I did not tell them everything.

I was very nervous throughout the interrogation. At one point, I could not stop quivering. My hands were shaking like leaves. I did not know whether they meant to torture me again. At the end of this session, I was returned to Steenkamp. He said he was satisfied I was not telling them all that I knew. He said he had a responsibility. And while I was a communist, he was a Christian, with moral principles. His final monologue ended with his telling them to *"vat hom weg!"* ["Take him away!"]. I was taken back to Durban North police cells and allowed to rest.

I remained there, in police custody, for six weeks until August 3, 1975, when I was charged. Throughout this period, I was allowed very little exercise, possibly an average of five minutes a day for the entire detention period, with no exercise at all on most days. At the same time, I was insufficiently inventive in devising exercise regimens within the cell — something I would learn to do during my second spell "inside."

I was allowed no reading matter at all, not even the Bible, which is normally provided to detainees. The lights were left on in my cell all the time. It was hard to sleep, because police would periodically come to check on the cells, after opening a courtyard gate very noisily. Then the outer and inner cell doors were opened — all making a terrifying, crashing noise. At the time, I took all of this to be conventional police station noise. I learned later, however, that some of it was "specially arranged" for me.

THE FOLLOWING is an extract from Laurence Kuny's unpublished account of his prison experiences (written after his release from detention in 1975):

"The guards there told me of him *[Raymond]*. As I didn't appear the hardened communist in their eyes they spoke freely to me.

"Raymond had not been treated like me. His light was kept on 24 hours a day — with no chance of it being turned off. He was left in his cell for longer periods than I. One guard told me that whenever he visited his cell, he would slam the door open to wake him up; when this man was on night duty. Raymond obviously didn't sleep. The guards disliked Raymond. They tried their best to make life unbearable for him. I'm not guessing this, the guards told me to my face.

"I was a potential state witness so they dared not show their true colors to me; kid glove treatment was reserved for me. Some readers may think prison was bad enough for me, it was hell, but compared to others it was paradise…"

At this time, I was able to see a magistrate, on two separate occasions, both of them in the Security Police offices. I felt South African magistrates were "in cahoots" with the government and saw no point in trying to get any remedy from them. They told me they were responsible to the minister, and just mumbled two or three questions and wrote "yes/no" answers on small pieces of paper. I knew of numerous cases in which people complained to magistrates, but nothing happened. Naturally, I was suspicious.

My doubts seemed confirmed by a case of the time, in which a judge referred to "wild allegations" of detainees being routinely tortured. General Geldenhuys, the then head of the Security Police, even claimed that "Moscow" had ordered detainees to make these allegations. The police knew the courts would back them up, so they could do what they liked, and administered torture to an extreme degree, stopping just short of death. Sometimes they went too far and detainees, such as ANC activist Joseph Mdluli, were killed. Members of the police hierarchy steadfastly supported their junior colleagues. A certain Lieutenant Senekal told me that an interdict could not stop them from torturing us. The police felt they were invincible. There was no real check on their power. In many instances, they were free to act completely outside the law.

CHAPTER 6

Awaiting Trial

I HAD never seen a door as massive and heavy as the steel one that shut behind me in Durban Central Prison. It shocked me in a way that the loudly crashing doors in detention had failed to do. There was something very final about the way it closed.

This door was at once a physical barrier to movement and symbolic of a change in my life. My previous life was now excluded, part of the "outside." In the years that lay ahead, my life now belonged to the "inside."

Normally, we close doors to provide personal security, comfort and safety. Behind the door of one's home there is usually warmth, harmony and contentment. A prison door, in contrast, locks you into a world that strips you of your dignity. Here, comfort is absent and there is no personal privacy. There is also a constant barrage of unwelcome sounds.

Although I did return through this door in 1975, it was only to be taken to court or another prison. My next opportunity to open a door for myself, away from prison sights and sounds, was not until my release in 1983.

At the same time as I was shut out from one life, I was, in a sense, publicly connected to another, that of the liberation movement. What was lacking in my period underground, when I had to hide my beliefs and connections, was now publicly known and asserted. I felt relieved about this, and a sense of pride in being seen for what I truly was. The courts might rule that I had acted disgracefully, but I could now declare myself — and be seen to be by those who shared my beliefs — a part of the struggle to provide a better life for all South Africans.

The prison door had shut me out of the privileged life of a white South African. For the first time, I experienced some of the discomforts that are the normal lot of the black majority. I was now shut out from privilege, and from my relatively esteemed position as a professional and university lecturer. My identity was now that of a prisoner, removed from society. There were, I knew, people who held me in high esteem as a freedom fighter. But they were far removed from the interpersonal relations that I experienced behind prison walls. The prison authorities saw me as a person who threatened the state and had to be held in secure prison conditions, away from other prisoners who might be influenced by my "terrorist perspective."

Being in prison does not come naturally to anyone. The concrete floors and walls and steel surroundings are alienating, and a cell is quite unlike the home of any person, rich or poor. Although one is "inside" one always feels like an "outsider."

That is why, at first, I experienced prison life as if I were an outsider looking in. On one level, I accepted that I was a political prisoner. In fact, I was proud of it. But part of me could never accept the "prisoner" tag, or having been thrown in jail because of what I stood for.

I had thought a lot about the political context of what I had done. I knew I was one of many people imprisoned for their beliefs. But I had now to deal with the reality of spending years inside. And I had not really understood what that would mean.

How does one describe the physical conditions of a prison? Much has been written about them, their peculiar atmosphere, and the impact they have on inmates. One thing I have been trying to understand is the symbolism, and psychological legacy, of their constrained spaces. I have thought a lot about what prison meant to me and continues to mean in my life.

My experience of prison is still with me, more than 10 years after I was finally released. It is something that makes me want to get out of claustrophobic, overheated rooms, to have access to fresh air and light, to avoid dark and dingy rooms and have a sense of space. It also resurfaces when I am forced to be with people with whom I have little in common.

What I found most oppressive was the absolute denial of everything I really wanted to do. This not only involved being confined to a physical space, but the imposition of sights and sounds that were unwanted and unwelcome.

Just as in the police cell, there was no raised bed in the prison cell. I slept under blankets, on a mat placed on the cement floor. But the cell did have a basin and was clean. I was also permitted, under South African law, to have reading matter, and soon collected a lot of literature. Obviously, the prison authorities had never encountered anything like this before, for they had no bookcases or were very reluctant to supply anything to house more than a Bible. I was supplied with very makeshift containers to accommodate my books.

I was the only political prisoner in the prison. Most of the other prisoners were awaiting trial. As remains the case today, many of these people waited months in jail before their cases were settled.

The prison was all gray and steel. These two words define the textures, the materials and colors I would have to deal with for a long time. In prison, there is little you want to touch or look at. The mat was rough, the blankets uninviting. There was nothing comforting or homely about what was to be my home. There was no garden and there was little time to see the sky. I was allowed out into a small part of a yard for half an hour in the morning and half an hour in the afternoon. If I had a visit, it substituted for exercise. The rest of the time I stayed in my cell. And I could see nothing outside of it.

The prison officials, however, treated me satisfactorily. Only one of them had had any previous contact with political prisoners. He had briefly guarded Rivonia trialist Denis Goldberg, who, he said, was in for *sabotation* [an adaptation of the Afrikaans word for sabotage]. In fact, at this time Denis Goldberg was serving a life sentence in Pretoria, where I would later join him.

I was charged under the Terrorism Act on August 3, 1975. But this was merely a formality. The actual trial would start two months later. Just before the trial, I was given fresh clothes and taken for a haircut. I also decided to have my beard shaved off, since it might make me look more respectable in the eyes of a white South African judge. I also wanted to appear as dignified as possible, as I was a representative of the liberation movement.

Two things changed after I was charged and returned to Durban Central. I now had access to lawyers and could see visitors for 30 minutes, twice a week. Although aspects of my conditions were better than I had expected, I was impatient to have my trial settled and know my sentence so I could adapt to the life that lay ahead.

It was pleasant, as well as unsettling, to be visited by friends, and for them to send me food and fruit, which was allowed prior to sentencing. This made life easier, but I kept on thinking that I should not get used to such "luxuries." At one point, I told people not to send special food because I had to get used to prison food. But I had a relapse after experiencing Durban prison food for a few days and rescinded the request. It was wonderful not to have to eat prison food for all three meals a day.

Although not yet a sentenced prisoner, I started to get a glimpse of what lay ahead of me. I saw the various ways in which prison rules try to rob prisoners of their individuality. There were constant invasions of privacy and attacks on the dignity of prisoners. One little thing that immediately struck me was the "Judas hole" on the door. Any passer-by could look into my cell whenever it took his fancy and sometimes other prisoners would do so, and shout obscenities at me. I felt, then, a peculiar sense of powerlessness. I could not see much of the outside from inside the cell, but anyone looking in could see as much as they liked and deprive me of any semblance of privacy. It was sometimes quite intimidating to have a person I could not see shouting threats at me from outside the cell.

From early on I noticed the prison noises, the occasional silences, broken by terrible noises, the banging of steel doors, jingling of keys, shouting and swearing of warders. No prison official speaks softly. Officers would shout at warders and warders always shouted at prisoners.

Sleep was difficult, since the young warders on patrol did not bother to be quiet. When they looked into my cell at night, they would switch on the light long enough to wake me and then go away. Sometimes a young warder would just stand around, apparently aimlessly, but lightly jingling his keys, enough to cause considerable irritation and make me realize how frayed my nerves were.

There were no direct-contact visits, and you had to speak through a glass panel. Sometimes other prisoners had visitors at the same time as I did, although they generally tried to keep us separate. I preferred it this way, because it was hard to hear above the shouting of other prisoners and their visitors.

At this time, I was preoccupied with preparing my statement from the dock. There was not a lot I could say in my defense. Purely in terms of the law, the case against me was cut-and-dried.

In a letter to my grandmother, which was dated August 18, 1975, I wrote:

"Generally I do not feel very depressed here. It is a great waste to have to spend this time locked away and conviction for a minimum of five years will mean that — but I cannot pity myself in this context: there are others who have far longer sentences and also went to prison around my age. Though I do not want to go to jail, this does not mean that I have any regrets for what I have done — I would do everything, but *more* again. That I have done insufficient is what I regret."

This passage is written in the tone of the revolutionaries I studied and tried to emulate. It is also a good example of my tendency to deny my own pain precisely because I knew others were experiencing worse. Nelson Mandela had been sentenced to life imprisonment. Therefore, I chose to say nothing about my own suffering.

At the time, I really did not understand what it meant to be put away for years — or know what depression really meant. I wrongly equated depression with unhappiness. I knew how to act, and how to take a defiant and unrepentant stance. But I did not foresee the real suffering that lay ahead, nor understand the toll that long imprisonment exacts. I am not sure that I fully understand it now, outside of recognizing that many of my present habits are conditioned by my prison experiences.

But perhaps my behavior was right at the time. Denying my pain was at least a strategy for coping, and perhaps an effective one. And I honestly did feel ashamed of complaining, especially when others had much heavier sentences. Complaining — as distinct from protesting — might have only wasted time, lowering my own morale and that of my comrades.

We live in different times now, and I am able to look back and be honest about how terrible it was. The letters that follow, typical of my attitude of the time, now seem a little naïve. But I was forced to draw on some basic beliefs to survive those difficult times. And my convictions were, in many ways, the key to my survival. I took a defiant stance, made no apologies for what I had done and stood with the liberation movement.

CHAPTER 7

Letters, Awaiting Trial

These letters were written from Durban Central Prison in 1975. Some have been abridged, and italicized explanatory notes, in square brackets, were added later.

August 7
Dear Ma [*my late grandmother, Debby Figg*],
It is clean in here... It has also been good to have hot water and feel clean... I did not know that I was being charged until that morning (August 3, 1975).

I was upset after having seen Mom today, that I had been a bit depressed. This is inevitable in new surroundings. I must stress that I am not worried about being in prison now and in the future. I understand very well how you must be feeling. I just want you to know that I am OK and equipped to deal with whatever happens. I don't say that it is easy — like in most things, adaptation is required.

I am strengthened very much by the support of my family.

I am strengthened and have been ever since June 17 [*date of arrest*] by the discipline that I have tried to maintain as a result of my beliefs. I know that I have small cause to complain when I compare what has happened/will happen to me, with what has been endured by others.

August 7
Dear Family,
I have just had a visit from Mike Olmesdahl, Peter Galt and Wendy Thorpe [*friends from Durban*]... It was hard to say much to them because we could not hear one another — the visit was not as they had expected, etc. — practice will make perfect I suppose...

The more I think about communications, the more disappointed I am. I had no idea that meetings were so seldom and carried out in this manner, at this stage...

I find it hard to adapt — I know that it is early — but I don't want to adapt to better things than I will have in the future; e.g., the food parcels. On the other hand, it seems that I will be here for some considerable time. Really, I need these visits, but everyone must plan what they are going to say — otherwise we just waste the whole period.

Re my reactions to the police and this experience: it is surprising, despite remaining relatively calm, etc., how much psychological distortion I seem to have experienced. The little things that are not happening now cause me anxiety — the unknown factors. If you know what it is, or how terrible something is, you can learn to cope.

I had no idea — I say for the hundredth time — that I would communicate under such conditions. I really looked forward to saying what I think, at length, etc. I wonder what the situation is during breaks at the trial. I hope that we can see one another then.

August 8
Dear Family,

It is nearly the end of the day, and I am rather tired. It is purely to avoid wasting a day's letter that I am getting this one out...

Bob *[Bob Youngleson, the Durban representative of my Johannesburg-based attorney, Raymond Tucker]* also brought in a lot of food and things I needed. I will prepare a list detailing when to bring food, etc., and days when needed, so as to avoid causing irritation here and to have enough for key times; e.g., weekends. I have no way of sharing the stuff so it seems people must really buy me minute quantities if they get things like cheese. I dread the thought of ants or cockroaches arriving because of my "pantry." I am very anxious to keep to a minimum the demands that I make here. I think that I can make a list, suggesting things I need, and the interested people can buy them amongst themselves, as they like.

It is hard to get used to being here after having returned briefly to some connection with my previous professional life — it all seems like my imagination rather than reality. I was correct about the privileged nature of communications with my lawyer — that is a very important example of how the type of experience that the attorney has had is so vital. I remember it more from actual trials, such as Rivonia, than from my legal training...

[Contact between lawyers and clients was privileged and prison officials were not allowed to sit in and listen (in theory). At first the prison officials tried to do this, and the lawyer stationed in Durban did not object, though I did.]

I feel very bad, being so helpless, being compelled to demand all the time. All that I can do is try to organize my requests for food and literature in a way that is least burdensome. I might try to go without most of these supplies, if it were not for my need to be alert and not depressed for the next few months. In that context, it is warranted, I think, to kill time by indulging a little in food and other delicacies that will probably not be available after my conviction.

I am not going to appear in court suggesting that this period has left any damaging impact on my personality. There are no scars left (literally) and have been none of other sorts.

Once the indictment arrives, it will be possible to get an idea of the length of the trial, just as we should know before the end of September when the trial will actually be. It is unlikely that it will be longer than a month, though the joining of the other two as co-accused will prolong matters. *[I was then under the impression that Kuny and Roxburgh would be co-accused and not state witnesses, as they turned out to be.]*

It is 5.50 p.m. This is, unfortunately, when I start to warm up — and then it is "lights-off" at 8 p.m. My mind, by that time, is usually ticking very well. The first night I got to sleep only in the last hour before "lights-on," at 5.50 a.m. The next morning, I was so tired that I fell asleep before lights out. Last night was again brief sleep. It is hard to get used to the surroundings — just as you have birds and crickets in some places, here there is constant shouting, clanging, banging, clinking, and jingling. Also, the typical Natal weather is getting me down. Lie in bed, and it is cold. No sooner do you pull up an extra blanket (they have supplied sufficient and good ones)... when it is boiling hot. You are allowed to fall asleep, only to wake up, frozen, with a blocked nose and an active mind. Soon it is time to get up and voices can be heard in the service singing, "What a friend we have in Jesus," or some such hymn...

I thought that my previous letters had gone through all right. It is strange writing about most things *other than* your daily experiences or the most meaningful ones. I suppose that I can tell you some very matter-of-fact, boring things in that respect, but the juice — including the humor — has to be internalized. There has been so much over the last period that I have wanted to tell you...

Saturday morning. Time changes on Saturdays and, I imagine, on Sundays; e.g., lunch at 10 a.m. I am getting used to things. E.g., I make my bed and, like the people in the army, I am considering sleeping with one blanket that is not in the "radio," to avoid the frustration of organizing the bed again in the morning... *[The "radio" was a method of folding your prison blankets and mat in a compact form, making it impossible to sit or lie on your bed until after inspection.]*

This is the first morning that I have woken up calm and collected. Things, such as having to make my bed precisely, throw me into a panic. I like to know what is happening and the most viable option in my present circumstances is to wait and be told. When I arrived, asking various questions of the SB, one of them remarked that I am "one of those who asks questions." I just like to know in advance what I have to deal with. What I knew about 17th June *[date of arrest]*, prior to its arrival, steeled me to deal with it. Nothing was a surprise — it involved all, or most of, what I had previously heard about. Even what they said was so hackneyed and typical of the experience of others. This enabled me to keep control of the situation, even if, on occasions, it appeared otherwise. Similarly, I would like to know about the rest of this journey, since this is just transit. However terrible the end of the road may be, I am now on it with — about five of — some of the best people, and that is bound to make things easier. In fact, I never lost sight of my connection with others, to things wider, during this whole period...

When reading about *[Maxim Gorky's]* birds I started to think that I have never really paid attention to birds. When one's view is limited (literally) and other things are restricted, the smallest little thing assumes a new importance. I think that Hugh Lewin *[a former political prisoner]* wrote a poem about a fly on the wall.) My senses absorb everything that comes within range at the moment, since I have been deprived and continue to be...

I started my account of dealings with "Monty's friend," et al. *[A reference to my torture, and to Dreyer, whom I believed referred to my uncle, Monty Suttner.]* It just spurts out. It is the sort of thing that you do not forget. I believe that, irrespective of proof, my account rings as being so authentic that it will be believed — and is so embarrassing that they would try to settle, if a civil action were brought.

I thought that I would get the chance to tell you fully of some of the conversations I used to overhear at Durban North. *[The police cell where I was held before being charged.]* I will have to give you an abridged account, which follows:

My cell was between two others, which usually contained people in for *kardiefstal en zol* [car theft, and slang for cannabis]. As "Angel van Niekerk," who seemed to have written all over my cell, wrote: *"Ek het zol en 'n man Hennie Viljoen lief — net een dag en ek is uit."* ["I love cannabis/dagga and a man, Hennie Viljoen — just one day and I am out."] On one side would be "Kleintjie" [little one] and "Christo." And, on the other, "Petrick" and the "twee Portugees" [two Portuguese]. Occasionally there would be a bit of swapping around, because of fights between them. Apparently, Christo, despite his vulgarity, in between conveying remarks between the cells, liked to spend his days reading the Bible and "the Portuguese" used to "worry" him. Petrick

seemed to get in a lot of food from his *murrer* [mother] and father so
that he was the one who was usually called:

"Petrick!" (No answer.)

"Petrick!"

"Yus!"

"Are you liss – ening? Come to the window, man."

"Okay."

"Listen Petrick: will you send over some food, man?" This would
go on for hours because it was difficult to convey the message
properly, and they had to send the food over with the policeman.
Occasionally, there would be a lot of music — banging against the bars,
the bench, floor, making sounds with their mouths like some sort of
instrument — as well as singing, between the two cells. At first they
used to disturb me. But after a while I used to long to hear them start
up about borrowing clothes for court the next day or to hear that
"another uncle" was taken in for "not paying at a hotel." Soon they all
left, all except Christo. And a new lot came in on the left. One of them,
Arthur, used to "check me out" every day — just to say hullo for a
short while. When I told him my name: *"That's lekker."* ["That's nice."]

When drunk African women were taken in, it was quite impossible
to sleep. Their voices could be heard for miles, mimicking the question,
"No complaints?"

*[Police and prison officials asked routinely of prisoners in the mornings,
"Any complaints or requests?" and usually moved past so quickly that even if
one were to raise a complaint or request, it would be too late.]*

August 10
Dear Family,

I am not worried about much, other than having subconscious
"romantic illusions." I think one sometimes remembers very selectively
and, in this situation, one can be taken by surprise...

When we are outside, we do not realize that there is so much that is
wonderful to look at, that we take for granted — particularly, other
living things. Right now, the movement of any insect is a matter of
great moment to me!

...I think that they must have decided what to do with the others
[Kuny and Roxburgh] by now. I think that there will be charges under
two acts, so that they can be found guilty under one of them, allowing
a lower penalty...

Monday, 8.50 p.m. My fingers still feel strange, though usually only
when it is cold or I have touched something cold, such as water.
*[Electric shocks, used in torture, had temporarily stiffened some fingers on one
of my hands.]*

I was delighted to get my first letter from outside — from Sally — a short while ago. I look forward to seeing her tomorrow...

Tuesday, August 12 (continued). It's 8.30 a.m., after exercises. I think that I am getting used to things, though I hesitate "superstitiously" to say so, lest there is anything unexpected ahead in this place. Lights off at 8 p.m. and getting up at 5.30 a.m. have, more often than not, been manageable over the past week. When I don't sleep, it has generally been because I am thinking about the case and not because of my surroundings, though I have found, not unexpectedly, that any tension is exacerbated by the situation — you will please understand why I use such cumbersome words.

The paper is again coming, morning and evening — since yesterday — and this makes a difference. Being closed-in here, I do not feel any link with what is happening outside my few feet of territory. Whatever happens, my general frame of mind, morale, etc., is OK — I am not *at all* vulnerable on that score. I am not in the least worried by the major "jolts" in my life. I wish to know what is going to happen — not so much during the trial, but in the subsequent period, when I will have to adjust again to small, trivial problems, which are bound to arise. I am not joking when I say that arranging my bed like a "radio" is more problematic than the fact of being here generally.

August 12
Dear Family,
This whole thing is so difficult — this situation — with you people doing your best to help but not knowing what can and cannot be done. In the meantime, I am trying to maintain a fragile type of stability — no matter how boring and empty things are, they can be dealt with when I know what to expect and have regular relations, causing no extra problems here.

August 13
Dear Family,
I have spent three or four hours with Tucker, together with Bob... I appreciated immediately that he knows what is going on... the specific nature of these trials. Normally one can bargain with the state over certain matters. The things that can be bargained about here are quite different. It is, in principle, desirable to go into the witness box because evidence can then be cross-examined. But that principle is not an absolute one and it is usually undesirable and can aggravate matters *here* — luckily we agree on this and on the low-key nature of our defense...

CHAPTER 8

Statement from the Dock

Delivered by Raymond Suttner in the Supreme Court, Durban, on November 6, 1975:

I HAVE furthered the aims of the African National Congress and the South African Communist Party. This [course of action] was carefully considered. I want to tell the court why I acted in this way and still consider it correct.

From my earliest encounters with black people I have been aware of the contrast between my own living circumstances and theirs. I felt, from the beginning, that it could not be right that some people, merely because they were black, should have to live with less than they needed.

In my home background, I was encouraged to treat all human beings with dignity and respect. I learned that a man's color is no indication of his worth. I learned that black people had hopes and worries like everyone else, that they needed health and security, food and shelter.

Nothing that I learned as I grew older seemed to justify the situation where the rights that people have, the disabilities they endure, the place where they live, where they can work and who they can love, should all be determined by the color of their skin.

At school, and especially at university, I used every opportunity to argue against racism and for a common society where black and white could live together in peace and justice. Despite what I heard from most whites, I came to feel that equal rights were not something to be feared but the basis of real security. With all that was claimed for apartheid, there were, nevertheless, few who would argue that it could benefit all people, or that it could benefit all people equally or that it could even provide sufficient for all people.

Notwithstanding its rechristening as "separate development," none of the main features of apartheid have changed. The black people have never sought "Bantustans" and similar unrepresentative institutions.

Their real leaders have made it clear that they consider the whole of South Africa to be their homeland and that they will accept nothing less than their right to share fully in its power and prosperity.

The suppression of the ANC, the Communist Party and other allies in the liberation movement has meant that we do not hear calls for equality — in one, undivided South Africa — as frequently as we should. Their banning may have created the illusion of a wider acceptance of apartheid than there in fact is. We do not hear the most outspoken critiques of apartheid nor what the liberation movement would substitute for it. It is hard to find out what the ANC and its allies stand for. We generally only hear what their opponents say about these organizations.

I have been cut off from information about the ANC and Communist Party for most of my life. I was told of the evils of these organizations and heard all the charges of their alleged villainy. I was never allowed to hear their answer. In trying to find a meaningful political role in our situation, I have sought information about the ANC and its allies. When I read their literature and heard their aims, I saw that they did not, as their detractors suggested, advocate indiscriminate violence or the setting up of a tyrannical regime. I found that they had simple aims — to make a new society that would benefit not a few, but all. "South Africa" in the words of the Freedom Charter, "belongs to all who live in it, black and white, and... no government can justly claim authority unless it is based on the will of all the people."

My own political experience, mainly as a university student, and what I knew of our political history, had led me to conclude that radical criticism, no matter how valid, is either ignored, rejected as illegitimate or suppressed. Even in pursuing quite legal activities, militants stand a good chance of finding themselves banned, arrested without trial or having other restrictions placed upon them.

When I studied their backgrounds, I had little doubt that the banning of the ANC and Communist Party were undemocratic and unjustified acts. There had been no evidence of these organizations using violence before they were made unlawful bodies. Similarly, their turn to violence could hardly be called unprovoked or without cause. What response did they receive for their many years' pursuit of non-violence? Chief Albert Luthuli, a man of peace, if ever there was one, gave this answer:

"Who will deny that 30 years of my life have been spent knocking in vain, patiently, moderately and modestly, at a closed and barred door? What have been the fruits of my many years of moderation? Has there been any reciprocal tolerance or moderation from the government? No! On the contrary, the past 30 years have seen the greatest number of laws restricting our rights and progress, until today we have reached a stage where we have almost no rights at all."

For many years, I participated in protest activities — organizing petitions, holding placards, marching — and various other demonstrations against racial discrimination. None of these protests, or any similar ones, had any effect. But, what is more, the government denied our right to oppose them — leaders were banned or arrested without trial.

Around 1969, I started to ask myself whether I was doing this out of habit or whether these activities were achieving anything. The minister of education had left few illusions about their impact when he said in one statement that student petitions went straight into his waste-paper basket. Every year, new laws made protest more difficult. Yet, each year seemed to make opposition more necessary. Although black people grew increasingly dissatisfied, it made little impression. The white people did not have to consider the views of those who were disenfranchised.

I could see no possibility of ending apartheid through appeals to the government, and that was virtually the only course open to opponents who accepted our constitutional framework.

I continued to read about and discuss ANC policy. What I heard and read strengthened the admiration that I felt for the selflessness and dedication of men like Albert Luthuli, Bram Fischer, Nelson Mandela, Walter Sisulu, Govan Mbeki, Ahmed Kathrada and Denis Goldberg — some of the leaders in the liberation movement.

I came to feel that I could contribute most by aiding the ANC and its allies. I came to believe that the course that they followed was the only way to achieve freedom in our country. It is true that this means supporting a policy that includes the use of violence. The law under which I am charged does not ask the court to enquire what precipitated the violence. The court cannot dismiss these charges because the ANC and its allies were forced to take up arms. It cannot rule that ANC violence is a response to the violence of the apartheid regime.

Yet there are factors in the ANC decision that make it abundantly clear that they did not desire violence, that they use it reluctantly. ANC strategies are aimed at minimizing conflict and promoting democracy. Violence is not seen as an instant answer to all problems. Certain types of actions, such as terrorism or undisciplined heroic acts, even if well motivated, are rejected as exacerbating the bitterness and hostility. I am convinced that this policy responds to suppression and oppression in the only way possible.

The work that I have done for the freedom movement has made rigorous demands upon me. It was not pleasant to spend my spare time licking envelopes, duplicating, typing, and sticking on stamps. Most of the time I did this work on my own. It is true that I need not have done this. But I honestly concluded that this was the best way of contributing to our future. The goals for which I worked warranted whatever sacrifices were required.

It is obvious that these activities had to be carried out in secret, that I had to conceal them from my closest friends and family. Though I am used to being frank and open, the nature of the work forced me to be silent. Though I would have been pleased to debate these ideas freely, I could not jeopardize the security of my organizations and others who were involved. Also, I did not want to endanger others who were not involved but who could have been prejudiced by knowledge of my acts.

With regard to the evidence of Kuny and Roxburgh, I acted on the basis of strong indications from them that they were willing to act in unlawful activities, that they knew the dangers and were prepared to accept the consequences of their involvement. While I strongly discouraged their withdrawal for practical and security reasons, I never said that they could not withdraw. Kuny has suggested that it was necessary to conceal from me his reading of a certain political work with which I would not have agreed. Since I would have considered a discussion of such a book valuable, in order to clarify his and my own views, I cannot understand that he had any reason for stealth.

Regarding the charge of training, this was for the most part ancillary to the production and distribution of the pamphlets...

I have no doubt that the policies of the ANC and Communist Party hold out a bright future for us. I know that the liberation movement is neither anti-white nor terrorist, that it works for the day when men and women will have all the comfort and security that they need. I realize that this is not the picture presented to South Africans. But because I know that it is true, I could not obey a law expressly aimed at suppressing these democratic forces. It was my duty, I believe, to act honestly and for the benefit of all our people, to inform them of their situation and the way to an alternative, free society. That was the aim of my work.

I am not the first person, nor the last, to break the law for moral reasons. I realize that the Court may feel that I should have shown more respect for legality. Normally, I would show this respect. I would consider it wrong to break laws that serve the community. But I have acted against laws that do not serve the majority of South Africans, laws that inculcate hostility between our people and preclude the tolerance and cooperation that is necessary to a contented and peaceful community.

For this, I will go to prison. But I cannot accept that it is wrong to act, as I have done, for freedom and equality, for an end to racial discrimination and poverty. I have acted in the interests of the overwhelming majority of our people. I am confident that I have their support.

CHAPTER 9

The Judgment: "Conduct Reprehensible"

AT MY first court appearance on August 3, 1975, the state announced that I would not be allowed bail. Under the Terrorism Act, it was not for the courts, but for the attorney general, to decide whether to permit bail.

One month before the trial, it was announced that Lawrence Kuny and Jennifer Roxburgh were being held under the Criminal Procedure Act. "They are not to be charged with allegations of participating in terrorist activities. They are being held in custody as witnesses in the trial of Mr. Suttner."

The indictment was broadcast on state radio. It tried to create an atmosphere of alarm, by referring to the revolutionary aims of the ANC and SACP, which it claimed were "...to overthrow the government of the Republic of South Africa by means which include violence, strikes, economical and industrial disorder or guerilla warfare and sabotage." The indictment stated that I had printed, published and disseminated literature to further these aims. Furthermore, I had recruited and trained Kuny and Roxburgh to assist in these tasks, by forming an underground cell.

My trial began on November 3, 1975, and I was sentenced on November 13. There was no chance that I would be acquitted. I decided to plead guilty, though I provided a justification for my actions in my unsworn statement from the dock (see previous chapter).

The state, however, wanted to build up an atmosphere that would justify a heavy sentence. They went through a laborious process of proving every element of the evidence, even though these points had already been admitted by the defense.

Kuny testified about the training he had received. He referred to small pink slips of paper, which were notes I had used during this training. The *Daily News* of November 5, 1975, reported Kuny as saying that I had instructed him not to cooperate with the police in the event of his being arrested. It also reported that Kuny was told how to resist possible police beatings during interrogations.

The *Daily News* said: "Referring to his arrest in June, Mr. Kuny said he believed that he was to be beaten up but, on the contrary, the police had acted like gentlemen and had not laid a finger on him."

During cross-examination of Kuny, my advocate, George Bizos, asked him if anyone were to interpret his evidence as being that of a young, ignorant, stupid man who had been pulled in by a much cleverer and intellectually superior man, would it be the impression he wanted to create?

Kuny responded: "I don't suggest that someone stood with a gun and said, 'You must do it.' I am not trying to create the impression that I was misled." Kuny admitted he was interested in Marxism before he met me, although he hadn't read any of the revolutionary books that I had given him in the course of his training.

He said that, when first arrested, he had protested his innocence. But, after the Security Police were "so nice to me, I decided to show them where the pamphlets were." (As reported in the *Natal Mercury*, November 5, 1975.)

Roxburgh's evidence was very straightforward. She explained how she came to accept the use of violence. According to the *Natal Mercury* (November 5, 1975), she said: "I had previously held ideals of anti-violence. The books (which Suttner had given me) reconciled my ideas regarding the use of violence. I read that the cost of revolution need not be as high as maintaining the status quo in a country."

Roxburgh said she had translated the Freedom Charter into Zulu, in order to distribute it in a pamphlet.

As was conventional in these cases, an alleged ANC defector also gave evidence about being trained as a saboteur. His name was allegedly "withheld for his own safety." The rest of the evidence was technical — showing typewriters and duplicators that were used, copies of the pamphlets and evidence about where various items were purchased.

Then it was my turn to respond, which I did through my statement from the dock (see previous chapter).

THERE IS a legal saying to the effect that every person has his or her day in court. If convicted, a criminal usually presents a plea in mitigation and tries to explain why the crime has been committed and to plead for leniency.

There were some cases in which political prisoners had followed this course of action — in line with conventional legal cases — possibly, to obtain a lower sentence, or because they were motivated by bitterness towards their comrades. In a well-publicized case in 1975, one of South Africa's foremost Afrikaner poets, Breyten Breytenbach, threw himself on the mercy of the court, pleading for the minimum sentence, with the prosecutor and Security Police investigator adding their voices in his support. (It did not work. The judge sentenced Breytenbach to nine years.)

In general, however, or in most cases, political prisoners avoided the mode of legal defense used in conventional cases. Their court appearances were part of a wider ideological battle. And by standing up against the state, the political fighter was ranged against the authorities in a way that was quite different from an individual offender, who had simply fallen foul of laws that are generally accepted as being in the interests of society.

The individual offender tried to escape punishment in terms of the existing norms of society. Unlike the political prisoner, he or she is not challenging the wider social order or the norms upon which it is based.

Different judges might cast varying glosses on the law, but in their oath of office had undertaken to administer justice according to the law. But the actions of political prisoners were directed against that very law — or, at least, those parts of it that we regarded as unjust and could not accept for wider moral reasons.

Thus, it was not surprising that judges and magistrates did not embrace our concept of justice. Instead, they described our actions as ones that no civilized state or authority could tolerate — equating our challenge to, and disregard of, the apartheid laws with a challenge to the very idea of law.

A politically motivated defense tended to be prejudicial to the personal interests of the accused. It made it harder to get out of jail and may have increased the length of our sentences. It tended to make certain types of legal defense impossible. In some cases, in order to safeguard our organizations or security, we had to conceal some of what might have freed us from jail.

There were some things I just could not say, even if they reduced my sentence, because they may have reflected negatively on the liberation movement. I first experienced this while an accused person; and then again in the 1980s, when applying for release from detention during the state of emergency. To some extent, we sometimes aided the process of legal conviction because we were unable to advance arguments to free us.

Appearing in court as a representative of our movement meant we had a duty to engage the courts and challenge the system under which we were tried. That meant attempting to get the lowest possible sentence, or to be released. But the courtroom was also a place where we could be heard, albeit to a limited degree — a place where we could make a public statement in defense of the liberation struggle.

Therefore, I could not align myself with the liberation movement to just a limited degree, and dissociate myself from "less tasteful" policies, such as the use of force. Some people, in the loneliness of their prison cells, might have found this course attractive — and selectively rejected liberation movement policies that were harder to explain in court. When you do have your day in court, you want people to at least understand why you acted as you did.

This meant, in the case of people involved with the South African liberation movement, rejecting the labels that the regime wanted to attach to us — such as "terrorists," and so on. We also wanted the fact of torture to be acknowledged, and that we had experienced various other losses, while undertaking political activities that had brought us no gain.

In many cases, people went to jail without the truth ever emerging. Deploying a maze of legalisms and moralizing, courts often de-legitimized what freedom fighters had done. We knew we had broken the law, but many judges denied the reasoning behind our actions, and thus allied themselves with the reasoning of the apartheid regime.

I WAS dissuaded by my lawyers from raising the matter of my own torture in court. They said it would not be credible, since there was not a confession before the court and I was not going into the witness box. I accepted this reasoning at the time. But I now think it was wrong. I should have described my torture. Even if the court had not accepted my account, the public would have known the truth.

The judge in my case gratuitously implied that the Security Police had surprised state witness Kuny with their "politeness." In case anyone were to imagine that terrible things happened in detention, here was Kuny giving state evidence, having found that he was dealing with gentle people.

As an academic, I had researched the ideological role of the South African judiciary, and how, in their judgments, they provided "authoritative" rationales for apartheid repression. (See, for example, my paper, "The Judiciary — its ideological role in South Africa" (1986), in the *International Journal of the Sociology of Law*, pp. 47-66.)

Twenty-four years after the event, when I read the judgment given in my own case by Mr. Justice Neville James, Judge President of Natal, it is clear that he went beyond the call of duty, in the words he used to convict and sentence me.

It was correct, in terms of the law of the time, that I should be found guilty. But James (like many others of his colleagues) also tried to assimilate moral and legal guilt. Thus, when considering the evidence given against me by Kuny and Roxburgh, James found I had manipulated my friendship with them, in order to induce them to take part in illegal activities. Thus, in regard to recruitment of Roxburgh, the judge stated:

"I have no doubt that the accused, as a result of his fairly close friendship with her, decided that he would be able to persuade her to enter his political orbit, and thus to make use of her skills for the purposes of his organization. And that he did so without paying any heed to the perils and anxieties which she would endure by joining into activities which he knew were completely illegal (even though, at the beginning, she did not). I consider that the accused's conduct in persuading his good and trusted friend, Miss Roxburgh, to help in his subversive activities was reprehensible and that he imposed upon her because of her regard for him."

Regarding Kuny, the judge said: "In passing, I should say that Kuny appears to have cooperated with the investigating police almost from the moment he was taken into custody. This apparently happened because he was quite unprepared for the politeness with which they treated him..."

In sentencing me, the judge said: "...he was prepared to allow his friends to risk their future for his cause."

The judge depicts this cause (for which I had risked my future) as some selfish venture belonging to me. The judge also uses the language usually deployed to convict someone for fraud, as if there was some gain involved. In reality, underground work entailed risking my professional career and the ordinary comforts of home life. The judge also ignored the prospect of Kuny's release, as an inducement for the latter's cooperation. Instead, police "politeness" is given the credit.

In passing sentence on me, the judge continued: "There is no question of his succumbing to sudden temptation or pressure... I consider that his reasons for breaking the law, even if sincerely held, afford little basis for mitigation of sentence. I have no doubt that many terrorists all over the world who have killed innocent people by the indiscriminate use of explosives claim that they were morally justified in so doing, but such conduct cannot be tolerated in a civilized community. And the motives of the terrorists are of minor importance when deciding upon an appropriate sentence, because the requirements of law and order are paramount.

"Similarly, a man like the accused, who promotes revolutionary change in South Africa and urges others, by means of widely distributed subversive pamphlets, to support that change by using every available means, including violence and guerilla warfare, cannot lay claim to special consideration from the Court because he asserts that he has acted from the highest moral principles. Although the accused has not himself detonated a bomb, he had endeavored to light a trail of gunpowder, which he believes will cause a bomb to explode...

"While it is true that he never disclosed to his colleagues, students and friends, or to his family, that he had embarked on an illegal course and, as far as we know, only recruited two assistants, that does not redound entirely to his credit. For it seems to indicate that he possessed the fanatical dedication of a resolute man who had embarked on a secret subversive course and had disciplined his life to prevent any sort of suspicion falling upon him.

"I am acutely and sadly aware of the fact that in sending the accused to jail, as I am obliged to do, his brilliant academic and legal career will be blighted and that his incarceration will bring distress both to himself, his distinguished mother and her family. But for the reasons I have already given these matters, although relevant, cannot be carried too far as a basis for mitigation of sentence. I am therefore not prepared to pass the minimum sentence permitted by law..."

As I left the dock and gave the ANC clenched fist salute, people in the gallery, led by Winnie Mandela, responded by raising their fists and singing the national anthem, *Nkosi sikelel' iAfrika*.

IN MY trial, Kuny and Roxburgh gave evidence for the state and, for that evidence, received indemnity from prosecution. For many years, people who did this were shunned within the democratic movement, particularly in the black community. Some who repeatedly gave state evidence were executed by Umkhonto we Sizwe.

While Jennifer Roxburgh tended to restrict herself to the evidence, Lawrence Kuny went out of his way to exonerate the police from any suspicions, both in court and after his release from custody.

In the *Natal Mercury* of November 14, 1975, Kuny is quoted as saying: "My attitudes, both to politics and the Security Police, have changed drastically since I was arrested... I now realize that violent struggle is not the way things are going to change in South Africa...

"When I was picked up by the police, I thought all sorts of dreadful things were going to happen to me but, to my surprise, discovered the Security Police are very warm, kindhearted people. During my time in jail, they were an enormous comfort to me and took pains to cheer me up whenever they saw I was depressed."

But Kuny gives a different account in his unpublished manuscript, written in 1975/6: "...I'd been in my cell, quietly thinking. Now, I was surrounded by all these men. The suddenness and formality of their actions threw me into confusion and panic.

"In the middle of this muddled state, Raymond walked into the room. For a split second our eyes met. Was that the man I knew? Gone were the twinkling blue eyes; they were tired eyes; dark rings contrasting with pale flesh. And the pale cheeks were puffed out; his lips hanging open showed his teeth. His hair was disheveled; but the eyes were the worst; they stared blankly, unaware of where they were, there was no reaction in their bright color. There was no mistake about his eyes; they were the eyes of a man who'd been to hell. He slumped forward like a lifeless doll; the men grabbed him by the shirt collar and dragged him out of the room. Raymond was too dazed to react.

"I looked at that face with naked terror.

"Since that night, I have wondered just why Raymond had been brought into the room where I was being kept. Did they want to show me what happened to people who didn't cooperate with them? Was it to show me that those who didn't talk were tortured? If this was their plan, then it succeeded. My terror was such that my whole body ached with fear. I will never forget that night, and those eyes; it was then that I understood what was meant by the word *fascism*." (Kuny's emphasis.)

While I still deplore the fact of anyone giving state evidence against freedom fighters, Kuny and especially Roxburgh were quite unlike some of the more notorious, professional state witnesses of the time. And, in Roxburgh's case, it was the last that anyone heard of her in public, as far as I know.

Kuny and Roxburgh had worked with me for only eight or nine months. They did not have time to assume the level of commitment and discipline needed to cope with detention, or to resist the threats, torture and blandishments of the police.

In the past, I would not have anything to do with former state witnesses. Now, however, I think we need to give these people a chance — to reintegrate with society, and contribute towards the building of the new South Africa.

CHAPTER 10

In "Maximum"

IMMEDIATELY AFTER my conviction on November 13, 1975, I returned to my cell in Durban Central Prison and was issued khaki pants and a shirt. The next morning, three prison officials transferred me by car to Pretoria Maximum Security Prison. I was handcuffed and my legs were in chains. I could live with handcuffs but always found leg irons particularly degrading. I think I associated chains with slavery. In any event, they were very inconvenient because they made normal movement impossible. Before leaving, one prison official told me he had a gun — just in case he had to shoot *dassies* [Afrikaans for little hares that lived in the veld].

I arrived at Pretoria "Maximum," but have only a vague memory of what it looked like, apart from its being huge and shiny, with mirror-like floors. Prisoners are not shown around the premises. You are whisked from one section to another and quickly deposited in whatever part of the prison your cell is located.

The Durban officials delivered me as if I was a parcel. The receiving officer looked down at me with the type of hostility reserved for a reptile. I found this kind of response hard to get used to. My own self-image was that of a person who was reasonably likable, yet, without us having exchanged a word, this official had apparently taken an acute dislike to me.

To report my arrival at the prison, a form dated November 14, 1975, was sent to my mother, which stated: "22028/75 was today admitted to this institution from Durban." The document went on to list my grouping and "privileges":

"Group D. One non-contact visit of 30 minutes, from one person, per month. Write and receive one letter per month."

Limited as my conditions may have been, they represented a considerable improvement on those encountered by the first batch of political prisoners in the 1960s, who, at that time, were allowed only one visit every six months.

I had expected to join the other political prisoners immediately, but instead was held in solitary confinement at "Maximum" for three and a half months.

"Maximum" is a terrible prison. It is where hangings took place before the new democratic government abolished the death penalty. Day and night, prisoners sentenced to death would sing hymns and, as the moment of death approached, the singing would grow more and more frenzied.

Death row was also used for prisoners who were being punished with solitary confinement. It was also used for holding those whom the authorities, for whatever reason, wanted to separate from other prisoners. This included people considered (or described as) mentally disturbed, such as Dimitri Tsafendas, who killed Dr. Verwoerd. The conditions on death row are well captured in Jeremy Cronin's poem "Death row" first published in 1983 and reprinted in his 1999 collection, *Inside and Out*.

At first, I was kept in a section on my own. I was in one of six cells. Above the cell was a catwalk along which warders patrolled. These warders were able to watch my every movement. When I was allowed into the small yard for exercise, warders armed with rifles stood guard on the walls above. I had no idea what existed outside of my cell and the yard.

Once or twice, I was taken into an office, off a passageway, to see the doctor. Sometimes my hair was cut in one of these offices. What existed beyond that, I did not know. Rumor had it that there were beautiful gardens where deer roamed freely. All I knew about were the awful sounds of death row. Not just the singing of the condemned, but the terrible banging and crashing of steel doors, jingling keys and aggressive shouting of the warders.

The anxiety I experienced was heightened by the resumed interrogations carried out by Security Police. One morning, I was taken into the exercise yard where some 10 or more senior police were waiting. I knew some of their names from court cases and reports of torture. They had an informal discussion with me. This was followed by questioning on two or three occasions, when they tried to establish whether I knew who was involved in underground cells in Capetown. I did not know — even if I had wanted to tell them. The way underground units were organized ensured that one knew what one needed to know and no more; or, at any rate, that was the intention. Consequently, I knew nothing about people working in other parts of the country.

These meetings with the Security Police, and the prospects of further encounters, aroused great fear. What could they do to me now? What protection did I have? Was there any law to protect me? When I saw my lawyer, he did not believe there was any law to prevent the police from questioning me after sentence, though he knew of no precedent. I had no idea how often they would come. When they stopped coming, I did not know they had stopped, whether they had finished questioning me or not. Any day, they might return.

One of the main interrogators was Spyker ("Nail") van Wyk, a notorious torturer from Capetown. I think he reveled in his reputation and wanted me to fear him, which I did.

Some warders in "Maximum," for some reason, felt they should do what they could to make life more difficult for me. I cannot remember what sparked it, but after a week or two I found myself enveloped in an atmosphere of total hostility and aggression. No one had a friendly or courteous word to say. Maybe I was naive to expect any such thing, but part of my upbringing was to say please and thank you and not to speak rudely to others, and to expect similar behavior in return. I quickly learned that such a code was not in operation here. In fact, I encountered continual shouting and threatening behavior, which, although it stopped short of physical assault, created much anxiety, as I imagined I might be assaulted. At one point, I remember one of the sergeants taking off his cap, which is often a prelude to assault — though he did not actually hit me.

Also, I was new to prison and there was no one to offer advice or pump courage into me — as there would be later, when I was moved from "Maximum" and joined other political prisoners in Pretoria Local Prison. During this period, I was thoroughly terrorized throughout the day. Some of these warders had developed particularly sadistic temperaments. Far from shunning the gallows, I learned that they would specially come to work on a day when a hanging was to take place even if they were supposed to be off-duty.

I remember seeing a doctor — but there was no such thing as a privileged doctor/patient relationship in "Maximum." You would see the doctor in the presence of all the warders and he would make jokes at your expense for their benefit. I remember asking for a sweater, because I was cold, but he ridiculed the request, gearing his response to his audience and hardly listening to me.

When I say I was given haircuts in one of the offices, I am not speaking of the gentle cutting and trimming of hair. Sergeant Arlow, who was in charge of the section in which I was held, cut my hair. He was very tall, thin, with a handlebar moustache. He was not very intelligent; but that made little difference to the great power that he wielded over the lives of prisoners. Arlow was left to his own devices. He appeared, to the officers in charge, to run things smoothly and none of us dared complain. Apart from the few moments when an officer would whisk through the section, Arlow ruled our lives. When he cut my hair, he would bang my head from side to side with the trimmer. The hair cutting process was a variant of being used as a punching bag.

I was very hungry in "Maximum." The food was not good, but I ate it all and needed more. But there was nothing to be had after 3 p.m., until the next morning. Even in this place there were, however, glimmerings of goodwill. On at least one occasion, a young warder gave me a piece of dried *boerewors*, pushing it through the wire mesh. *Boerewors* is literally sausage of the *boere* [farmers], traditional sausage made by Afrikaners.

I had no idea how long I would remain in "Maximum." One day, after I had spent three and a half months there, they came and told me to pack my things. The prison officials never said where you were going, whether it was to the doctor, to see the police, to a new cell or, as in this case, to a different prison. You would find out only once you arrived. My way of getting some idea of what was happening was to ask whether I should take my toilet paper. If not, that was a sign that I was leaving the prison. If you were merely changing cells, you would take your blankets and toilet paper with you.

The following (abridged) letters were written in the Maximum Security section of Pretoria Central Prison in late 1975 and early 1976.

November 30, 1975
Dear Family,

I think often of you and my friends outside. It has been good to have support over this period and to know that you are thinking of me now. It is rather hard, but, somehow, the days seem to pass. My present cell is reasonably quiet, so I sleep quite well.

I have some worries, small compared to my normal life, and I hope that these will disappear in time. I am hesitant about stating my feelings since things may change again (as they have recently) for better or worse. I was recently moved to a more difficult situation but having experienced a few days, I cope more easily. I gather that I will stay in this part of the prison for about two months, after which I go to "Local."

Almost my whole life is, now, in this cell. It is lonely and empty. I speak only to officials, mainly when they open/close the door. It is hard to get my bearings, since I can see nothing of the outside (Pretoria) or the rest of the prison. There are few indications of time. I cannot obtain the necessities of life or control anything on my own...

But this is, I suppose, characteristic of prison life — a dependent and stripped-down existence. I have not contemplated anything but cooperation. It is the only practical thing and does not, in itself, cause me any difficulty. There are naturally many jarring and irritating incidents, but I try to see beyond them rather than becoming bitter.

Naturally I cannot strike the right approach immediately and do often get upset. Generally, however, it is OK... So do not worry.

December 11, 1975
Dear Family,

I have sent off the six Xmas cards allowed. I may receive 12, so, if not too late, please try to regulate.

I have enjoyed the visits and I hope that the last one relieved some of your worries. While I see little point in my present type of confinement it is not a source of misery. I just have to come to terms with it. It is lucky that this did not happen 10 years ago, because I probably would have been much less prepared, psychologically. People are best able to deal with this situation to the extent that they have sorted out and convinced *themselves* of their priorities...

So far, I have been able to get very good books. Nevertheless, reading only occupies a few hours — with a maximum of two books a week. It is not so much idleness, but constant confinement in a cell that is difficult.

Most school principals would be horrified at the suggestion that their hostels are like prisons. Yet most of the unpleasant things that I have experienced here, I recognize from school. There is a similar structure of authority and power.

I lead very much of a double life — thinking and feeling one thing, yet acting differently. I behave as they expect a prisoner to behave. It is sometimes very disconcerting since you never *do*. Things happen *to* you. You do not generally know when or how, and it is best to save your questions for more important occasions. There is no room for *individual* personality. You are part of a situation in which only a certain (narrow) range of responses are possible.

I can handle this — just as long as the basic things like medicine are organized. Though a month has gone by, the time has not dragged as much as I had anticipated.

January 12, 1976
Dear Family,

I realize how difficult and very limited you must find our present opportunities for communication. It is hard to say much of consequence, and almost impossible for me to make a meaningful contribution to the discussion of family problems... But nothing can be done about this.

CHAPTER 11

Serving my Sentence

THIS CHAPTER covers more than seven years of my life, yet it is comparatively short. This is due, I think, to the sameness of prison life. All days in prison seem alike and it is difficult to accurately recall when things have happened. Outside, there are various rites of passage and landmarks that fix the phases of one's life — the achievement of certain goals, changing relationships through marriage, parenthood, divorce and so on. This is not the case inside prison.

Even when one does have knowledge of a significant event — such as the birth of a child to a relative or close friend — it is impossible to relate to the event directly. The child, in the absence of a personal relationship and direct experience, remains just a name — like the name of a person in a novel or history book. While I was in jail, two of my brothers and one sister married and became parents. Over time, I received photographs of my new relatives, but it was impossible for me to relate to these changes as I would have done under normal circumstances.

The entire framework of prison existence is aimed at turning the prisoner into a passive object — an object whose every movement, whether inside or outside his or her cell, is either determined by others or severely limited. The prisoner's number was said by officials to be the most important part of his or her identity and there was a pre-numbering period when prisoners were deemed to have no identity at all. To be allocated a prison number was to be saved from this nothingness.

The language of prisons expressed the view of prisoners being regarded as things — as objects whose management was in the hands of warders. Thus it was common to refer to prisoners in Afrikaans — the language of the prisons and police force — as *eenhede*, or units. You would often hear announcements directing a particular warder to come and collect his "units." The words used for "collect" and "to bring" are *afhaal* and *aflaai*, and both are associated with the delivery or loading of things. Many of the ordinary criminal prisoners conformed to these expectations. They waited for their cells to be opened for exercise — and said nothing if this was later than regulations demanded. They waited to be asked before speaking, went back to their cells when told to do so, showered at the times allowed, accepted food when it was given and ate it hot or cold, all without complaint.

In "Maximum," they returned to their cells at night, first putting their shoes and spoons outside the door, as was required for security reasons.

In February 1976, I was transferred from the Maximum Security section of Pretoria Central to Pretoria Local, where I joined a number of other political prisoners. Together, we challenged this dehumanized concept of prisoners and the prison world, and generally prevented it from being applied to us.

For example, we did not hold out our numbered prison cards at "inspections." In most prisons, a daily feature of life was to have the head of the prison inspect the prisoners. This was to see that everything was in order, that all the prisoners were present, that the prison had been cleaned and to hear complaints. Most prisoners stood to attention and held out their cards at these inspections, with their clothes neatly ironed and shoes shining. But the hearing of "complaints" or "requests" was generally a formality.

Denis Goldberg tells the story of how, when he was in Pretoria Central, he responded to a request for complaints. The officer was moving so quickly that he skidded some yards down the passage before he could come back to hear Denis.

As political prisoners, we were very conscious of our dignity and any attempt to undermine it. We expected, and demanded, respect. If they called us we would go, but we would not run or move with undue haste. It was common for warders to shout *"Kom, kom, kom!"* at prisoners; which in English literally means "Come, come, come!" But in Afrikaans it sounds much harsher and more degrading. If a warder shouted this at us — and new warders would sometimes try — we would normally object to being summoned as if we were dogs. The prison regulations made reference to treating prisoners in a civil manner — as we would never fail to remind officials who deviated from this rule.

Prisoners were expected to stand to attention when speaking to an officer. Our version of being at attention was by no means a military one. We would not fawn or beg; though we adopted various stratagems to win concessions that might improve our conditions.

I came into an environment in which, after long years of struggle, some of the conventional ways of treating prisoners had been reversed and the prisoners ran many aspects of their lives. This was a reasonably attractive environment, which included a lawn and garden. It also included a kitchen, complete with stove and a table, where we ate our meals on plates, using knives and forks. All of this was quite different from my experience in "Maximum" or in Durban Central Prison.

Our cells were much better than those occupied by Nelson Mandela and other black prisoners in places such as Robben Island. Ours were slightly bigger, were fitted with basins, and had hot water and flush toilets — which was not the case on the island. However, we heard odds and ends, via the International Red Cross, about the conditions of women prisoners in Barberton and Kroonstad, and these seemed always to be very hard, worse than for most of the men in their various prisons.

In some ways, we were a community that owed a massive debt to the early pioneers who had cleared the way for progress. Some of these remained with us — people like Denis Goldberg, who conducted most of our negotiations in the prison.

Denis, who had been jailed for life during the Rivonia trial — at the same time as Nelson Mandela — was very inventive and knew how to do numerous things to make our lives easier. There was nothing he couldn't fix. That was an important skill, because it was hard to replace the things that one takes for granted outside. (Or, it would take some time before the replacement arrived and you would have to do without something necessary to your well-being.)

We played tennis with *tennissette* (wooden) bats, which were not strong enough for robust games. Denis would reinforce the bats in the prison workshop so they could be used on a three-quarter-sized tennis court. If books fell apart, he would simply rebind them. At Christmas, the Prisons Department allowed us to buy 500g of sweets, 500g of fruit and 500g of biscuits. Denis, and another fellow prisoner, John Matthews, would supplement this ration by making additional sweets. In the plain, unvarying prison environment, with its unvarying diet, something that tasted a little unusual made a difference.

John Matthews was in for 15 years for his work in the Communist Party and Umkhonto we Sizwe. He came from a working-class background and had spent decades in the struggle, unobtrusively making things happen. One such thing was building, with his own hands, a temporary wooden stage for the 1955 Congress of the People, at which the Freedom Charter was adopted. Unlike many of us, John enjoyed doing woodwork. Marius Schoon (who was serving 12 years as a political prisoner after being trapped by an agent provocateur) used to say that John created a lot of "surplus value."

Jeremy Cronin has recorded aspects of John Matthews's life in his memorable poem "Walking on Air," in his collection *Inside and Out*.

David Kitson, who had been operating deep underground, was sentenced to 20 years in the "second Rivonia trial" for acts of sabotage. Dave used to divide and dish up our food, something that he had apparently done in the army, during WWII. He was always in good humor and that is important when things are tense.

For a short while, just after my arrival, Marius Schoon was also held at Pretoria Local. Raymond Thoms, who had been sentenced with Marius, was also an inmate. But, when I arrived, the other prisoners had not been speaking to him for about 10 years. Thoms had given evidence for the state against Harold Strachan, after Strachan exposed prison conditions in *The Rand Daily Mail* newspaper.

The Prisons Department had lined up a whole troop of *bandiete* [the term used by the prison authorities to describe people convicted of criminal offences] to contest Strachan's allegations. But their real prize was to have one of the political prisoners give evidence against Strachan. Perhaps Thoms had hoped to be freed for this, but he served every single day of his sentence.

Isolating him was a very harsh response. But the community of political prisoners depended on trust. It was a very vulnerable group. It depended on mutual support and solidarity in the face of the authorities. What Thoms had done had made it impossible to keep him within that community. But he remained there, physically, which meant that his own comrades were, in effect, administering additional punishment over and above his sentence.

Others among us were Alexander Moumbaris, a citizen of France, who was serving 12 years for Umkhonto we Sizwe activities, and Sean Hosey, an Irish citizen, who was serving five years for assisting MK.

Jeremy Cronin and David Rabkin also arrived while I was in Pretoria Local. Jeremy and David were serving seven and 10 years, respectively, for issuing illegal pamphlets, just as I had done. David Rabkin was later to die in a MK training accident in Angola. Anyone who met him will know that his death was a very great loss to our struggle. He would have made a substantial contribution to South Africa in the present period of rebuilding.

Later, Tony Holiday arrived — sentenced to six years for pamphlet distribution. Guy Berger arrived and served two years for ANC activities. Tim Jenkin and Stephen Lee were sentenced to 12 and eight years, respectively, for pamphlet distribution. And Renfrew Christie was sentenced to 10 years for acquiring some of the apartheid regime's nuclear secrets for the ANC.

As I have already mentioned, the earlier political prisoners in Pretoria Local had fought and won many battles, making life a lot easier for those of us who came after them, in the 1970s. Hugh Lewin's book, *Bandiet*, gives some idea of how difficult things were in the beginning.

Hugh Lewin had spent seven years inside for activities connected with the African Resistance Movement, a mainly white group with roots in the Liberal Party. All those from this particular group had been released by the time I arrived in the prison.

By that time, most of the worst excesses were no more and some of the most extreme personalities among the warders were merely part of folklore, and no longer our tormentors.

The terms boers and *boere* [farmers] were used to describe prison warders and police, and the authorities as a whole. These were Afrikaans words, but used to describe even English-speaking people. The words were applied to warders, police and Nationalist Party politicians.

Dave Kitson liked to say the early prisoners had tamed the boers. An example of how they had subdued the elements became evident a few days after my arrival. One Wednesday afternoon, I came down to the yard after being unlocked and saw a strange scene. There was, at that time, a boysenberry bush in the yard and, behind the bush, prisoners were sunbathing or lying on their backs. Others were idling around elsewhere. The warders were minding their own business in other parts of the yard.

This was a Wednesday afternoon, and both senior officers were off-duty. Everyone else acted as if they had the afternoon off, too. The warders were "tamed" in the sense that they did not consider it their duty to ensure that we were kept working. They did not mind what we were doing, so long as they did not land in any trouble themselves. If an officer was to have turned up unawares, the alarm would have been sounded pretty speedily, but short of that, nothing seemed to disturb the idyllic scene.

This may also illustrate something about the prevalent mentality of prison warders, as I experienced them, as opposed to the Security Police. The police tended to be fairly dedicated and did all they could to ensure we had a hard time and were put away for long periods. They were quite energetic about their work. They were fairly politicized and, in some cases, reasonably knowledgeable about politics. Warders were quite the opposite. They seemed content to lounge about, day after day, catching as much sleep as possible, doing as little work as they could. If there was an instruction to make life hard for us — for example, by carrying out regular searches — they would do this for a while, but never had much staying power.

Some warders were vicious, most were simply lazy. There was

something about the job of being a warder that dulled the mind. Warders might arrive at the prison young and fit, but, over the years, they grew paunches and learned how to sit. It seemed to be a sign of maturity, to be able to just sit, with eyes closed, yet sense when a superior officer might be about to arrive, and not be caught out. For the most part, they lived in a twilight zone somewhere between being asleep and awake.

A type of peaceful coexistence reigned most of the time, with neither the boers nor the prisoners seeking confrontation. For our own reasons, and in order to reduce their involvement in our lives, we kept the prison clean and did most of the things expected of us. It was rare that prison officials would go around scraping their fingers on the top of doors to look for dust, as one found in other prisons. We did not polish the floors because we convinced the warders that the tiles were made of a material that did not need polish.

Through this "balance," we managed to achieve a sense of tranquility most of the time. I remember how, during breaks from the prison workshop, we would sit with our backs to the wall in the prison yard and there was a sense of peace that I prized.

It suited both sides to reduce conflict and avoid situations where we had no option but to fight. We could not be at their throats every day. We did not have the energy for that. Conflicts drained us more than in normal life. The dullness of prison life made it harder to deal with sudden changes and it suited us to let some things pass, even when they were unjust.

Before I joined the others in Pretoria Local, I had conjured in my imagination some sort of idealized version of what the other political prisoners would be like. Being in solitary and having worked with very few people before my capture, I had ample time to amplify this fantasy. Consequently, I imaged that the liberation movement comprised figures such as one finds in revolutionary novels, people who had managed to eradicate all the normal human weaknesses.

It was a rude awakening to find that many of the men that I was to spend years with possessed various habits and traits that were not only contrary to what I had imagined but were downright irritating and difficult to live with.

We were together because of our common allegiance to the liberation movement. Outside of that commonality, a great deal divided us. And personality differences often made for serious incompatibility.

We were from different generations. Our life experiences and the character of our involvement in the struggle were very different. In theory, these differences might have enriched our community, but they often led to tensions. Every individual has his or her way of coping with extreme conditions. Sometimes one person's coping mechanisms disrupted another's. Some of us required solitude at times, when others wanted company in order to deal with a difficult situation. Some wanted to play while others were more inclined to read and study.

Prison life comprises a number of petty interactions that make up social life. Just as people may fall out over major issues outside prison, great anger could arise over minor issues within prison. For example, how someone dried a floor, or whether or not a mop was adequately rinsed, or dishes properly cleaned, could cause ill-feeling. Most of us had gone through some sort of training, but nothing prepared us for being thrown together in the way that we were — for so long, and with people we would not have chosen to be with in the normal course of events.

A recurring theme, in my early letters, is my sense of some loss of confidence. Barbara Hogan — a comrade who was sentenced to 10 years in a women's prison for her ANC activities — later revealed, in conversations with me, that she had similar experiences. Why was this so? I am not sure to what extent this "loss of confidence" was a factor on Robben Island, where there were large numbers of prisoners; but I suspect that it was less of a factor there.

My feeling is that it had something to do with small-group dynamics; and with the fact that our primary identity was that of "prisoner," an identity shaped by the environment of the prison. In our inter-personal relations, even the fact of being a *political* prisoner seemed less significant than other factors that were more to do with the constraints of living within the prison environment. (Though the fact that we were political prisoners was very significant to the boers.)

Being a political prisoner, being in jail because of your beliefs — and having made sacrifices that few others, and especially whites, had made — may have been exceptional in white South Africa, but it was not exceptional in our yard. It was something we simply assumed and took for granted. We did not find it unusual or even bother to mention it. This may have led us to value one another less than we should have done.

On a day-to-day basis, the identities that were significant — concerning one's inter-personal relations, as opposed to one's relations with the *boere* — were all prison-related; and they depended upon what one did, or failed to do, within the prison environment.

We had come to prison with a variety of identities — as husbands, brothers, uncles and so on. We had been professionals, or workers in a particular field. Our various skills and qualities had been recognized by the people with whom we socialized in the world outside. In prison, some of these qualities seemed totally irrelevant. The esteem you once enjoyed — as someone successful outside of prison — might be totally absent inside. Your former identity might have little or no relevance to life there. There was no way you could act out the old identities and they remained more or less "dormant."

Tensions between us were magnified by our mutual confinement. They were also heightened by the extreme censorship practiced inside prison, which limited contact with people outside. Bare and limited as our rights and privileges may have been, even these were not secure. There was nothing to which you were entitled that you could count on with certainty. The letters you might receive — even a single monthly letter of 500 words — would not always arrive; and if a letter did arrive, it might be cut to ribbons.

If you complained about not receiving letters, the authorities (such as the notorious Brigadier du Plessis) might suggest that people were simply not writing to you — that is, that your family and friends had abandoned you. Unsubtle as this may have been, it was meant to feed into real anxieties that some people harbored. (See my introductory notes and *Letter of complaint to the Commissioner of Prisons* in the following chapter.)

Insecurities about censorship added massively to the normal tension of being locked up in jail. Much of the day we looked forward to 4 p.m., when the post was supposed to arrive. We would wait anxiously, hoping to be in luck. We would try to recognize hand-writing or a type of envelope before the name was called. And a good letter would be treasured. I still remember how Jeremy Cronin received letters from his young wife, Ann Marie, who died while he was in jail. He would not open her letters until he was upstairs and could enjoy them in his cell.

And if it was your lucky day, and you did receive a letter, would it be intact? I remember cries of anger as prisoners discovered that letters had been cut to pieces.

The same insecurity was induced by the censorship of books and other literature. I was particularly vulnerable, because books were a key to my survival. There was much time for uninterrupted reading, and I wanted to use it to the full — so I would come out knowing more than when I first went into prison.

The first problem was one of sheer prison inefficiency. There was actually a well-stocked prison library. But in all the years I was inside, I must have received fewer than a dozen of the books I requested, though they were actually in stock. I remember how David Rabkin specified, in his library requests, that he wanted "no historical romances," but continually received *only* historical romances.

After much effort, we got hold of the library catalog and some of the entries revealed why the officials couldn't find our requests. *The Tempest*, for example, was listed as "science fiction" and *Romeo and Juliet* appeared under "author anonymous."

Some books, acquired by prisoners as part of the "privilege" of being in Group A, had been collected together, but I remember one day returning to my cell to find that half of these had been confiscated. I recall a sense of horror and powerlessness. We fought to get these books back. Some were returned to us, but most were not.

Study was a very important part of many prisoners' lives. The attraction was not so much to sit for examinations, but to have access to the University of South Africa library — albeit, subject to prison censorship. But the future of one's studies was always subject to great uncertainty. Where one had permission to study, the prison authorities would usually take their time in ensuring registration and obtaining prescribed books. This also meant — at least, until you were registered for study — that the lights in your cell would be switched off at 8 p.m.

But study was not only administered haphazardly; it was also sometimes under threat. At one point, studies were phased out, and we were given a limited period to complete whatever we were doing. But, a few years later, we saw their full reinstatement, together with an extension of possibilities, which allowed us to do postgraduate work, from 1982.

Tensions were also associated with the few visits to which we were entitled. Those present consisted of the prisoner and the visitor, plus a warder on each side. And the warders did not try to make their presence discreet. They stood right next to the prisoner and the visitor — and were very much an unwelcome part of the experience. Visits could be interrupted, or concluded, after only a few minutes, if the discussion was deemed to infringe upon prison regulations. One visit with my brother, John, was stopped after a few minutes, and I still do not know why this happened.

It was not that we were innocently complying with the regulations. We did try to smuggle in news via visits or letters. We expected the warders to try to stop us. But the prison regime extended even into stopping what was quite legitimate and innocuous. They stopped much more than political news being communicated, and there was always the anxiety that a potential interruption — signaled by the body language of the warders present — would take place, whether it was justifiable or not in terms of the regulations.

A visit was generally our only contact with outsiders, and this often made us tense. The anxiety we felt about impending visits was heightened by the hopes, held by our comrades, that we would get political news from our visitors. One went into a visit feeling that one had to deliver the goods afterwards.

Seemingly minor things would "throw" us, making it difficult to focus or to enjoy the visit in a relaxed manner. And, before one realized it, the time was up. Prisoners and visitors would sometimes make notes, to make it easier to remember points we wanted to raise during our limited time together. Sometimes the authorities would unsettle us, and unsettle our visitors, by preventing us from taking notes into sessions, or preventing visitors from taking their handbags into the visiting room.

Gradually, we improved our access to news. During the 1970s, we unsuccessfully challenged prison censorship in the courts. After winning their case, however, the Prisons Department slowly relaxed censorship in prisons, first allowing censored radio broadcasts, and then, in the early 1980s, allowing daily newspapers. This made a huge difference to our morale.

Under the conditions of substantial peace and tranquility that prevailed, the possibility of escape was also discussed from time to time. But no clear or concrete plans had been made in the first years after my arrival. And no high priority was given to escape plans — as we conducted our political seminars and set about our daily routines. When ANC activists Tim Jenkin and Stephen Lee arrived, however, the question of attempting an escape was tackled with renewed urgency. The pair had smuggled in some money, and Jenkin started to make duplicate keys and soon had as many as the warders.

Some of us were concerned that the issue of an escape attempt was not being considered politically. That is, that Jenkin, Lee and Moumbaris were not discussing their escape plans with the rest of the prisoners. In our view, it was crucial that any escape attempt should include Denis Goldberg, who was serving life imprisonment.

After further discussions, the question of escape became one of broader concern. We agreed that all except Matthews and Holiday, who were soon to be released, might escape. In addition, that we needed to ensure that outside logistical support be secured for escapees, to ensure they would be ferreted to safety. We did have contacts with the ANC outside the prison — although it took time to get answers from the ANC and to convince them that we were serious.

In the meantime, Jenkin, Lee and Moumbaris became impatient. On the basis that there was some reported change in the guarding system, they wanted to make their escape as a group of three, without waiting for the confirmation of outside support. The rest of the yard did not support their view, as we still felt a larger group should escape, including Denis. We also felt it crucial not to leave their "reception" outside the gates to chance. We didn't want lives to be risked unnecessarily. But Jenkin, Lee and Moumbaris could not be persuaded. In the end, Denis Goldberg helped distract the guard so the three could make their way downstairs. But Denis remained behind.

The escape of the three was successful and rocked the prison establishment. Being experts at shutting the stable after the horse had bolted, they increased security massively and all our routines were dislocated. After a month or two, we were all moved to "Maximum" for some three years. We only returned to the old prison in 1983, just before my release. And when we did return, we found the old prison environment was unrecognizable. It had been totally changed. There was no more garden, only concrete and steel. And the new, mechanized doors were not susceptible to lock-picking.

CHAPTER 12

Letters, 1976–82

THE FOLLOWING letters were written during my first term in prison as a convicted prisoner. They cover the period from 1976 to March 1982, when I was in Pretoria Local, and from April 1982 to the end of that year, when I was in "Maximum." Other white political prisoners were also serving sentences at this time.

These letters were subject to stringent censorship. It was strictly forbidden to write about certain subjects — in particular, prison conditions and political matters.

We took pains to avoid some topics. We did not want to write about tensions between fellow political prisoners, or divisions in our ranks, or difficulties that we might have had in coping with prison life. We did not want to give the authorities any ammunition to use against us. Nor did we want to sow or increase divisions within our ranks, or demoralize fellow comrades.

In fact, there was very little we could write about. And, often, we would decide not to discuss much of what remained. So, we wrote from prison without writing much about prison. We were writing as if we were abstracted from our surroundings.

Before I arrived in Pretoria Local, I had been in Pretoria Maximum. And I remember very clearly how terrible it was there. But I could not say so in my letters. Nor did I want to alarm my family. I could not have told them about these conditions in any case, because the authorities would not have allowed such a letter to get out. They would have refused to post it, or would have told me to rewrite the letter.

In order to prevent the suppression or non-delivery of our letters, we also practiced self-censorship, or used a variety of contorted allusions that passed the censors but were sometimes very hard for our correspondents to decipher. We were desperate for information from the outside, but we had to solicit this news in innocent-sounding and indirect ways. It was only the most obscure references that escaped suspicion. And the more successful we were in fooling the censors, the more difficult it might be for our correspondents to follow our meaning.

We were generally not allowed to write to those who might most easily have understood our oblique references. But it took *years* to get a *decision* from the authorities when we requested permission to write to someone new, particularly when the new person was not a close family member. And usually these requests were refused.

Because of the conflicting pressures mentioned above, the following letters might also sometimes seem a little awkward. The letters selected here — like those in later chapters — have been abridged, while italicized explanatory notes appear in square brackets.

Letters, 1976

March 17
Dear Family,

You will have gathered from Alan some of the peculiarities of visits here. I got the impression that he may have been given a "pep talk," which made things more inhibiting than usual. But we will have to adapt and it may get easier. I really despair of a method of keeping in touch with even some of you. And, as regards friends, by the time I am allowed more letters, it will have been years without contact. Any person who is not a family member will require head office permission to visit...

I have been at Pretoria Local since February 26. It is pleasant to have company again, to hear a wide selection of music, to have work, better food, facilities and space, space, space.

You either work on the land or in the carpentry shop. While I am in the garden now, I may be sent to the shop later. Apart from this, we share cleaning and other chores. We eat in a dining room with knives and forks — imagine that.

It has been hard to adjust to this new world. Nevertheless, it makes me feel much healthier. Since the work is tiring (in my unfit state) I sleep well and am learning to appreciate the after lunch lock-up, as a time to rest.

I am in good health and am receiving the medicine that I require. I have seen two specialists — eye (no change for better or worse) and ear, nose and throat (prescribed something, but nothing serious). Basically there is no need to worry — there is enough hypochondria without your worries. We have so much time to study all our bodily functions that it is easy to persuade oneself that something is wrong (always the most serious possibility). Because you are on your own so much of the time, you notice so many things that are of no consequence outside, where there are so many other things to hold attention.

Please write your address on any letter that you send me — otherwise I won't receive it.

I am altogether happier, though the last few months have had considerable effect on my nerves. I do not know enough about the present situation to tell whether I will be able to relax properly. Until now, every "pleasure" seemed precarious and liable to interruption.

I imagine that this is all that I *can* write.

September 19
Dear Family,

I very much enjoyed Mom's visit and John's letter... Although this is my normal quota of contacts with the outside world, it has sometimes seemed a lot harder this month, than normally. You can judge how desperately I need changes when I say that the change to summer uniform was a source of some excitement. But we never miss the slightest change and anything that happens is analyzed and reanalyzed till every possible factor of interest has been extracted.

Although I have been here for a short time, by our standards, some changes in my habits suggest that it is actually quite long: I am thinking, for example, of my changed attitude to escapist films and magazines. Before I came here, I had never opened *Darling* or *Fair Lady*. Now I look forward to my turn to read them. I think that we need this "escapism." We can't think about our situation the whole time and this sort of literature and film fulfills a purpose that cannot be done by anything else in the circumstances.

I seem to be reasonably fit since I have been running every morning for three weeks. It is one of the advantages of a monotonous, regular life that you can more easily start something like this without having to miss much of importance. I am also playing a lot of tennis. This has become a lot more important to me than I should have imagined, since I seem to "hit out" much depression in a hard game.

We are finding it hard with so few of us, irritating and boring one another. *[There were only six political prisoners at this time.]* Yet there is no serious friction between us...

I seem to be plagued with diarrhea. I have had it on and off just about all the time. I think it has something to do with the degree of tension here...

I am sorry if this has not been interesting... But this is all there is.

October 12

Dear Family,

Had I written last week, my letter would probably have reflected a more despondent mood than I am in now. It has been a lively and interesting week because of the arrival of two newcomers. *[Jeremy Cronin and David Rabkin, who were arrested in July, 1976.]* It makes a tremendous difference. I must say that I was finding it very hard with a "world" of six people, despite my having the advantage of comparative newness. We are forced in our situation to focus on one another's weaknesses or to see them in an exaggerated light. Similarly, we take for granted one another's most important qualities. That is, the things that have brought us together. And quite naturally so, because there is nothing remarkable about them — here.

The arrival of two others has eased the pressure of our continual contact with one another, going over more or less similar topics. It has also expanded our social life since we can now play volleyball. It is the first time that I have played and it is very enjoyable. I seem to be getting rather fit and I suppose that it is a good thing, making it less likely that I will fall ill. We now have five out of eight running in the morning so that there is some pressure to continue.

Certainly, I can do a lot of things here that I couldn't do outside (and, equally, the other way round!). I imagine that many of my circumstances are healthier than they were outside (just as many are, psychologically, very unhealthy).

I still have diarrhea — but they are taking tests now. Otherwise my health is fine.

My visit with Sally was a bit difficult. Any extra tension, like the instructions about the notes, seems to make things more difficult. *[Sometimes prisoners or their visitors would take notes into sessions, to help them remember points they wanted to raise and make better use of the available time. Sometimes, warders would confiscate these notes, or not allow them to be taken into the visiting rooms.]*

Because one is inhibited, or may not say what one wants to say, it is easy to end up saying what isn't intended. I hope, therefore, that I said nothing hurtful.

We have some tomatoes growing — one or two have ripened so far — as well as mealies and boysenberries, which should be ready in a month or so. The garden is looking lovely. The rain has helped the grass a lot — I now spend a lot of time mowing. When there isn't rain, there is usually a full day's work in garden, these days. My other work is washing towels, dishes and generally cleaning, including the gramophone records.

It is now some 16 months since my arrest. I feel a bit dazed when I think about that — it is hard to see these months as real. So much of it has been part of a world that I previously imagined that I do not yet feel that it is really happening and going to continue for another 79 months.

November 20
Dear Family,

...I wonder whether you would mind writing earlier in the month — say after the visit, so that I can write my letter in reply to yours. Think about it, because it is becoming more and more difficult to extract something new out of my circumstances.

I have been working hard, reading Balzac, Gorky, Shakespeare and a lot of historical works.

I think that being here longer enables one to get a more and more objective view of our situation. My first reaction, which occupied most of the first months, was just to survive. Now I am trying to take stock, to ask myself, "What psychological effects this has had, what have I done to myself, consciously and subconsciously, in order to cope?" I often wonder how drastically my self-confidence has been impaired... We are so exposed and often feel inadequate.

I worry, personally, since I often seem quite different to the self-image that I had outside.

A lot of this is mitigated by our behavior as a group. Despite arguments, we are generally very creative and mutually supportive. We are all conscious of one another's needs, loves and disappointments...

It is terribly hot, much like Durban at night. It is uncomfortable during the day in our new overalls, which seem to absorb the heat. The overalls have the advantage, however, of making us look like workers (very much in contradiction to reality). Also, they will be good in winter.

We still play sport — mainly volleyball, during every free moment of the weekend. My fingers are sore — but it's a good game.

December 22
Dear Family,

Thank you for the last two letters... especially the first, which was full of news about my friends. Letters that express ideas are less welcome, since I need to hear things that connect me to people outside.

I am glad that you have written about John's visit. I wrote to the commissioner protesting and requesting a substitute visit. I was told, verbally, that this had been refused — which will not be the last word on the matter... *[A reference to warders having stopped a visit from my brother John for no reason that I could understand. See also "Letter of complaint," below.]*

We are allowed 12 Xmas cards. I have received eight, and some are very pleasant surprises. It is generally very exciting to suddenly be inundated with mail. It seems ages since I have had normal contact with people, though the time nevertheless goes quickly.

Please thank Judi for looking at the books for me — but, please, they should be in English, especially from the "angle" that interests me...

I have not applied for any magazines, since I try to negotiate one request (to buy records) at a time. I usually apply (unsuccessfully) every three months or so. We are generally restricted to specific magazines, such as *Darling*, that are published in South Africa...

Things are very peaceful now. This is a strange place with terrible contrasts.

Sometimes I feel more relaxed than I can ever remember being outside. In a moment all this can be transformed and everyone can be on edge. There are often causes for the sort of fright that one doesn't usually feel outside. But the evenings are usually completely peaceful.

The increase to our numbers has made a great difference. If this were the sort of place where you do research, you could make a very interesting study of the effect of pressures and slight changes on our behavior patterns and relationships.

In some respects, I must admit that I don't regret being here. In the areas where I do have choice, I use my opportunities as effectively as I can...

I confront, as practical questions, issues that would usually only arise on a theoretical plane outside. That we should live according to our beliefs is a necessity here.

I think that I will also develop intellectually. I am discussing a variety of relevant issues, and reading widely, including novels by Stendhal, Zola, Fielding, James, Gorky and Dickens.

I just feel I have got to work hard, so I will be better equipped for the future.

* * *

[The following letter was written after a dispute with Brigadier du Plessis, who was the most senior prison official dealing with political prisoners in Pretoria. It is one of the many letters of complaint that I (in common with many other prisoners) wrote over the years. Sometimes the prison authorities

just noted these complaints, but usually they provided some form of reply. This may have been because prison regulations required them to respond to requests and complaints. We were under the impression that our letters were placed in the file of the official concerned, and could possibly affect their promotion. In this case, Brigadier du Plessis came to the prison from Head Office to reject my allegations in person.]

July 26
[Letter of complaint, written to South African Commissioner of Prisons]

I wish to protest against the conduct of Brigadier du Plessis, in response to questions that I put to him when he visited this prison on Tuesday, July 20.

I asked the Brigadier why I had not received any letters since receiving one written on May 20. I also mentioned that one letter sent out by me, and another posted to me earlier in the year, had not arrived.

The Brigadier said my people no longer cared to write to me. I said that I knew this to be wrong because one of my brothers had recently visited and told me that letters had been sent.

Instead of indicating that he would investigate, Brigadier du Plessis asked: "Is he also a communist?" The Brigadier then made various provocative remarks about my political beliefs. I explained that I did not wish to continue the argument that he had instigated because I felt that he was relying on his official position to protect himself from a frank response to his remarks (which were, to say the least, in very bad taste).

I also asked when I would be promoted to Group B, adding that being able to see two people at a time would help me to see my family (which is large) and friends. The Brigadier responded with the remark that I could not see friends — unless they were Afrikaners.

It may be that these above remarks were intended as jokes. Quite apart from their non-humorous nature, I strenuously object to my legitimate questions, about matters that concern me deeply, being used as a basis for the Brigadier's crude and divisive political propaganda.

I also object to this type of exchange being made in front of junior officials. Is it right that an officer should set this type of example, that he should taunt a prisoner in this way? The junior officials seemed to enjoy the Brigadier's remarks. What is to stop them from also trying to bait prisoners?

What the meeting indicated, quite clearly, is that Brigadier du Plessis is not prepared to consider the substance of any inquiries or complaints. Quite apart from the unpleasantness of the remarks, they show that the Brigadier is not able to consider applications without bias, that his personal feelings and attitude to my political convictions are the determining factors.

Are political prisoners, therefore, to conclude that they have no right to put complaints or queries to an officer, and, if they do, that it will be interpreted as an empty gesture?

Letters, 1977

January 28
Dear Family,

Yesterday I received a slightly abbreviated *[censored]* letter from Sally, dated 12.01.77. I have registered this and suggest you do the same. Please also send photos. *[We registered letters, to help prevent them from "going astray."]*

Psychologists would really love to study our situation. I find particularly interesting the way in which our tensions get resolved. You can't "escape" from irritating people and reappear when you have recovered control. There is no opportunity for the discreet behavior that reduces personal conflict outside. Over here it is likely that you will find yourself working with, eating and playing tennis with a person immediately after an argument or something that has irritated you in someone's behavior.

It is astonishing, the number of ways in which tension is generated — relations with authorities, family, one another, general conditions, etc. This means that any person's anger is very often caused by factors stretching quite far back.

February 2
Dear Family,

It will be a lot better when I can write/receive more than one letter and need not always write to all of you at once...

I wonder to what extent we prisoners are fully conscious as we do our daily tasks. A lot of the time I feel in a daze and just drift along. I suppose it's necessary, in that it makes life seem normal. What I hate about the situation, is that you have to consciously foster illusions or delusions for yourself (something that I would never do outside) to avoid continually facing the reality. That is, of being stuck here, surrounded by bars (and something else that alliterates with bars) for so many years. Therefore, we view our creative or meaningful activities as preparation for a life that we will live outside, which is in contrast to living for "now." There is very little that attains meaning here and now. It is a strain here — I must confess that I am a bit tired of being a prisoner. But, otherwise, I am in good spirits, making what I can of the situation...

March 3
Dear Ann [*Perry, a friend from Durban*],
Please reply, by registered post (keeping a copy of the letter), to a maximum of 500 words, without overt political comment or reference to political news, before the end of March.

I hope that I will soon be made Group B (two letters a month) so that these letters can be more frequent...

My situation has generally not been as bad as it must seem from outside, though in some ways (which one does not anticipate), it has been worse. The main pleasant surprise has been how quickly the time passes. Naturally, this does not leave me absolutely happy, since it is time that I can never make up. And, in a place like this, you become more conscious of growing old and feeble, etc. Yet, I don't suggest that the time is wasted. The time that I spend with the others, freely (mainly meals and weekends) and on my own (lunch hours and 4.30 p.m. to 7 a.m.) is certainly used carefully. I am learning a great deal, filling some serious "blind spots." In some areas of knowledge, this is the first time that I have also had the opportunity to discuss things with people who share a similar world view.

Where one learns most, if you are willing, is morally. It is quite a problem dealing effectively with the tensions of our situations — our relations with one another, while living in close proximity, the additional tensions of our situation as prisoners, and in relation to our families. Tempers often flare over small issues, because there are many factors continually working on your nerves.

It is often pure chance when something erupts. But this is a situation where there are many temptations to act selfishly at the expense of others. I have seen that it is naive to suppose that it doesn't happen. It is easy to slip into an "I'm all right Jack" attitude, far easier than it seems in theory. Yet, in a community as small as this, it is equally obviously necessary to keep disciplined and get rid of one's anti-social and disruptive whims.

We have good music, though we are a bit thin on S.A. jazz. Please think of suggestions — especially groups like Malombo jazzmen... Also, book suggestions... Generally I'm OK — the others make things a lot easier. The pace is not hectic, but I try to use my time effectively, so that I will come out better equipped for whatever must be done...

April 18
Dear Family,

Recently, we had a more exciting time than usual with the arrival of the Red Cross and also our Pesach parcel. *[Twice a year, on Passover and Jewish New Year, Jewish prisoners received parcels of food, which we shared with the other prisoners.]* We are now back to normal and it is hard to foresee anything of interest occurring in the next week. This is the worst thing — having hardly anything to look forward to. Even Unisa circulars telling of printing errors in lecture notes are more interesting than nothing. *[Unisa is an acronym for the University of South Africa. We were permitted to study via correspondence, subject to various restrictions.]*

The films are a mixed blessing. Usually they are very disappointing, especially because we look forward to them so much. But when they are at all absorbing, they tend to drain us emotionally.

I find that it is often quite jarring to come back to "reality."

One faces this problem continually — to what extent, and how, do you take your mind off your situation as a prisoner? While it is desirable to find ways of occupying one's mind, some of these tend to make it even more difficult when you resurface. Others, such as excessive studying, tend to have anti-social effects, etc.

Most of the time I find it OK — quite bearable, sometimes enjoyable and stimulating. Sometimes it is depressing. This whole experience seems to be structured with a view to shaking one's confidence and I think that it has had some effect. I am not as confident as I was, before I came to prison, of my general ability to cope with problems in life. I often marvel at the responsibilities that I used to be able to shoulder and the things that I used to achieve. This may be quite illogical, but it does disturb me.

Anne Marie's death, as you can imagine, was quite dreadful for all of us. We do what we can to make things easier for Jeremy. We all have so little that is ours, that we all appropriate one another's friends and relatives. So, we can genuinely sympathize and comfort most effectively — but what a thing to have to bear! *[Anne Marie was Jeremy Cronin's wife, who died of a brain tumor while he was still in prison.]*

Some new photos would be nice (they must be posted — hand deliveries of letters/photos are not allowed)...

May (precise date unknown)
Dear Mom,

I am doing some worthwhile work. It is frustrating however, because one often has to read about books without being able to get the originals in Unisa; e.g., Althusser *(Reading Capital)*, Poulantzas *(Political*

Power and Social Classes and *Classes in Contemporary Capitalism)* and Hirst and Hindess *(Pre-Capitalist Modes of Production)*...

I often "fantasize" that someone may present them to the University, so they all become available.

July 26
Dear Mom,

Writing without something to reply to is especially hard now because we have been experiencing a fairly long period with little of interest happening, very little "input." Whenever this happens our personal relationships become strained. Ideological and personal differences merge to make life difficult.

Despite this, I sometimes sit in my cell after lock up, the day's work, arguments etc., eating my bread while listening to the music — and I wonder what more one could want of life. It shows how accustomed I have become to loss of liberty, how these relative comforts seem like some sort of summit.

Still most of the time it is hard to have these illusions. I wish I could feel some connection to any world other than this yard. For us, the existence of a city, somewhere out there, is hardly a real factor. We never hear or see people out of uniform. All we know of the city is one or two sounds — shunting trains and the city hall clock...

I am now in the workshop, making toolboxes. They look impressive, joined with dovetails.

Luckily there are ways of covering up every conceivable error, which is a relief to me since I had feared that I would ruin all the wood. It is rather tiring, but generally better...

August 18
Dear Sally,

...Our situation here is very complex. Analogous to Fanon's description of a colonial situation; the overall framework turns us on one another. Despite a fundamental unity (which is often difficult to achieve) there are serious conflicts between us. What to one person is a useful way of adaptation is often a source of tension to others. Generation gaps affect ways of viewing situations — people who have been here longer are often more attached to what is than the newer ones who find what is (amongst us) one of the chief sources of discomfort.

It is very difficult to examine arguments or discuss truthfully when one's attitude is so conditioned by one's general attitude to whoever puts the argument. All of us are probably at our worst here. While I never feared prison, I did not have any idea of what it would be like in fact. Reading about the tension can give very little idea of the actuality. Sometimes, like wet days, it gets "a bit much."

Yet I do achieve some things... through discussions with a couple of others... and that is what gives my life meaning.

September 20
Dear Sally,

[Referring to messages from friends.] ...I am usually so emotionally starved that messages from people whom I have not previously heard from, who matter to me, or a card from someone new, excites me for days. Our entire day revolves around, or our thoughts are oriented towards, evening post and Unisa books, etc. Sometimes a worthwhile book is an exciting substitute for a letter.

My life here is very disciplined and regular... I don't waste time or, at any rate, my own time, if I can help it. There is a tendency in many cases to merely survive, i.e. not to try and develop oneself here. This is manifested in personal behavior and reading. There are some people who spend almost all of their time reading real rubbish, since they reason that they have a rough enough time as it is. The rubbish consoles them. Another wing, while rejecting this, gets lost in studies and the need for academic achievement. When I arrived here, I was less critical than I am now of the dangers of escapist literature and films. Although I periodically escape for a while (e.g. reading *Darling* and *Fair Lady*) my reading is generally very disciplined and single-minded. The possibilities of discussion make it often much more fruitful than outside. While there are very many difficulties, I have also had real opportunities.

The same goes morally and socially. Things are very difficult and they are likely, over the years, to grow more problematic. Yet I am close to those who try to avoid competitiveness, selfishness, etc. It is rewarding having relationships such as these, where no envy is felt, where there is no conflict of interest between one another, where each one's disappointments and joys are shared by the others.

November 1
Dear Pete, Wendy and Dean *[friends in Durban Peter Galt and Wendy and Dean Thorpe]*,

I still listen to music here (*Missa Solemnis* at the moment). I am much more in to pop than before. I think that it has something to do with my emotional state, my need to feel linked to things outside.

Somehow this music connects me in a way that Prokofiev doesn't, since I didn't grow up hearing Prokofiev at parties.

It has sometimes been rather difficult, especially during this second year, when a lot of the novelty of prison life has worn off. You cannot conceive how small is our connection with the world outside...

Unfortunately, there are various constraints on what can be written. I can't write exactly as I feel all the time. Yet many of the constraints of outside have been removed. Though the overall atmosphere here is often difficult, we can generally be ourselves amongst ourselves. I don't have to hold back as I often had to in my relationships outside...

Date unknown
Dear Scilla [*Rayner, a friend in Durban*],

I have been finding it very hard to write letters, whether to family or friends. Mine have tended to be very detached accounts of prison life. Consciously or unconsciously, my letters seem to be more concerned that people understand my prison life in a particular way rather than trying to communicate my feelings.

Yet I actually need to get through to people on an emotional level. But, in this situation, there is no way of edging gradually to a more frank relationship on the basis of responses that you observe. You just have to be prepared to take the plunge in letters. With you, I am prepared to do that. I need to write to someone... who doesn't view me as a "figure," who knows my faults and feels for me in spite of that. If this embarrasses you, tell me.

December 12
Dear Pete, Wendy, Dean,

We are going through a rather unsettling period because of changes, whose immediate effects are not clear. Ultimate effects are to phase out studies. Now, must just wait and see. Be patient, keep your cool — that much I have learned here.

December 17
Dear Mom,

We were actually disappointed in the "improvements." All I gain is 15 minutes per visit, the prospect of censored news broadcasts (when?). And concern over studies. While the ultimate aim is clear (to end studies) its immediate effect is not certain. What worries me about this is not only the particular problem, but also the general feeling ·of insecurity that it engenders. What can you regard as a permanent part of your environment? What is the next thing to be threatened?...

One change that was sprung on us, and we are very happy about, is that we now have an extra hour for tennis on weekends. I get a fair amount of pleasure from the game. You just have to throw yourself fully into whatever is offered — reading, music, sport. I get more and more out of the music and have extended my interest a fair amount. Three or four of us discuss the programs, which is an incentive to listen carefully...

Letters, 1978

January 9
Dear Mike and Elfrieda *[Olmesdahl, friends in Durban]*,

Photos are important because we see nothing besides our yard and cells. Yet the yard is fairly pleasant as prisons go — we have a Pride of India, a plain tree, a stretch of grass and a number of flowerbeds. We can't receive seeds or slips (or anything else) from outside — thanks anyway. I am no longer in the garden. Although I spent a year or so "outside," most of my duties were in the dining room and bathroom, etc. — cleaning...

I feel a bit remote from a lot of the faculty happenings of which you write. You cannot visualize how completely I have been cut off from everything in the last two years.

It has often been difficult. Yet, being able to study, albeit in a limited and unsatisfactory way, has made it possible to be constructive. Yet now that is to be stopped. All of those who are registered for degrees have been given three years to complete whatever they are doing, irrespective of their stage of study. In my case, that is 13 courses, including three majors, one of which is a four-course major.

It is hard to see this as unconnected with our court action. After the judgment, we heard that there would be improvements in our conditions. The study changes were embraced in new regulations with other "improvements," such as the introduction of censored news broadcasts at some unspecified future date; 15 minutes extra per visit; and Group A now being called Group I.

Censorship of magazines and correspondence is unchanged.

Prohibition of newspapers, etc., is an old policy. We are used to that, hard as it is. The object of the new regulations on studies is to remove the main compensation, the thing that has contributed most to coping with the boredom of prison life.

Letters, 1979

August 28
Dear Judi *[Kalk, a long-standing friend]*,

We've just had a season of visiting personages. First, the prison board, then, after two days of washing and scrubbing floors, walls etc., the new minister. Finally, last week, we saw the Red Cross. We made various requests concerning studies, access to newspapers and remission of sentences. We hope that some will be successful.

September 4
Dear Stan and Lesley *[Kahn, friends from Johannesburg]*,

I'm quite pleased to have passed the halfway mark here. Although I've gained much from this experience, I sometimes feel that it is costing me quite a lot, emotionally. I have no choice in the sense that I have to handle it. All I mean is that I won't be sorry to forego some of these gains for a different experience. Yeats writes about people like us, who, through having "one purpose alone" become "enchanted to a stone." In this situation, there's a combination of repressing and suppressing what you want but can't immediately have, plus an overall view of things that keeps you going.

You can lose a lot of your spontaneity and ability to respond emotionally, because you just have to keep yourself in check. Where I disagree with Yeats, is that I think most of us will be able to recover our spontaneity. In fact, this "enchantment" is cultivated — a defense — and the restraint repeatedly breaks down.

October 2
Dear Lyn *[Stonestreet, a friend from Durban]*,

Thank you for your last letter. I'm pleased that mine proved OK — it was hard to find a way of expressing what I thought, without being ambiguous. Because you are restricted to one method of communication, you cannot easily convey your tone or clarify your intentions...

Normally, I only see my family. It's hard to find friends who would be allowed to visit and also be suitable (and female — I'd like to refresh my memory on what it's like to talk to a woman again.) Fortunately, time is flying. I'm getting "wonderful" insights into the meaning and implications of confinement in prison. A lot of things I would never have known — without actually experiencing it. All the same, I'll be happy to understand less about this and experience other things. Although it is a quiet life, usually at a slow pace, it is a great strain to keep oneself under a continual, rigid self-discipline. Because you live in a community, you can't always do what you feel like doing, and the fact of being in prison means you try not to let your imagination wander to things that are just not possible.

October 2
Dear Barbara *[Harrell-Bond, an academic friend from Oxford]*,
   You ask whether we get news or newspapers, and therein lie two or three years and thousands of pounds spent in litigation. Until 18 months ago, we got no news whatsoever and we unsuccessfully challenged the legality of this ruling in the Supreme Court, and on appeal to the Appellate Division (where one out of five judges agreed with our contentions). Despite losing in law, our de-facto situation has improved dramatically.
   Apart from one major setback (formal studies are being stopped once existing *[undergraduate]* courses are completed), we've seen some welcome innovations. These include (censored) radio bulletins, improved magazines — including *Time, New York Review of Books, Ms, Sight and Sound* — and better and more films. Requests for newspapers have been refused. You ask if books can be sent to me — generally, no — though they might be prepared to make exceptions in the case of books that are hard to come by ordinarily — if a case is made out...
   Now that I'm a Group I prisoner, I may order three books a month — since that's not all that many, I take a lot of care before choosing.

October 11
Dear Judi,
   We used to play cards a bit here when I first arrived — mainly on rainy weekends. On the whole, it doesn't serve the social function that it might do outside — to enable you to get away from things, relax, etc. Here, it transfers the normal tensions to cards instead of (say) tennis. (The same people who "poach" or serve before you're ready in tennis seem also to have infuriating ways of dealing cards.)
   "Passing the time" is not the main problem here. Most of us can keep occupied with reading, sport, and music. This doesn't mean that we're not bored, but it's a special type of boredom, quite interestingly discussed by Gramsci (in Joll's brief biography). This special boredom is born of lack of contact with the outside world.
   Apparently the old religious hermits had this problem and

practically used to crack up around midday (the "noonday devil" they called it) — so great was their desire, at that time, to break away from their isolation. So what we need is more of other people's company...

October 29
Dear Ann,

It was good to see you again though these brief visits are rather frustrating. There is always too little time to discuss all that is important, yet I often find enough time for ambiguity or misunderstanding...

Thank you also for the birthday card and for remarking on my seeming "together" — it's useful to hear such things over here. I'm not always able to handle things with as much equanimity as I'd like...

What I find harrowing is to derive most of my sustenance from interaction with nine (and soon, eight) other males in a prison yard. While I continue to gain a lot from this experience there are aspects of our personalities, which just never come out here. I've never previously been aware of the way my personality has been split into areas shared with women and children, on the one hand, and the predominantly male world of politics (in my experience) on the other. The way it finds expression here, is that there are some things that I just won't be able to say until 1983, and it's nothing to do with censorship.

Right now, I have a reminder of Durban — when I look out of my window just over the wall, I can just make out a row of jacaranda. They don't look as deeply blue as in Durban (the others say I'm talking nonsense when I say that) — but it's nice to see. Our garden is looking good — had a bit of rain, but usually very hot and humid.

Every few months, I run into a new "landmark" in my sentence — four years completed mid-November — not bad? Like Elvis in "Jailhouse Rock," I tick off the weeks. Whenever I move towards self-pity, I just need to look around at the plight of others, and I can feel quite lucky with my "parking ticket."

November 11
Dear Scilla,

I've spent almost four and a half years in prison since my arrest and I think I've learned a lot of things ... most situations here throw up complex issues, which don't present simple "right-wrong" choices... What I've really had to learn is a more flexible and patient approach, the ability to compromise — and to recognize when it is necessary.

December 3

Dear Lyn,

Things are unchanged. The run-up to Xmas is always a bit heavy. Tempers are shorter than usual... People generally feel a bit depressed. It's not because of any special attachment to the festive season, but the general slowing down of an already slow life. We seem to get fewer letters than usual. Unisa is closed, so fewer good books, etc., arrive.

To deal with this lack of input, I'm trying to work on a few projects. For example, I'm going through the Wiehahn (government) report on labor relations. I'm also trying to improve my German — one of the useful things that I learned in my first year here.

December 31

Dear Celia, Josef, Deborah-Marie *[Netolicky, relatives in Australia]*,

...You probably know that we've had a more than usually exciting time over here. *[A reference to the escape of Tim Jenkins, Alexander Moumbaris and Stephen Lee.]* We are down to six people, which is a rather small number to spend so much time with. It's not been easy, but luckily we have the advantage of being fairly united and disciplined at the moment...

We've been out of the woodwork shop for the last month and perhaps security reasons might keep it closed. There are only three of us (pretty mediocre) carpenters left and it's hardly worth keeping the shop open for us: this probably means that we'll help with cleaning and gardening and then read. There's been a lot of cleaning lately — a sort of ritual purification after disaster.

December 31

Dear Binks *[Belinda Bozzoli, a long-standing friend in Johannesburg]*,

You probably know that we've had something of an upheaval here. Everything's been tightened up, ranging from the installation of bordello-style mirrors in the cells to extra bars, doors, and guards. It's hard to deal with the pace of things. We've learned to take things slowly, since everything usually stays the same for years. Suddenly, much that was normal in our life is no more...

Otherwise, things have general been improving. All six of us are in Group I now, which means more visits, letters, books and 17 rand of groceries per month. Together with improved films (including one a month from the Capetown film society) these material benefits have made things more pleasant than in earlier years. It's nice to be able to have coffee when you wake up, or to make muesli with Jungle oats, raisins, etc., instead of eating prison pap *[porridge]* every morning. We eat most of our things communally, taking turns to "cater" on Saturdays. Recipes would be useful — just attach — separately...

Letters, 1980

January 14
Dear John *[Schlapobersky, a friend in London]*,

Our studies situation is not clear-cut. As it stands, we're allowed to complete existing courses (undergraduate, in areas not previously studied) and then no further studies. This is, however, under review. I'm a student of "library science," which fortunately allows a certain range of BA courses. You can visualize what they're like. But the library is very valuable and has a fairly good coverage in some areas. I've been able to do some useful reading on South African history, the Middle East and Eastern Europe.

On "promotion" to Group I, we're also able to buy three books a month, which, despite restrictions, has enabled us to assemble a good range of works. It can be rather frustrating, however, in that it's hard to follow up things — at a certain point, what you feel you need is unavailable. In some areas (philosophy, contemporary South Africa) we have practically nothing. I try to use my time constructively. I dread coming out and feeling that this whole period has been a "write off." In consequence, I work hard and fairly consistently...

January 22
Dear Jonathan *[Shore, a cousin]*,

My first eight and a half months were in solitary, and one of the key ways that I drew psychological strength was by reminding myself of my link with others who understand my situation, or who are experiencing similar situations themselves. (Unfortunately I'm forced because of the conditions of correspondence, to discuss such things rather vaguely and superficially.) Now I'm with five others and my social/psychological relationships with them are more important to me than any inward reflections. Our relations are sometimes very difficult (as can be expected) but in problematic situations there is a great deal of mutual support and solidarity...

February 25
Dear Lyn,

We've had a difficult couple of months. A lot of things have changed — any alteration in our "normal" life is hard to deal with.

I try to keep calm and disciplined — but there are numerous "irritants." Sometimes things just snap and you have a vast reservoir of anger and bitterness that just wells up. It's great at the time! — but (unfortunately) not worth it in the long run. Things work better if you unnaturally repress your feelings. This is the unfortunate thing — that the most appropriate mode of adaptation seems to require all sorts of personality contortions/distortions.

March 17
Dear John *[Schlapobersky]*,

Books — we do share the three-a-month books, and I do read a lot of fiction... My choice is conditioned by what is likely to be allowed and by specific psychological needs over here. Psychologically, we have needs that can't be fulfilled in real life, and reading is some sort of substitute. I prefer books that raise problems that concern or move me...

You ask about relationships. We start with a basic unity and substantial agreement on how we should live together. Anti-social behavior is disapproved of, though what "sanction" ensues for "contraventions" is variable... In prison, you have to conserve your emotional energy. You can't just let loose and have huge flare-ups on any/every issue. Some people are fairly set in their ways, so it's practical to develop the more compatible aspects of our relationships...

We still have some heavy arguments, but, as in disputes regulated by "traditional" courts, after some slander, the disputants have to be reconciled — in the interests of the cohesion of the wider community. It sometimes amazes me how quickly we are reconciled. It is necessary. We have no escape from one another.

There are also many positive sides to our living together. We need one another and from some relationships I have gained a lot.

March 24
Dear Al and Jenny *[Suttner, brother and sister-in-law]*,

Sometimes I get into my cell completely wound up, angry and completely, helplessly, frustrated. I then have to "talk to myself" and handle things in the best possible way and not according to my first impulse. Otherwise, it's a joy to be here.

April 3

Dear Scilla,

Since your letter arrived we've been through a time of many changes. If you "adjust" to prison, you learn to dread any change. Most radical of the breaks in routine was our transfer — last week — to "Maximum" (where I started my sentence) I believe that the change is temporary. In the meantime, it is easier to be here with others (last time I was alone). It is a much more functional prison than "ours" is, since the objects (and facilities) are much more limited. They have nevertheless taken some trouble to "jazz up" the place and provide facilities for our most important activities — music, films, reading, exercises.

Still, because it is cramped and there's less to do, we're going to have to take care to minimize tensions among ourselves.

Next month, I will have three years still to go, and I'm rather pleased about that. I feel like I've been holding myself back, suppressing and repressing a great deal for very long time. Sometimes, I feel pretty brittle. Because I can't react against the really basic things, I find that I tend to overreact to the minor ones. I am often consciously or unconsciously so tense that there's a flood of emotion just waiting for an occasion to be released.

Luckily, I'm generally fairly practical and realize that there's no alternative to continual self-discipline, and that I just have to pull myself together and handle it.

April 9

Dear Binks,

I find that I'm much more conscious of "aging" than I was outside. This may be because you have far more time to look at yourself and little else seems to happen besides getting older. My hair is thinner and pretty gray. Still, I'm keeping fairly fit, after a lot of running and other crazy things.

Re: the move. Unlike last time *[in "Maximum"]*, when I spent 23 hours a day in my cell, we can move into our yard or stay inside during the day. It makes a difference to be able to choose — however limited the alternatives. We had sensed that something was going to happen and it was almost a relief to have it done with. Still — it's rather cramped and more depressing, so we look forward to returning to "our" prison.

April 29
Dear Celia, Josef and Deborah-Marie,

We have a small yard around which we run 26 times (to make a mile), and we do exercises. We had sensed that something was on the go and, after our speculations, it was almost a relief to end up here.

Life here is even more uniform than before. There is no way of distinguishing the days from one another, except for those on which one sees a flick *[movie]* or a visitor. Parts of this are preferable — such as no workshop, which means more reading. I don't like to lead such an entirely "cerebral" life — but work with books is the only way of getting something out of this experience. At the old place, I had learned to like watching birds (we saw 30 kinds) — but here, birds can't get in, apart from one or two wagtails that slip under the wire. So, I'm basically tied to my books.

May 5
Dear Lyn,

I'm writing this on a Sunday night — feeling rather tense. I had a visit today. And, as often happens, after a glimpse of the outside I feel a bit less reconciled to my environment. Where we are now (see address) is much more confined and, consequently, acts more intensely on our nerves. We moved six weeks ago. Apparently, it's temporary...

I miss the odd signs of the outside world (birds, sky, etc.,) that were part of our old place. But that's how it goes. Human beings can adjust to all sorts of things — so we just handle this...

I took your advice and read and enjoyed *Tree of Man*. Over here, it's good to read long novels, from which one can extract a lot. For you, reading fulfills a different function. For us, books (together with films) have to substitute for a normal social life. Reading of emotional and social problems is the closest I come to experiencing them. I seem now to analyze most things with prison analogies, as if all my years outside were peripheral experiences. I think that I'll be a huge bore when I get out — full of reminiscences of these times, inflicted on all.

June 11
Dear Judi,

Nothing distinguishes the individual days and, visually, one confronts hardly anything but concrete. I feel this especially when locked up for the night at 3.45 p.m. Sometimes, I just don't feel like reading and there is nothing else to do, nothing you can look at. Many of my letters have not arrived and it is harder to write...

June 30

Dear Stan, Lesley, Rebecca *[Kahn]*,

I've been gradually working towards writing, waiting for something interesting to happen since some new "input" makes it easier to write. Now, I've been fortified by our weekly film, *Ms, Time* and some prison bread and jam — so it is a bit easier. Where we are now, very little happens. This is very nice — if you like all things to be precise, regular and predictable. Nothing is ever extraordinary, nor very far from your reach; that is, nothing that you can hope to see or experience. Without the distractions of birds or much of the sky, one gets a pretty single-minded appreciation of what prison means.

I have been here before, but it is easier this time — with others, and more facilities. Still, with so few of us, we have to keep a tight control over ourselves. Fortunately, our general relationships seem to have grown much stronger. I'm starting to feel as if I've spent all my life in prison. All that I used to do seems like something that I've read somewhere, rather than actually experienced. It's the same with people's lives. People tell me things, but it is hard to picture. When I was outside, I knew things about people, not merely because they told me, but because their life was part of my experience. Now, much of what happens outside seems like what I read in a novel. I'm therefore not at all sorry that time is passing. In fact, I find that I spend a lot of time these days calculating days/months, etc., that I still have to spend enclosed in this way.

June 30

Dear Celia, Josef and Deborah,

I've been inside for more than five years now and it seems like this is the only life I've ever known. My own previous life seems like something in a novel or cartoon.

Letters can be very important, in providing a link or degree of involvement in the "other world" outside. I suspect that you might feel reluctant to talk about ordinary problems, for fear they might sound banal? Yet, it is these everyday problems, and apparently trivial issues in people's lives, that give us some idea of how people live...

We have been in this place for more than three months now. From a work point of view, it suits me. I've been able to get through a lot of things. Without tennis and many other communal social activities, we tend, over here, to do our "own thing" much more. And this is harder for the more gregarious chess/bridge-playing types, who need to take part in more activities with others, and sometimes resent those with "their noses always in books," who might be unwilling to make a fourth for bridge (if they know how to play at all).

All our pleasures and pains are very interrelated. Hardly anything that you do here is without its effect on others. We expect to make sacrifices for the general good, but it is often hard — outside of textbooks — to draw the line between legitimate social demands and impositions.

July 16
Dear Lyn,

It's nice getting pictures with lots of odds and ends in them like cats, firewood, candle, colored socks, chickens — all things belonging to a world that we just don't see. I've got so used to prison garb and hairstyles that any deviation seems quite dazzling. Whenever they do alter some aspect of our dress or other aspect of our lives we always feel a bit put out and resistant to change. It's a mixture of conservatism and suspicion. In an insecure existence it often seems safer to stick with what you have rather than risking worse through changes.

PS. Rules:

1. Where more than one person writes, it is now required that they write directly after one another — not on separate pages. They may write in their own handwriting — but the letter must be continuous — otherwise it is counted as more than one.

2. The length is to be no more than 500 words — in the body of the letter. No politics; address at top; writing on one side of the page only.

July 22
Dear Scilla,

Following your advice I read and enjoyed *Tree of Man* and have just got *Voss*. Doing a lot of novel reading — I finish one and immediately pick up the next. This environment leaves few alternative ways of getting through the hours in the cell...

That I now have less than three years to go, the "outside" is no longer so remote — so I think a bit more about it. At the same time, I'm starting to feel how long this has been. All that happens to friends and family outside often seems part of an unreal world...

Dear Kate [*Scilla's daughter*],

It was good and strange to hear from you again. Strange, because you are no longer the little girl that I knew and it's like writing to a quite different person. You must please send photos of what you see. Where I am now, I see some grass surrounded by cement, concrete walls, bars and some sky in patches between wire. It feels like winter, but, visually, it could be any season...

September 16
Dear John *[Schlapobersky]*,

Over here the "situation in general" has been a great deal more depressing, this year, than previously. Yet we now seem to be breaking into the "dawn" with the announcement — just now — that Group I prisoners (all but our newest one) may each buy one paper a day. This may not seem much to you — but to us, it's the most important gain that we've made regarding our conditions. It has been an issue for so long, it's hard to believe that it has been resolved. Just to have more information reduces the amount of fantastic speculation that goes on here.

You ask about when I get out... I intend to go to London. All this is presuming that I am not confined to some magisterial district or house, etc.

What I want most from the outside is just ordinary relationships — particularly with women. It's not so much sex, as the things that one talks about in an emotional relationship, which just don't figure here...

November 3
Dear Judi,

Right now, it's terribly humid and stuffy — much like Durban. It's been raining, but not hard enough to make much difference. There's really no way of getting relief, since you can't fan yourself the whole night.

December 29
Dear Luli, Eddie and family *[Luli Callinicos and Eddie Webster, long-standing friends]*,

This time of the year is normally the most difficult period. Possibly because we all knew this place would make for an extraordinarily grim festive season, we have made efforts to be in good spirits — and it hasn't been as bad as all that. The nights in the cell are, however, terrible — like being in a sauna. Whatever you do, it's impossible to get cool. It's been raining now, and, like Durban, gives little relief.

Letters 1981

January 12
Dear Lyn,

We've had a rather heavy festive season. I prepared myself psychologically for it to be worse than usual because of this place. But it's been the weather, more than anything else, which has brought such "preparations" to nought. Until the last few days, it has been terribly hot, humid and airless, making it difficult to work or sleep. The pillow gets hot, everything gets sweaty and there is no way of varying these or most other circumstances.

January 12
Dear Merle [Shore, cousin],

It is very depressing, with little to look at besides walls and bars, and even the sky is seen through little cracks in the wire.

Most of the time I try to "ignore" where I am and just read. It's OK when life goes on along a smooth, predictable path. Sometimes, however, factors in our environment make us insecure and tense. Prisoners are very conservative. They like to know what to expect and sudden changes or, worse still, the threat of them, is very upsetting...

They let me out in May 1983, which is soon enough to lead me to do a bit of fantasizing. Actually, it is a bit fearsome to contemplate suddenly rejoining humanity after eight years inside. I'll be 37 then...

March 4
Dear Luli, Eddie and family,

Our censorship position is becoming closer to ordinary censorship outside — though we'll have a better idea exactly what's going on when they tell us the fate of various books and magazines that have been held back for some time.

March 23
Dear Wendy, Dean,

We now get newspapers and try to spread our subscriptions over a wide range... We have gone from receiving no news to being among the best-informed...

April 1

Dear Al, Jenny,

As you can see from the address, we are still at "Maximum" — a year now. The summer has been particularly unpleasant and it has generally been a rather depressing time. I am, of course, one of the lucky ones — with only 25 months to go.

It's a surprising thing how much of survival in prison is a psychological matter. Muhammad Ali tries to "psyche" himself into a winning frame of mind and to get his opponent to believe he will lose. (Unfortunately, it didn't work with Holmes.) It's the same here. I sometimes have to "talk to myself," to sit in my cell at night and just get things in proportion and not get too upset, say. Most days there is something to get you upset or angry. But you can't afford to just let go... It doesn't help. I can't get up, ask for the bill and "stalk out." You learn a lot about patience and diplomacy here...

I'm trying to keep fit — but it's rather difficult here. There's not much that you can do in a very small yard. Running round and round gets pretty boring and I just try to force myself. I'm much more conscious of this sort of thing, because it's not the best place to be sick in — and I find that, being fit, I have fewer colds, flu, etc.

As you can see, there's not much to write about. Nothing much happens here...

April 1

Dear Stan,

I've done all but 25 months of my "stint." Most of the time it has not been too difficult. The first eight to nine months in solitary were hard and the last year — spent in "Maximum" — has been difficult. This place is very cramped and depressing — geared to the modest needs of terminal cases. Apparently, we are returning to "our" prison after it has been modified...

May 1

Dear Barbara,

Thank you — but you are not allowed to send me books or anything other than letters, photos, Xmas and birthday cards. I have to buy books through the authorities — subject to various rules, or order them through the University of South Africa library...

One of these days I'll have to start applying for an exit permit or some type of travel document. If not allowed, I'll presumably be under some form of house arrest or other restriction in Johannesburg...

June 2
Dear Al and Jenny,

We remain in the same place and it's getting very cold. I don't know when we move and what it will be like. Our numbers have recently increased to eight — which makes things easier and more interesting...

With less than two years to go I'm already at the stage where I'm watching what I say about my future, to avoid upsetting those who must remain here.

June 12
Dear Ann and Eugene *[Gerson, sister and brother-in-law],*

We now have one more "resident." *[Guy Berger, now a professor of journalism at Rhodes University.]* Apart from liking the bloke, it is nice to have more alternatives in our "social life." If X is driving me round the bend, I can now choose between six (instead of five) others to talk to...

It is freezing cold. *The Star* says it was nine degrees centigrade yesterday. But I'm sure this place is much colder — as a result of its location and type of construction. I'm trying to continue running, but it requires a great deal of willpower to go out in this weather.

July 1
Dear Wendy, Dean,

I don't think that you should envy my reading... It's to a large extent a substitute for an interesting life and very frustrating. I lie here working out how things in (say) Latin America should be "sorted out" (and don't get to sleep in consequence). And it all remains in the realm of thoughts. I am pleased, however, that I have not wasted my time here...

August 4
Dear Barbara,

While I sit here, we are playing some 16th Century love songs, which seem to suggest just about any place in the world — other than the atmosphere in the cells. We've just had a "hectic" day with stocktaking. Anything out of our familiar and very regular pattern is very exhausting. I can't imagine surviving the ordinary stresses of life outside!

September 1
Dear Wendy,

Yes — our relationships here are pretty close. I'm not equally close to everyone — but there is, nevertheless, a basic mutual supportiveness that we all share. Probably, we have tighter bonds than we realize. It seems to happen when you go through difficult things together. Through two or three close relationships, I have learned a great deal and, I hope, also grown more flexible and tolerant. The analogy of a lover is valid because there is no other situation that I can imagine where one gets to know people so well, and where one's relationships grow and change over years. Yes — I'll be sorry to leave people behind (not to leave). Also, I don't regret having been here. Had I just stagnated and only grown older, I would have found it much more difficult to handle. But I think that most of us have worked actively to get as much as possible out of the experience.

September 1
Dear John and Myrna *[Suttner, brother and sister-in-law]*,

We saw the film *Coming Home* last Friday — about problems of Vietnam vets and wider issues about male/female relationships. Any film that makes a serious attempt to deal with problems of human relationships makes a big impact here. We can't experience some things except through books or films — yet so few films make the effort to discuss relationships, except in a romanticized form. This one doesn't quite come off, but at least they try.

September 28
Dear Lyn,

It is very hot and airless. Being stuck in here one is quite powerless to modify such things — there is not even a window within my reach. So, my problems… are of a very basic order.

October 5
Dear Stan, Joyce and family *[Levenstein]*,

We normally have music every night but our amplifier has broken down. Not that it is quiet. There are a great many distinctive Pretoria Maximum sounds. But it feels very strange having any break in our routine. I am "programmed" to responding to a set pattern and I don't know how I'll respond to the ordinary stresses and strains of a variable life outside. For your own psychological survival here, you adapt to the pace and expectations of prison life. That way, all goes well — until some change leaves you "dumbfounded."

October 26
Dear Barbara,

Thank you for you letter of 28/8. The authorities won't let me send a curriculum vitae "at this stage," so I have asked my family to send what they have... It will help me a great deal if it were to become possible to have some idea of job/scholarship, or whatever opportunities — on the one hand, in order to get permission to leave, but also for my own peace of mind. Right now, it's impossible to make plans or to even imagine what direction most aspects of my life will take.

November 6
Dear Ann and Eugene,

It has turned very hot in the last week and it feels like being locked in a sealed cupboard. It's difficult to study or get to sleep and one wakes up with a headache and sore throat. How much longer we'll be here and what it will be like afterwards we do not know... It seems ages ago — or more like a dream — when I was a "respectable" member of society. But I have no regrets and, on balance, I think I've gained from being here.

November 6
Dear Lyn,

This weather is making me feel very fragile and ill-tempered, which is not a desirable state of mind in prison. You can't avoid the company of others here, and, when in this state of mind, something that someone says, that would normally seem innocuous, easily sparks off a completely disproportionate reaction...

December 1
Dear Mom,

Another Xmas has come around, in the sense that we are now putting in our Xmas orders: 500g sweets, 500g biscuits and 500g fruit. It is incredible how the time has flown. I can still remember the first days very clearly. Yet, in some ways, I'm starting to feel that it has been a very long time. This is mainly when I try to picture how I used to live outside. I can't remember the physical surroundings very clearly. For that matter, everything outside of these walls now carries an air of mystery, when imagined from here. Whatever problems we still have and are on the horizon, the restoration of studies and the new permission to do postgraduate work, plus being able to get newspapers — have all made everything else a lot easier to bear. I spend hours a day reading and discussing the news. In the early years, there was no such fresh input — we had to generate interests from within these walls and from one another's company. I have ambivalent feelings about moving to the old prison. It is physically very difficult and depressing here — but there is no workshop, so you can use your time doing what you consider worthwhile. Some of the more gregarious people find it difficult, because there tends to be a lot less socializing here — but that part suits me. Even if one wanted to, it would be impossible (psychologically) to just sit in the cell and swot the whole day. But I find it advantageous to be able to withdraw from company — here — more often than it was possible at the "old" place...

Letters 1982

January 28
Dear John and Myrna,
   Apart from some eye trouble — an infection that returns on a weekly basis — I'm in good shape and high morale, especially as a result of the short time left.

February 16
Dear Celia, Josef and family,
   We remain at Maximum Security — though we've repeatedly been told various dates, long since past, for our return to our old (now renovated) prison. This place is pretty grim and also jarring on the nerves... Whatever happens now, it is for a short time only.

February 18
Dear Ann and Eugene,
   It's still hot and unpleasant. There are new rules, with some gains and some losses. For Group A there are now 40 instead of 36 letters a year, and 30 visits instead of 25 — but these are now 30-minute, instead of 45-minute, visits. We can't buy books any more, apart from study books. And only magazines registered at the GPO, etc...

February 22
Dear Raphie and Cath *[Kaplinsky, friends of long-standing, then based in UK]*,

Many thanks for your letter... I am very grateful to you for finding out so quickly what the position is with regard to possible scholarships (Jeremy also sends thanks). The closing application date... is a bit problematic. It would be very difficult and, I think, undesirable, for me to make an application before I get out of prison (in May, 1983). And I would, in fact, prefer to wait till I get to England. If all goes well with obtaining an exit permit (about which my mother has begun inquiries) I should be there in July/August 1983...

March 1
Dear Scilla,

Additional Rules.

We have been instructed to convey the following to our correspondents:

That letters (outgoing as well as incoming) containing references to one or more of the following "aspects" will not be forwarded or handed over:

Administration of the Prisons Service.

Discussion of films, as well as books, narrative poems or any report of whatever nature, read, or heard on the radio/television, or any quotation thereof.

Particulars concerning structures/locations/measurements of any prison buildings or parts thereof.

Complaints regarding treatment.

Life stories or biographies, or any part thereof, concerning himself or any other person.

Politics.

March 30
Dear Al and Jenny,

I am fairly switched off as far as prison life goes. There have been some substantial changes in prison rules — some of them improvements. But basically this sort of thing is no longer the center of my life... I am pretty absorbed with my studies and in reading the papers. Still, I have to be very careful to play as full a role in communal life as before, so as not to hurt the feelings of those who must remain...

I'm trying to keep fit by running most days. Unfortunately, it is incredibly boring and hard on the heels and knees, going round and round in a minute square. Still, I think it makes a difference. I have had very few health problems inside...

It will be strange returning to a more normal life. For years, I've had to spend most hours of the day alone in a cell — learning to make out on my own... It may be hard to break the habit. I don't mean that I'll set up bars and locks around my bedroom at 4 p.m. — but that I may have become anti-social...

It's going to be a great relief to get out... Just getting by with one another is quite difficult. We're not all equally suited to one another's company, and it requires a lot of self-discipline, which I'll be glad to relax.

March 30
Dear Lyn,

For some reason, I'm working pretty badly now. It affects all aspects of my prison life. I sleep badly if I feel that I have wasted a day, then I work badly again, because I've slept badly, etc. My studies are psychologically very important. It's a way of affirming that you are still a creative individual — physically restricted, yet still able to create something meaningful in your life.

March 30
Dear John and Myrna,

By the time this reaches you, I will have 13 months to go... This is something of a problem, in terms of my relationship with the others who are staying behind. (Half of our present lot leaves in the next 18 months.) I have to be very careful not to think aloud too often about what I'll do when I get out...

April 12
Dear Brian [Figg, cousin],

Apart from studying, there is not much that you can do on the average day here. (Once a week we see a film, which is a pleasant change.) I run most mornings. The yard is so small that 26 times around makes a mile...

May 19
Dear Wendy,

I passed the six-and-a-half-year mark last week, but it doesn't excite me all that much... If one gets worked up about how much or how little time is left, it is more difficult to cope with the practicalities here...

They have recently announced that we may now be eligible for remission and parole. We do not, however, know on what conditions this is based. Consequently, it is not clear whether this has practical consequences for anyone here...

June 25
Dear Ann, Eugene,

I am thinking of leaving within a week of my release — provided I get the exit permit. I will just sort my books, clothes etc., which will take four or five days, and then leave... I'm more aware of this imminent release — these days. I don't spend all my time thinking about it, but sometimes I spend an hour or so day dreaming. In earlier years, there seemed no point in this — it was so far away. The time goes very fast. Basically, I think this is because I keep very busy and have tried to use every minute... I've started to look older, with my hair getting pretty thin in front — and grayer... I'm more conscious of these things than I used to be, possibly because there is more time here to notice them...

July 26
Dear Barbara,

Since I last wrote, my mother has been negotiating to get an exit permit for me (my passport has been withdrawn). Before they'll consider giving it, another country must indicate willingness to accept me. My first choice — the UK — has refused me permanent residence or asylum. We are still working on that, as well as possible entry to Australia or the Netherlands...

Meanwhile, I am working hard and constructively here. I've completed a 25,000-word piece on customary law and a 35,000 word one on the South African judicial role in the social order. Although not completely satisfactory, I think that I'm doing some new things in these papers. Now, I'm working on my thesis on South Africa and the UN.

August 9
Dear Celia, Josef, Deborah, Joey,

Don't worry about the new regulations. They are, I think, aimed mainly at disguised allusions concerning South African or prison matters. Since this is not the sort of thing that you could refer to anyway, just write normally, in a relaxed way.

We've heard nothing about the application of remission or parole to any of us here. It seems unlikely that it will apply to me... though it could perhaps become routine "after my time."

August 30
Dear Judi,

Our circumstances remain very difficult... being able to get newspapers and do a wider range of studies has proved some compensation and raised our morale...

I've been doing yoga for a month or so — from a book. It seems to help a bit... to unwind.

October 4
Dear Wendy,

We are expecting to move from here to our old (now new) prison any day now. It's very unsettling not knowing what is happening and what lies ahead. As unpleasant as any cell may be, it's our world and it is very threatening to fear that suddenly everything will be uprooted, overturned, or whatever. It's going to take me very long when I get out, to get over the constant feeling of insecurity about all sorts of things that seem to characterize life in prison.

CHAPTER 13

Out, Then on the Run

WHEN I was released, on May 11, 1983, my mother fetched me from Pretoria Local. I was given a couple of cardboard boxes. One contained personal belongings, and the other books and papers that the prison censors had not allowed me to have while in jail. In the margins were written remarks, such as "pure Marxist formulations," which the prison censor must have jotted before holding the papers back.

I wore clothes borrowed from one of my brothers, because I did not yet have clothes of my own. We drove from Pretoria, a place I had only known from prison vans and prison walls, on to the highway to Johannesburg.

At first, I stayed with my mother at Jubilee Hall, the women's residence in the University of the Witwatersrand, where she was dean. Throughout the term of my incarceration, my mother had worked tirelessly to try to improve prison conditions and expose various threats to our "privileges," such as the attempted ending of our studies.

On the way to the residence, we stopped to buy newspapers because I wanted to follow what was happening in some local by-elections. For the first time in eight years, I was able to go into a shop and buy something myself. I worried that I might make a mistake in doing this simple thing. From the moment I arrived at Jubilee Hall, the pace of things seemed very intense, compared with what I had become accustomed to in prison. I was not used to seeing so many people. My senses felt bombarded. I was not in the habit of making decisions for myself on many aspects of my life and it was quite disorienting.

A lot of comrades came to greet me. I remember seeing Professor Ismail Mohamed, soon to be a leader in the United Democratic Front (UDF) and Tiego Moseneke, one of the leaders of the student movement. I also saw Ismail Momoniat of the Transvaal Indian Congress, and Lesley Schermbrucker and Issy Heymann, comrades who had served sentences for refusing to give evidence against the Afrikaner communist leader, Bram Fischer.

Some journalists conducted interviews and this weighed very

heavily on me. I did not want to say anything that implied any form of contrition. I knew that what I said would be interpreted as coming from someone in the liberation movement. At the same time, I did not want to be audacious enough to invite a banning order. Finally, I wanted to use the press to refer to those who remained behind in various prisons in the country, especially those on death row. I insisted that all the reporters read their copy back to me, so I would know exactly how it would appear in print.

When I was released, I had at first planned to leave the country on an exit permit. Many political prisoners had left the country after serving sentences, because they immediately found themselves placed under close police surveillance and heavy restrictions, and had great difficulty finding work or playing any political role. That is why I made initial inquiries about studying overseas and obtaining permission to enter the UK and other countries. Since my passport had been withdrawn on my arrest, I would have had to obtain an exit permit from the South African government.

But there had been a shift in the political climate, as we had noted in newspapers legally obtained in prison in the early 1980s. We had observed important political changes in the first years of P.W. Botha's rule. There was some attempt to "normalize" politics and some space had been won for open, legal democratic activities. Independent trade unions had been formed and they were well organized and engaged in impressive strikes. A public campaign to release Nelson Mandela had begun and this had seen a renewed popularization of the ANC. Many of the symbols of the Congress movement had started to reappear and popular organizations were being established.

The government was perhaps tolerating a broader range of opposition activities, to create the impression that whatever constitutional dispensation was arrived at, it would be in an atmosphere of free debate. In reality, however, the constitutional dispensation being developed in the 1980s was being imposed on the people of South Africa. It sought to incorporate Coloreds and Indians, as junior partners, while continuing the disenfranchisement of the African people.

For me, these changed conditions meant it was no longer inevitable that I would be banned on release. And it seemed possible, if I proceeded cautiously, that I could play some constructive role within the country.

This was a position that we, after discussing the matter as a collective in prison, had reached at a very late stage. We changed our position at the end of 1982, and decided that I should remain in the country.

This was a political choice. But it was also a very difficult personal one. I knew and feared the implications of the decision to remain in South Africa. I did not intend withdrawing from politics. I did not intend taking unnecessary risks, but I did foresee the possibility, indeed likelihood, of experiencing further state repression. I did not want to go back to jail. I did, in many ways, long for peace, quiet and a contented family life. I dreamed of a tranquil home life, uninterrupted by police attention or the threat of it. But, I asked myself this: "If I were a black South African, without any opportunities to take up a professional career or emigrate, would I then consider withdrawing from politics?"

Having been in jail once, having been tortured, I knew what might well lie in store for me. But I saw no other way. I had made my choice in the late 1960s to throw my lot in with those wanting to change South Africa. I considered it important that I, as a white person, should not demand less of myself than did my black comrades.

I was also influenced by the choices made by Joe Gqabi, the ANC militant who was assassinated in Zimbabwe in the 1980s. He, too, had been in jail, but came out and continued to struggle, first inside the country, until he was rearrested; and later, after he was forced to leave. I saw very clearly that my end could be like his. I did not want that, but felt I had no alternative. The decisions were my own. The consequences flowed from what I had chosen.

A few months after my release, the United Democratic Front (UDF) was launched at a gathering of some 10,000 people in Capetown. Its leaders included people who had been active in the Congress movement since the 1950s, as well as many newly emerging activists. The Front became a coordinating body for hundreds of organizations representing all manner of sectors of society — political, religious, youth, sporting, women, students, educational, housing and workers. From the beginning, the UDF consciously adopted the principles of the Congress movement, although it did not initially adopt the Freedom Charter — in order to be as broad as possible and with the hope of drawing in elements from the Black Consciousness Movement. But the UDF spoke the language of the Congress alliance; that is, the language of democracy, nonracialism and peace.

For some time, I was very cautious about my political role, operating in semiconspiratorial fashion, for fear of inviting police attention. I met with various activists and engaged in discussions, but this was with a fairly low profile.

Jeremy Cronin was released shortly after, and we were in close and regular contact, able to compare our impressions and seek one another's advice on how to proceed. I also met and formed a close relationship with Billy Nair, who was released shortly after me. Billy had served 20 years in prison for sabotage. But he came out more militant than anyone else and was always ready to take on the regime. He usually had a twinkle in his eye, but behind this there was steely determination. Billy is minute in physical size, but the police could never dent his determination. They arrested him twice within the first year of his release and, on one occasion, punctured his eardrum. He won damages in court and just carried on.

I also started to work closely with people such as Laloo Chiba, who had served 18 years on Robben Island for sabotage and is now a Member of Parliament; and Amos Masondo, now the executive mayor of Johannesburg, who had spent time on the island for activities related to the June 1976 uprising — and had then been redetained repeatedly. I also worked with Murphy Morobe, who had spent time on the island for activities related to the Soweto uprising. He is now chairperson of the Financial and Fiscal Commission. And Mohamed Valli Moosa (of the UDF), who later became South Africa's minister for the environment and tourism.

I got a job a few weeks after my release, first as a researcher in the African Studies Institute and later as a senior lecturer in law at the University of Witwatersrand, and thus quickly became integrated once more into the academic community.

At that time, a lot of debate was taking place within the emerging democratic organizations. Many participants did not hesitate to quote Marx, Engels and Lenin and cite the ANC or SACP in support of their positions. Jeremy and I were more cautious. Laws were still in place that could be used for bringing charges against people who tried to further the aims of illegal organizations. Even when we felt that our opponents were misrepresenting the position of the liberation movement, we did not feel free to make this fact clear by citing the movement's illegal publications, as this could attract prosecution. Having previously been convicted for promoting the aims of the ANC and SACP, we were more likely to be charged if we did so.

I gradually emerged from seclusion, particularly after being invited to deliver the T.B. Davie Memorial Lecture at the University of Capetown in 1984, published under the title *The Freedom Charter — The People's Charter in the Nineteen-Eighties*. My objective was to promote the Freedom Charter as a unifying vision of the future, democratic South Africa. By doing this, I hoped to help popularize not only the demands of the ANC but also the principles of popular involvement, consultation and mandated leadership. The Charter had been adopted at the Congress of the People on June 26, 1955, after a massive campaign to collect peoples' demands, to hear what type of South

Africa they wanted after the demise of apartheid. The consolidated demands were embraced in the Charter.

The Charter had a unique legitimacy, because it contained basic, democratic aspirations shared by the majority of South Africans. It also had great weight because the document emerged not from textbooks but from listening to the hopes and grievances of ordinary people. The Freedom Charter crystallized the points of consensus amongst very many democrats opposed to apartheid.

The approach that I adopted was to argue that the Freedom Charter was a people's document, emerging from popular demands and reflecting the aspirations of a wide range of South Africans who were being oppressed under apartheid. While it had a working-class bias, it did not cater to any single class or stratum exclusively, but tried to broadly embrace the aspirations of all democratic South Africans.

The attention given to this lecture drew me further into UDF activities and, in 1984, I was elected Education Officer for the UDF in the Transvaal. Together with Jeremy Cronin and other contributors, I also wrote the book *30 Years of the Freedom Charter* (which appeared when I was in detention in 1986). In preparing this book, I had the opportunity to meet older comrades, such as the late Dorothy Nyembe, who had served 15 years in prison for MK activities; A. S. Chetty, who was a veteran Congress activist; and Martin Ramakgadi, who had served a long term of imprisonment for sabotage.

In mid-1985, I was invited to a legal conference in Washington. My passport, which had been withdrawn on my arrest in 1975, was returned. On the way there, and again on my return, I met secretly in London with Joe Slovo and others. It was our first meeting since my release, and I reported on the situation in the country and discussed my future role. We sat down for a full day, analyzing developments in the country and discussing how best to go forward.

On the day I was booked to return to South Africa (July 21), funerals were being held in the Eastern Cape for Matthew Goniwe, Fort Calata, Sicelo Mhlauli and Sparrow Mkonto, four activists who had been murdered by the police. Thousands of people openly marched in the Eastern Cape under the banners of the ANC and SACP. A state of emergency was declared, covering most of the country.

While waiting at Heathrow Airport, I talked with a group of people, including Gill Marcus (then active in the liberation movement, and now Deputy Governor of the South African Reserve Bank). Gill, without the others noticing, indicated with her eyes that someone wanted to talk to me at the bookshop about 200 yards away.

I walked across and found Joe Slovo, who was pretending to look at books on the shelf. He asked me whether it would not be wiser for me to remain behind in London rather than go back to South Africa and risk arrest. I said I was worried that if I did not go back it would always be difficult to return. Since I was in the UDF leadership, not to go back could demoralize others and I did not see my role as remaining in exile. He left it for me to decide.

When I arrived at Johannesburg airport, I wondered whether the police would be waiting for me, but they were not there. My sister, Sally, who was obviously anxious, had come to meet me. She dropped me at my flat in Muller Street, Yeoville (Johannesburg), where I had been happily settled for two years. I packed my things, never to return to that address again. I then spent some seven or eight months evading arrest and moving from place to place.

A large number of the comrades with whom I had worked had been arrested on the way back from the Eastern Cape funeral. Thousands of people who ran the various affiliates of the UDF were now in prison. Some had escaped arrest because they left on different routes in the days after my arrival. I set about finding them. Mohamed Valli Moosa was out and we conferred with comrades like UDF activists Barbara Creecy and Lisa Seftel, who had come back from the funeral on the bus, but were not arrested.

I went down to the Western Cape and made contact with Jeremy Cronin, while Valli went to the Eastern Cape. In these situations, we had to find people who were making it their business to be inaccessible. We had to "dig them up," as Valli would put it.

Then Valli and I went down to Durban, where the state of emergency was not yet in operation, to meet Curnick Ndlovu, who had also served 20 years on Robben Island for sabotage and was then national chairperson of the UDF; and also Billy Nair. Gradually, a network was pulled together and we regrouped to continue the work of the UDF. All of this was in secret.

I did not return to my lecturing job. Instead, after consultation with Professor John Dugard (then a very senior member of the Wits Law Faculty), I wrote to the university, explaining that I had gone underground to avoid arrest. I said my political activities had been within the law, but suspected this would be no bar to being arrested. The university did not fire me but reviewed my appointment on a month-by-month basis and did not confirm my tenure while I was underground.

I was in disguise. All I had learned from Ronnie Kasrils in the 1970s, simple as it may have been, now proved of use. I had to watch out in earnest, to see whether I was being followed on foot or by car, and carefully applied what I had learned. I had to study my own habits and form an identity that appeared quite different to my normal one. I changed my walk. I combed my hair straight back and grew a very severe and ugly moustache of the type that one finds amongst prison warders. I smoked. Few people recognized me in this more extreme disguise and I escaped police detection throughout the first emergency.

There had been no safe houses prepared for me, or by me. Seldom do you know exactly when you will be forced underground. For the first few nights of the emergency, it was nightmarish, as I moved from place to place, staying with people I did not know and in circumstances that were very inconvenient and unsafe. I had to borrow a car or exchange my own car, and try to find more permanent accommodation.

It is interesting to note how many people were prepared to take the risk of offering refuge. There were many unsung heroes and heroines who, despite the dangers, gave me — and others like me — a place to stay.

Eventually, I found fairly stable accommodation. I managed to settle down in a house found by UDF activist Catherine Hunter, through her contacts in progressive sections of the Catholic Church. Together with Barbara Creecy, I produced a long pamphlet analyzing the role of the democratic movement during the state of emergency. This was issued by the UDF a few months later.

In general, during the 1985-86 state of emergency, we regrouped and carried on. We escalated our activities against the regime and advanced calls that raised the level of resistance.

However, this was a period when I felt considerable fear. At the beginning of the emergency, I really did not want to be caught. When I heard the way people were being tortured, I believed I was not ready to face that again. I remember one night driving with Khehla Shubane, who was an activist in Soweto (and is now a researcher at the Center for Policy Studies, in Johannesburg). We were discussing what would happen if I was arrested. He quite practically assured me that I would, definitely, be tortured. I did not resent his frankness, but I wondered if I still had the same single-mindedness that had carried me through my earlier detention.

Nevertheless, through applying myself to political activities, I was not obsessed with the prospect of arrest. I just carried on, causing as much trouble for the regime as I could. To do so was the policy of the ANC.

After about nine months, on March 7, 1986, the government lifted the state of emergency and we gradually surfaced, though not completely. I took various precautions to conceal where I was staying, although I was not always in hiding. During this period, before the reimposition of the emergency in June 1986, the ANC call to make

apartheid unworkable and South Africa ungovernable was coming into
effect.

In my own area of activity, political education, we held many
discussions and workshops, explaining and advocating the formation
of organs of people's power, particularly the establishment of street
committees. I met with many activists from all over the country to try
to understand their experiences, the difficulties they had encountered
and the successes they had achieved. I wrote various papers on
questions related to people's power — both for activists and academic
audiences.

Some real gains were made in this period, in terms of popular
political involvement. One aspect that impressed me greatly was the
way in which many communities took steps to control crime and
disarm people who carried knives and other dangerous weapons; to
recover stolen property and resolve disputes in the community. In
these situations, where communities had little confidence in the South
African police, street and yard committees gave a measure of
protection that would otherwise have been absent.

There were, however, cases of serious abuses, such as the
"necklace" killings (execution of alleged collaborators through placing
a burning car tire around their necks) and kangaroo courts, in which
youth and sometimes gangsters took control and executed harsh
punishments. We condemned these abuses, perhaps with insufficient
vigor.

While not excusing them, these negative phenomena should be seen
in relation to a situation of severe repression and fear and the arrest of
leadership figures. In some townships of Port Elizabeth, for example,
many of the structures that had previously been run by a leadership
representing all sections of the community fell into the control of a
small group. Very often, youngsters who had little discipline filled the
leadership vacuum. Without the benefit of experienced comrades to
advise them, such abuses could more easily occur.

This was nevertheless an exciting time, when I saw living examples
of "mass creativity," a phenomenon I had previously known only as a
phrase from books. It was also a time when police repression led to the
killing and arrest of thousands of people. Because of the level of this
repression, which was aimed at the top level of our organizations, it
became more necessary than ever to organize at every level of the
community — in particular, at street and yard level. Organizing on a
local level brought us closer to the needs of ordinary people. But this
objective was only partially achieved, and not evenly throughout the
community.

The 1980s were a very important period in many people's political involvement. The struggles of the 1980s forced the apartheid regime to negotiate. We need to study this period and build on its lessons — both positive and negative — in order to secure mass involvement in our new, democratic society.

CHAPTER 14

Underground Letters

The following letters were written during the 1985-86 South African state of emergency to my mother, Mrs. Sheila Suttner, while she was based in Perth, Western Australia.

September 23, 1985
Dear Mom,

I do not know what reports you have heard. There was a massive swoop on all UDF leaders, and the police rounded up most people who had not already gone underground. They also caught those who had returned home or to work. They came for Jeremy *[Cronin]*, but he got away. Police treatment of arrested people now seems worse than ever before. The indemnity provision seems to have obviated all their usual inhibitions, if there ever were any. We understand that the Protea police station *[in Soweto]* is being used to torture just about everyone. The police are using car jump leads to apply electric shocks to many people.

In Durban, they tortured Billy Nair so badly that they perforated his eardrum. They also gave him a black eye. Fortunately, there was some evidence and an interdict was brought.

I'm telling you this so that, should I be caught, you can get the Australians *[government and lobby groups]* to put immediate pressure on the South African government for assurance regarding my treatment. We *[the UDF]* intend mounting a general campaign and possibly bringing further interdicts to highlight the extensive — even by South African standards — use of barbaric methods.

You are wrong in imagining my "frustration" in being where I am. We *[the democratic movement]* are by no means smashed, and have mounted an offensive in a number of different directions — to protect our organizations, but also to take the struggle for democracy to a higher level. We have got out quite a lot of propaganda and the people are resisting, often spontaneously, right around the country. In this situation, I do what I can. We are a legal organization — even within the laws of this state. We are not giving up our role. If I were merely in hiding, and not carrying on the struggle, I *would* be frustrated and depressed.

You ask: "What joy does life hold out for you?" Obviously, this is a very difficult experience. Every day, every moment, one is on one's guard...

I can't see the people I would normally see. I cannot do my normal job. I am staying out of reach to avoid the immediate danger of being caught and detained (for however long), possibly as an accused in some cooked-up trial. Even if I were eventually acquitted, it might be after awaiting trial for some time — and, possibly, after a difficult detention. Perhaps I will be caught tomorrow, though I do not think so.

I will continue with the struggle as long as I can. I can't simply opt out in order to lead a happy life. This alternative is not open to black people. If I identify with the majority of South Africans, I have to demand of myself what they demand of themselves.

I am not happy about the continual fear and tension and the horrific prospect of being taken. But, in a deeper personal sense, this is the most valid way of maintaining my commitment.

On the job front — the University *[of Witwatersrand]* has until now been understanding about my situation. They have paid my salary until the end of this month and I will hear tomorrow whether it will be paid after that, for another two months. The big problem will arise when the emergency is lifted. They may then expect me to return to work, but as far as the UDF is concerned, the danger exists whether or not there is a formal emergency. In other areas, there is a de facto emergency. *[A degree of repression was already being practiced because of the formal declaration of a state of emergency.]* And even up here, the police have been distinguishing the UDF detainees from the rest by holding them under Section 29 of the Internal Security Act.

So, I will have some problems later this year, or early next year. I think that they will lift the emergency and claim to have put the uprising under control — even if that is not the case. They have to do something that will increase business confidence. Otherwise, they will face a huge crisis at the end of the year, the date when they have pledged to repay all their short-term debts...

I cannot say that there is nothing to worry about in regard to me. For the foreseeable future, I intend to be safe. Hopefully, if they get me, it will be in a period when they will have been forced to exercise more restraint. Maybe I will not be detained at all. There is no point in dwelling on it. I just have to get on with things and I hope that it is possible for others to do the same.

December 11, 1985

Dear Mom,

I have returned to work, though I do not have to be there at fixed times. At this time of the year, there are no lectures. But I am still not home.

Jeremy is being sought. They have his mug shot all over the police stations in the Western Cape. He had surfaced before they declared the state of emergency in Western Cape. He had to go underground again in great earnest. On this occasion, like the previous one, he just managed to get away when they came for him. They are very stretched, so it is quite hard for them to mount huge searches for one individual.

I am playing safe because, although I am not being sought, there may be a new swoop.

This whole thing has had a serious effect on my whole life. It seems like a new phase has begun. (I do not think that things will ever return to P.W. Botha's conception of normality.) It seems that a normal life, uninterrupted by the possibility of detention, is no longer possible for me. Periodically, I am going to have to be on the run, as is the case now. This will, of course, be very problematic for my job. On the other hand, the police may realize that they actually have nothing on us and try to build up towards some big trial in a few years' time and leave us in peace for now. Who knows?

I do not think that they can lift the emergency, though the press clamp is an attempt to create an atmosphere of normality by concealing what is happening.

This period has altered so many things for me. For example, I do not know if I can think of using the university housing grant. Nor do I think it is safe to live on my own. If they can't get you one way, they may try more drastic means. So I may move out of my flat and share a house for rent, or some such thing.

The university had hinted that they might not have paid me after last month. I took that as symptomatic of the weakening of my situation, and it made my — very cautious — reappearance a necessity. The university would not try to get rid of me, but promotion is out, in the light of this underground stint...

I am planning to go away for 10 days. I am in very good physical shape. I run between 20 and 30 minutes every day and have lost weight. According to everyone, I look very healthy. I am, nevertheless, very exhausted and emotionally drained.

I have been keeping such strict control of myself for so long that any "easing" seems to unleash all sorts of things. David's death was quite shattering in that respect. *[David Rabkin died in a MK training accident in Angola.]* While I was not totally shocked, in the light of death being an occupational hazard, I feel that I have lost an important part of my life. Although he has not been with us, Jeremy and I have always thought in terms of David being involved in what we do. This is partly because many of the ideas that we are propagating were worked out with D.R. inside.

The Johannesburg Democratic Action Committee (JODAC) organized a small (because of the emergency) memorial meeting for David, which was advertised by word of mouth. I have sent you a tape of it...

CHAPTER 15

John Vorster Square

"That's how it goes, my friend.
The problem is not falling a captive,
it's how to avoid surrender."
(Nazim Hikmet, from "That's How It Goes," Selected Poems, 1967.)

JOHN VORSTER Square, the notorious police headquarters in Johannesburg, is a terrible place. It was named after Balthazar Johannes Vorster, who, when minister of justice, initiated long-term detention without trial. It saw the deaths of numerous people, including Ahmed Timol in the 1970s and Neil Aggett in the 1980s. The police relished this reputation and would threaten detainees with the same fate as Timol, that is, falling from the 10th floor. When Prema Naidoo was interrogated, they told him they would rename the building "Prema Heights" after he had fallen. Even if one were fairly experienced, the name John Vorster Square evoked fear. I hoped I would never find myself there.

June was always a dangerous time in the 1980s. We commemorated the Soweto June 16 *[1976]* uprising annually. The Security Police expected heightened political activity and would take preemptive steps to prevent problems for themselves. To avoid falling into their net, many political activists moved into hiding.

I found a fresh hiding place, but I could not be fully underground. I wanted to hold onto my job at the university and felt that I should, at the end of the first emergency, reappear at work. One morning, as I left my place of semi-hiding in Houghton (Johannesburg) and drove towards Empire Road on the way to Wits, I saw some men get out of a car and hastily move to the door of a house. I thought they were police. I drove on to Empire Road and, as I turned, a second car came off the curb and followed me. I went into Wits and parked. That evening, I swapped cars with a friend and left the university with the intention of finding somewhere new to stay.

I went to a house in Westdene, a suburb of Johannesburg, where I had stayed eight or nine months previously. I was about to go in when I noticed a dark Toyota behind me, a car I had seen a number of times, with a number plate I recognized. I immediately got back into my car and raced off, with the Toyota behind me. I sped around corners and through red lights, but the car followed me. I went onto the highway and off the highway, on again and off again, round and round. I felt the car on my tail was faster than the Honda I had borrowed but it did not try to cut me off. They just remained behind. What did they want? Were they trying to force me off the road? I had to stop at the traffic lights at the road opposite the zoo. The Toyota was right behind me. A second car, which had not been there at first — a Ford Escort, then a favorite vehicle with the police — wedged itself on one side of me. But the occupants of these cars did not attempt to arrest me.

I did not know what was happening. I raced back onto the highway, sped along before turning up again at one of the off-ramps near Rosebank. This time, I was in luck. I managed to slip in between some cars. The pursuers could not immediately force their way in. I drove a short while, then turned right, down one of the side streets. I rushed down the street, which ran parallel to the highway in the direction of Sandton.

I had been told that you could turn off your lights, but still see ahead of your vehicle, by pressing the bright switch. The rear lights would not be illuminated, or seen from behind. I did this and managed to shake them off. But I drove around for some time just to make sure.

I had to find a completely new place to stay. Certain people had once assured me that I could stay at their house if I was ever in trouble. I arrived at about 10 p.m. When I told of the car chase, however, they were not brimming over with pleasure to welcome me. I, nevertheless, settled in for the night.

The next morning, they explained that the husband's business involved various government contracts and they could not risk my being caught there. I had to change my car again and find somewhere new to stay. I had enough money to hire a car for a short while. I think a colleague, Cathi Albertyn, helped me with this. She had started to lecture at Wits but had found herself, uncomplainingly, having to fill in for me for months on end while I was on the run.

That night, I met with a number of comrades in a house in Doornfontein. Mohamed Valli Moosa was there. He was then acting general secretary of the UDF. Rev. Frank Chikane was there and this was shortly before he became general secretary of the South African Council of Churches. He is now director general in the office of the president. Laloo Chiba was also present. Ismail Momoniat, known as "Momo," secretary of the Transvaal Indian Congress and now in the

Ministry of Finance, was in the group. Amos Masondo ("Ambie") was there, too, between one of his numerous spells in and out of detention. He was centrally involved in the rent boycott, which was then having a devastating effect on the Soweto collaborationist structures. Khehla Shubane was there, too.

We discussed the rent boycott and Ambie did not speak as if he had much to do with it, but Khehla said that everyone mentioned Ambie's name as a key figure. We knew the police would be hunting for him. In the light of the car chase, I wanted to know whether I should still go to Zimbabwe the next morning. Professor Reg Austen of the Law Faculty had invited me to give some lectures at the university. But the main reason for going was, really, to meet Mac Maharaj — who was then a leading figure in the ANC and SACP — to discuss the possibility of expanding underground structures. Ambie felt I would be picked up at the airport and should not take the chance. The consensus was, however, that I should go. It was important to coordinate our work with the ANC outside South Africa. Frank Chikane also wanted to know what the ANC could do to protect people inside the country from the threat of assassination. I was not happy about going but abided by the collective view.

Valli, Momo and I spent the night in a hotel room in Hillbrow. Valli was to take me to the airport early in the morning. I had made no secret of my trip, applying openly for a visa, on the legitimate grounds of giving university lectures. At this time, I was constantly operating in this ambiguous way, partly underground, partly openly. I wanted to assert my professional identity as an academic. I had hoped it would provide me with a measure of protection, but this hope was to prove unfounded. Being a lecturer also meant my hands were tied in ways that did not apply to many other activists. People who worked for "struggle organizations" could simply go underground. That was part of the understanding of the job, especially for people in the UDF. But those who did not have "struggle jobs" could not simply abandon their work.

The three of us were so tired, that we did not hear our alarm clocks and had to hurry to make the plane. Unfortunately for me, because of the rush, no one read the headlines of the *Citizen* before we set off. The government was to declare a new state of emergency on that very day, June 12, 1986. I found out about this much later.

As I arrived at the airport and was heading for the plane, a man called out: "Mr. Suttner, Zimbabwe plane?" And, for a moment, I thought it was a helpful airport official. Soon he waved to two or three others to come and join him. I was under arrest. I hoped Valli would guess what had happened. He did, and managed to get away.

I had dreaded this moment. I was back in police hands. I wondered how I would handle it, now that I knew all of what it entailed. I asked a question of the arresting officer, Major Oosthuizen, and he answered me rudely. I immediately felt angry at being treated this way. I think that anger was also a surge of strength flowing back into me and this made me better prepared to deal with what lay ahead.

On the way back into the city, they spoke to someone on the police radio. They first asked this person to look for Valli's car. Regarding my arrest, I also heard the person on the other side saying, *"Gaan jy hom 'n ding of twee wys?"* ["Are you going to show him a thing or two?"] That is, were they going to beat me up? I said nothing. I just waited.

They went to a house in Mayfair, where I had stayed for some months, and searched it. Then they took me to Wits.

Some of the police did not know how to behave in this environment. They wanted to appear different from the image we had of them — as being thugs. But on arriving at a security barrier, they simply got out, displaying their guns, and lifted the barrier. After they parked, just before going into the law faculty, one of the policemen came out brandishing a huge rifle. Oosthuizen, slightly embarrassed, told him this was not necessary.

They took me to my office. This is where their problems started. I am not very neat and tend to accumulate a lot of paper. There were lecturing and research notes going back to 1968. There were also political papers. The police had no idea where to start, what was relevant to their task and where this mass of papers should end up. In the meantime, people were knocking on the door of my office. Eventually they let in Professor June Sinclair, then dean of the law faculty, and decided to bundle me out, abandoning their search.

In the passage, I told those around my office that I had heard the police say on the radio that they intended to beat me up. I said I had been tortured the last time I was in detention. I asked them to bring an interdict preventing similar assaults.

The police then pushed me away. The late Etienne Mureinik, who stood by me very loyally throughout this period, raced after us to get the exact words I had heard on the police radio.

The police were furious. Oosthuizen turned to me in the car and said, "Now we are seeing the real Raymond Suttner." It was as if I had betrayed a sacred trust, by taking steps to avoid being tortured.

I was then taken to John Vorster Square. We had often driven past the square on the highway to Soweto or Lenasia. We would look to see if lights were on. They always were, and we would wonder who was being interrogated. I had never been inside. On entering the building, I met Colonel du Toit, then deputy head of the Security Police, whom I had known from my Durban experience. Referring to my mention of possible torture, he said, "This is not Durban."

I was taken to the cells after seeing a doctor — which was then a routine procedure (following various inquests into deaths in detention). After Aggett's death, various precautions had been taken to prevent suicide attempts. All cells were openly monitored through video and audio systems. The police had three video screens, which they rotated in order to monitor all the cells. One could do nothing in private.

There were two types of cells. The better ones had windows, out of which one could see what was going on outside. I later took advantage of this view, until the police stopped me. The other cells, in which I spent most of my time, had no access to the outside. The bars, windows and door were covered with Perspex, which was perforated with small ventilation holes. When the police brought food, they did not open the door but shoved it through a gap in the Perspex — similar to the feeding of rats in a laboratory experiment.

There was a toilet, mat and blankets in the cell. There was no pillow. They gave us drinking water in unhygienic plastic containers. You could not wash or brush your teeth in the cell, but only when taken to the showers. There were only two showers, located in separate parts of the building, to service all the prisoners. There were probably about 60 prisoners at that time. Officers were supposed to let only one prisoner go to the showers at a time. We were not supposed to have contact with other prisoners. One practical result of this was that some would have showers at 6 a.m. and others during the rest of the day, right up until after 2 p.m. One never knew when one's turn would be. You just sat in your cell, feeling dirty.

Often, the police said nothing and, even if you addressed them, would leave without answering. In the first week or two, I was in one of the cells without the Perspex on the windows. I tried to make out what was going on outside, especially whether there was a successful "stay away" [*general strike, and non-attendance of classes by students*] on June 16.

Having a "view" was an advantage, but these cells were very far from the office where the police sat. That meant it was a complicated process if you needed something and wanted to contact them. Generally, the bells did not work and you had to shout. There was a terrible sense of insecurity and dependence on the police for everything, and you could go for 12 hours without seeing anyone.

According to the state of emergency regulations, which took some time to extract from my jailers, detainees were supposed to leave their cells to exercise. In my first 19 days, I had exercise on only two occasions. In reality, John Vorster Square could not comply with the regulations regarding exercise without breaking the rule that we were not allowed to see or talk to each other. This was because the only exercise yard adjoined one of the showers.

I, nevertheless, bombarded the authorities with letters of complaint about the lack of exercise. After 19 days, they did allow Azhar Cachalia and me to take our exercise. (Azhar, who is also a lawyer, was then UDF national treasurer and, until recently, South Africa's Secretary for Safety and Security.) The rest of the prisoners were not taken out to exercise. We tried to communicate this to them, so they could also claim their rights.

Once I had established my right to exercise, one of the policemen would take me out of my cell. The first day he said, "It is 25 to four now. You have an hour's exercise. You finish at 25 past four." I thought that perhaps I had not heard correctly. I did not argue. The next day, however, he said, "It is 20 to four now. You have until 20 past four." So I asked myself, "What would happen if he were to take me out at five to four, would the exercise end at five past four?" I explained that an hour was the period from 20 minutes to one particular hour until 20 minutes to the next hour that followed it — not until 20 past the first hour. He looked at me suspiciously and called another policeman *"Jacobs, kom hierso!"* ["Jacobs come here!"]. Jacobs confirmed my version.

In many situations, the police control would break down slightly. Sporadically, the different prisoners did have contact with one another. Some of the police were less vicious than others and were prepared to let us speak to one another, provided they did not land in trouble. And we would try very hard to avoid bringing any trouble on their heads.

I had not met Moses Mayekiso before. He was then a leading trade unionist and civic leader, now director of the investment arm of the South African National Civic Organization. I spoke to him in John Vorster Square. He was returning from the showers. I was on my way in, and we compared notes about interrogation. We discussed the question of organs of people's power, which later formed the basis of charges against Mayekiso.

I remember also seeing Zwelakhe Sisulu, then editor of *New Nation*, now a leading businessperson. Back then, I did not know him well. He was walking down the passage with a towel around his shoulder, much like someone going off to the beach. He seemed completely at home. Indeed, he knew the place well from his various spells inside.

Some of the police stationed at John Vorster Square made things difficult for us. Most were fairly easy-going, uniformed police. They had no special reason to give us a hard time. Nor did they go out of their way to make things any easier. They mainly made things easier for themselves; for example, by not worrying whether we got our food hot or cold, taking their time about coming round to the cells to take us for showers, and so on. But one or two were quite decent. I remember one day, early on, a policeman arrived with a red apple and said, "This is from your friend Azhar." I had not known until then that Azhar was inside.

One night, my lawyers brought me some fruit. I asked the policeman on duty if I could take one to Zwelakhe Sisulu, one to Azhar, one to Mayekiso and one or two others. He said he would take them. I replied that I wanted to take them myself. He said: "You are section three and they are section three, OK." The fact that we were held under the same emergency detention section was good enough reason to keep us apart, but I did not say so. I walked down the passage, greeting the various prisoners and then returned to my cell.

I always wanted to do my own washing. But there were no facilities — you could only wash clothes at the showers. And they were normally in use. At about 6 p.m., if one of the more reasonable police were on duty I would ask if I could do my washing. Since no officer was likely to come around then, they often agreed. I could walk around the yard and look out onto the highway while my clothes were soaking. I tried to imagine it was not the road to Braamfontein but really a Seapoint beachfront.

While strolling around, I would always peer into offices, reading what notices and correspondence I could see. As a sentenced prisoner, I learned the habit of reading "upside-down correspondence" while standing before the desks of prison officials. In one of the offices looking into the yard, I saw someone tuning a radio. He turned around and it was Azhar. He had persuaded the police to allow him to listen to the World Cup soccer, while he was actually trying to pick up some news. We were able to share information about our detention; especially in regard to what questions people had been asked. The police came upon us doing this, and we did not deny speaking to one another. We said we were friends. And they just let us be.

I remember Azhar said, "We are going to sit here for months." I did not agree. Azhar was wrong in his own case, too. A week or two later, I was in the passage and I saw them releasing him.

Not all relationships were amicable and sometimes one had to do something to remedy the situation. When I first arrived at John Vorster, the constable who took me to my cell was fairly cordial and he said, "You Regulation three. Yes, no that is OK. Section 29 very serious." He then allowed me to take soap into the cell. The next day, a new young constable arrived. The first thing he did was to take the soap away.

While we were walking back from my shower he said, "You are going to have to learn this is not a five-star hotel." I thought to myself, "I don't need to be told this by a young fool." But I decided to wait. This was not the right moment. I knew that in dealing with conflict in jail, it did not help to take these things up on a one-to-one basis with a junior person. It was best to wait for a senior officer.

Every day, at about 5.30 a.m., an officer visited the cells. I would be half-asleep and he would have left before I could offer a complaint. On one occasion, I tried to raise a complaint and he just said, *"Lees jou Bybel man!"* ["Read your Bible man!"] And I consequently did not get a chance to complain in the morning. But, one day, a brigadier came around later in the day. The young man who had been rude to me was with him. I said, "I have generally been treated in a professional manner, with the exception of this young man." The young man was also there and I told the brigadier what had happened. Usually, when officers reprimand their staff, they are supposed to call them aside. But he delivered the reprimand there and then, saying: "You must treat him in a professional manner! This man is in trouble. It is not your job to make it more difficult for him."

In the beginning, there was a general state of ignorance about our conditions, the prospects of our release and how long we were likely to spend in detention. Thousands of people had been pulled in and the officials had not sorted out who would go and who would remain. I was not interrogated at all for the first 19 days. I had expected to be interrogated immediately. But once the expectation of being interrogated was removed, I used the time to rest. I just lay on the mat in the cell and reminisced about what I had done in the three years I had been out of prison — all the interesting things, as well as the errors I had made. I did a little exercise. I did not think I would be in very long.

From inside the Perspex-sealed cells, cars outside on the highway made a "whoosh, whoosh" sound. I tried to imagine it was the sea. I felt alone and abandoned in the cell. Sometimes, the only social interaction the whole day would be rudeness from a policeman. Most of the time, I felt powerless.

After 19 days, I was interrogated by two policemen who did not seem to know much about politics and kept on bandying clichés, such as "You act as if you are as innocent as a lamb," and giving me their own view of politics. If this were the standard of interrogation, I thought, there was nothing to fear.

During this period, many people were being held for just two weeks, although they had no idea that was the case. In fact, many only knew they were in jail, but not the provisions under which they were being held. One day, I bumped into the unionist Bashir Valli in the showers and he said to me, "Raymond, what is this about a state of emergency?" I said, "Yes, there is a state of emergency." He said, "Does this mean we will be in for long?" I said, "I don't know." Bashir was out a few days later.

Even in John Vorster Square, in the middle of this awful place, there was defiance. When I walked round the small exercise yard one day, I saw scribbled on one corner, "Long Live the ANC/SACP alliance," then "Long live SACTU/COSATU! Long live UDF!" And in another part of the building I saw "Free Mandela!" One day I saw someone had written "Long live Azapo! Long live the PAC!" Unfortunately, we had not done enough to rid our ranks of sectarianism, for the next day that had been crossed out, while the pro-ANC slogans remained.

Back in the cells, however, there was evidence of private soul-searching. On the walls, written in penciled script that could not have been seen from the door, there was a dialogue between successive inhabitants in the cell. One wrote: "This place is hell." He added that he just wanted to get out. And then someone else wrote: "Look here, comrade, don't despair. Despair leads you to forget your beliefs. Next thing you are a state witness." Someone else being held under Section 28, which was a state witness provision, wrote: "Comrades, just know I will never give evidence for the state." These brief notes reflected the private agonies of people who, faced with hard choices, were trying to pump courage into themselves.

While I was sitting there, I did not know what was happening in most places outside my cell. Suddenly, one day, a man in a suit arrived and gave me part of a court record. It was an undertaking that the police would not assault me. From this, I worked out there had been an interdict. They denied they had said, "Are you going to show him a thing or two?" They claimed they had said, "Is he going to point things out to you?" That is, reveal the whereabouts of arms caches. Since no such question ever arose, they were obviously lying. Although this was not an absolute guarantee that I would not be assaulted, it was sufficient to give me some sense of security.

I did not look for trouble in John Vorster Square. I took risks only where I had to. I was not prepared to invite unnecessary attention. In the cell opposite me, there was for a time a person who had been arrested for holding a poster saying: "State of Emergency or State of Bankruptcy?" I knew he would be out in about a week. I hoped I would be in for only a short time, but knew it could be months or even a year. This person wanted to have running conversations with me. It was a risk I did not want to take, just for nothing. On the face of it, I may have appeared more cowardly than he was, but I was not prepared to get into confrontations with the authorities over nothing. I was prepared to "make waves" only over matters that were important to me, such as rude treatment or failure to give me exercise time out of the cell.

While at John Vorster Square, I had two or three visits from my brother, John, and my sister, Sally, and was visited twice by lawyers. These visits took me completely by surprise. I told my brother they had arrested me under the Criminal Procedure Act. I understood I was then being held under emergency regulations, but had never been formally redetained under the state of emergency provisions. I doubted whether they had followed the correct procedure. In fact, this was how one detainee obtained his release — by pointing out this lack of procedure. My lawyer, Peter Harris, came to see me with a draft for an application along these lines. I was called for this visit by a Lieutenant Gordon Brookbanks, who had been a police spy on Rhodes University campus and I think had a lot to do with my remaining in detention. He is still in the police force as a colonel. He insisted on sitting in on the lawyer's visit, which was illegal.

Pete said to me, "It seems you have got a good chance of getting out on this." The next time he saw me he said, "What they are doing is trying to avoid your release at all costs. They are saying this is a very important case. Even though there has been a decision in the Pretoria division, they say we need a full bench (that is, three judges)." But they would still have had to reverse an earlier court decision, which had released someone on the same grounds upon which I was basing my case. So, I had a glimmer of hope. I did not want to have illusions about the court case, but it raised wonderful possibilities.

CHAPTER 16

"Pack all your things!"

"How long will it last...
serving my country like this
no one knows."
  (Nazim Hikmet, from "That's How It Goes," Selected Poems, 1967.)

LATE IN July 1986, on the day I expected to hear the result of the court application for my release, a policeman came to the door of my cell and said, "Pack all your things!" I asked: "For release, or for moving to another place?" He answered: "For moving to another place."

I was taken by elevator from the top floor of John Vorster Square (where detainees were held) to the ground level. I was then transported to Johannesburg prison in Diepkloof with a group of black detainees. Both black and white prisoners were held at John Vorster, unlike in conventional prisons, where they were completely segregated. I knew some of these comrades were in John Vorster but had not been able to speak to them. We made the most of the trip, laughing and joking as if we had no concerns in the world.

When we arrived at Diepkloof, I was separated from the black prisoners and taken to a different part of the complex, where whites were held. The prison officials searched my belongings very slowly. My books and the fact that I was a university lecturer fascinated a certain Captain Marais, who was in charge that day. He was a student at the correspondence University of South Africa (Unisa), and later would periodically ask for my help with study assignments.

He did not know how to deal with me. He had no previous experience with detainees. He took me to my cell, where very loud music was being broadcast from Radio Highveld. I asked him to turn the music off and he replied, "No, it's impossible," which we both knew was a lie. It is the reflex action of many prison officials to say no and tell lies, especially when a new prisoner makes a request. Later that evening, I got the warder on duty to turn it off.

There are prison regulations concerning hygiene, and I asked for clean blankets. Marais said those in my cell were the only ones available. I requested the medical superintendent to inspect the blankets to assess whether or not they were hygienic. The captain started to waver and, a short while later, new blankets — many more than I could use — were delivered to my cell.

I had learned that officials need to get used to new arrivals. In the beginning, I tried to be as neat as possible. Once they were used to me being around, I could relax.

The combination of my being an ex-convict and a lawyer evoked considerable fear and they treated me well under the circumstances. A sergeant who had responsibility for the detainees told me that if ordinary prisoners made requests he just said *"fok jou"* ["fuck you"] and locked them up. But, he said, "With you people, it's the United Nations, the United States and the Supreme Court."

Among prison officials, there was a great fear of the law and lawyers. It was common for officials to say they were charging a prisoner, until they heard he wanted to see a lawyer. If they found the prisoner had funds to pay for one, the charge might be dropped and changed to a "warning."

I spent some two years in Diepkloof prison. I had company for about eight months of this time. The remaining 16 months were spent in solitary confinement. This did not literally mean I had no conversations or contact at all. I did speak to the warders who guarded me. Many of them were supporters of the right wing Conservative Party or even the militarist Afrikaner Weerstands Beweging (AWB, literally Afrikaner Resistance Movement), but we got along well. They were youngsters who were ignorant of politics and had inherited political allegiances from their parents. I also had some semi-legal contact with convicted prisoners, to which the prison officials turned a blind eye.

My cell was in a separate section, but close enough for me to speak to, or pass things to, convicted common-law prisoners. This contact enabled me to smuggle newspapers, in exchange for cash. It seemed strange that prisoners were now allowed to hold cash in their possession and this made smuggling much simpler. The *bandiete* used the cash primarily to obtain dagga. There was so much dagga smoked in the prison that I could get high from opening my windows.

In the prison, the ethos of the criminals was hegemonic. If a prison section was not clean, which meant shining floors, the warders would be in trouble. To get it cleaned meant the warders needed the cooperation of the gangsters. They could not afford to be on a collision course with the big criminals. The warders earned very small salaries and the gangsters would get them to "bite," that is, bribe them. First, there would be small things like making them tea but gradually the warders would become more and more ensnared in relationships with the prisoners. Soon, they would begin smuggling for them. It was not unusual to see warders, who had been absent for a while, returning to the jail as prisoners.

It was not simply a practical issue of commerce in contraband items. It was also that the moral values of the *bandiete* became the hegemonic values of the prison. On one occasion, I was standing with a warder and a particular gangster, who had asked us to call him "the godfather," or "GF." GF pointed to the warder and said: "This is the boer who saw me stab X, and when they asked about it he said, 'I saw nothing.'" The warder's chest swelled with pride at the mention of his silence on witnessing a crime.

Being alone was difficult. But being with other detainees could be both supportive and stressful. The dynamics of small groups within prison are always very intense and difficult. Some comrades were determined to get by, while supporting others as much as they could. But some detainees felt a sense of despair and gave up finding ways of surviving. Instead of remaining occupied and doing things to keep up their spirits, they threw in the towel and left it to the regime to show mercy or not. When someone was not coping, it made it harder for all of us. (By "us," I mean detainees under the state of emergency provisions.) It meant that – in addition to coping yourself – you also had to carry the other person on your shoulders.

To get by, you had to do things that made life still seem meaningful. These included exercise, reading and writing, study and watching movies. After years of prison, I was experienced with various strategies for survival. And I knew what would drag me down. As another prisoner once observed, when the warders opened my cell doors, I flew out like a rocket into the fresh air. I was not much of a sports person but I kept at table tennis and running and, on occasions, billiards and whatever else was going.

Gradually, all of the other white state of emergency detainees were released and I was on my own. The last to go was Tom Waspe, chair of the Johannesburg Democratic Action Committee, an affiliate of the UDF. He was released on June 10, 1987, the last day of the 1986-87 state of emergency. They released him in front of me, in the passage of section of the prison where we were housed. Almost simultaneously, they redetained me under the new state of emergency of 1987. I had known this was coming and was thus able to handle it "without visible emotion." In fact, I argued with the police, and that made me feel better.

They asked: "Are you satisfied?" I said I was not. They asked why not and I said my continued detention was illegal. They asked why and I said I needed to consult my lawyer before I formulated my position to them. This continued without my conceding it was a valid redetention.

I hoped to be out the following year, in June 1988, at the end of the second year of the emergency. But I also had to prepare myself for disappointment. I remember that I tried to emulate Nazim Hikmet, the Turkish poet, who spent decades in Turkish prisons, by showing no fear about being hanged. He writes to his wife that if the hangman puts his noose around his neck:

"Well, those who're waiting to see fear in my blue eyes / will look at Nazim in vain."

When they called me down to the prison reception area, a policeman said: "We are releasing you under..." I hoped he would conclude: "...under restrictions." But he went on to say, "...under the old emergency." And he concluded: "We are detaining you under the new emergency for the same reasons."

As the months went on and on, solitary gradually wore me down. Very many letters people wrote to me never arrived. There was hardly anything getting through the prison walls. Near the end of my period in detention, the prison officials started to worry about my psychological condition. They were not concerned about my health, but worried that they might land in trouble if anything happened to me. I took advantage of the situation to apply to have a pet, confident it would succeed. I had seen how sentenced prisoners were allowed pet birds and I successfully applied to have a pet lovebird/parakeet.

One day, Sergeant Joubert, a warder who was always very kind to me, arrived with this beautiful little red-cheeked parakeet in a shoebox. GF explained how to clip the wings so the bird could not fly away. It was then a question of training it. I held the bird and it bit me. I let it carry on biting, even though my hand was very sore, just to get it used to me. After a few days, it relaxed, and spent most of its time under my tracksuit or on my shoulder. It was wonderful having this beautiful little live creature with me. Its head smelt like a baby and it had no one else in the world besides me. I called him Jail Bird or "JB."

We bought a cage. When I put the bird inside, it would pace up and down, much like prisoners did in their cells. When it was time to sleep, I would put a towel over the cage and JB would sleep.

We were inseparable. The bird would eat out of my mouth. I used to buy granola bars and the moment the bird heard me open the packet it would stick its beak into my mouth. When I exercised, the bird would sit on my shoulder. If it was angry with me, it would retreat into my tracksuit, and sit there. If I tried to touch it, JB would bite me.

One day in the third year of the emergency, they told me I was being moved to Pretoria prison. This was shattering. I was used to Diepkloof and prisoners are very conservative people. We hate to change things. It costs a lot to adapt to a particular prison environment, no matter how unpleasant it is. Once one has worked out a pattern, one does not want to alter it.

The Security Police had not realized that I had accumulated quite so many books and papers and other odds and ends. They were unable to fit my things into the car they had brought. They had to take me back to my cell and return the next day with a more spacious van. Many things were stolen on the way to and from my cell. This is part of the price I paid for being in an ordinary prison.

That night, I was full of anguish about the impending move. I lay on the floor doing relaxation exercises, trying to calm myself. I have seldom felt such severe anxiety. I lay shivering until I was calm.

The next day, we arrived at Pretoria prison, which was familiar territory but not where I wanted to be. I wanted to be out.

Still, here I was, in the most secure of secure prisons — for how long, I did not know.

My cell was in a separate part of the prison, away from all convicted political prisoners and those awaiting trial. It had a huge steel frame in front of the window. Air came in but I could see nothing. Music was being played in a section of the prison where I was housed during my first period here, and that was OK. I was in an old and simultaneously new situation again. This time, contact with other prisoners of any sort was very difficult. It was only JB and me.

I sensed my time in detention might be ending. My lawyers were engaged in various efforts to secure my release, but when would that be? People, such as fellow prisoner and UDF activist Maurice Smithers, had heard they were to be released, but waited weeks before it actually happened.

People were detained for various reasons. Sometimes, it was for charges to be brought against you. Sometimes it was to elicit information about others, and torture was used if you did not talk. But I had hardly been interrogated at all. I had been interrogated intensively by Lieutenant Brookbanks and Major Oosthuizen of the Security Police for a couple of days in the first year. They asked me about people's power (and had two tape recorders in operation). Then the interrogations stopped.

Perhaps the police had wanted to press charges, but were unable to do so. Consequently, they may have been holding me, and some others, just to keep the UDF leadership indefinitely out of the way. When we were arrested, we had taken the previous emergency as our measure and assumed we would not be in jail longer than eight or nine months. Once they kept on reimposing the emergency, however, we had no idea when it would end. We thought of the Zimbabwean struggle, when political leaders such as Nkomo and Mugabe had been held for more than 10 years in preventive detention. There was no saying when we would be out. It just went on and on. It was impossible to adopt the frame of mind of a prisoner serving a fixed sentence. It was equally impossible to anticipate returning to normal life.

In my own case, the detention acquired punitive connotations. After a while, the police released all the other white detainees and I was left on my own. It may not have been their intention to hold me in solitary confinement, but that was the result of being continuously detained. I was on my own for 18 of the total of 27 months I had spent in detention, first at John Vorster, then at Diepkloof and Pretoria. My conditions were not comparable to those of convicted prisoners. Although conditions in the detention areas of Johannesburg and Pretoria prisons were better than at John Vorster Square, I had no access to facilities that one normally enjoyed as part of a settled community of prisoners. Everything was makeshift — and meant to cater for people spending a very brief period awaiting trial or serving a short sentence.

I became very depressed. Perhaps I had been depressed in my previous period in prison without realizing it. This time, there was no doubt. I would go to sleep at 11 p.m. and wake up at 1 a.m. Waves of gloom would descend over me. As the months of detention continued, I felt more and more exhausted and found it difficult to concentrate. I relied much more on physical exercise than intellectual work to get me by.

If it was suggested to me that I was depressed, I became quite angry because I equated depression with self-pity and self-indulgence. I did not appreciate that my situation could induce depression quite independently of my will. My capacity to deal with it was gravely impaired, until I came to recognize and understand it properly.

I exercised every morning till the aches in my shoulder muscles were relieved and I had reached a frame of mind adequate to get me through the day. Every day in prison, one must recreate the conditions for one's continuing survival.

In my days as a sentenced prisoner in Pretoria, the conditions for survival were social, had to do with my relationships with the other comrades and my intellectual endeavors, such as reading and research. In this second period, it was strange to find that I was depending on physical exertion to get by — as I had previously been so much involved with intellectual pursuits. At one time, I ran so much that I damaged my knee and had to have surgery. GF taught me how to skip the way boxers do. I also rode an exercise bicycle and used a "Gymtrim" exercise system.

I never considered giving up, although there were times when I definitely would have liked to have been released into some form of confined existence, restricted to some quiet spot where I would never again risk redetention and could quietly retire. I remember leaning out of my window and talking to Maurice Smithers, who was in for about eight months as a state of emergency detainee, and how we both expressed our longings for this quiet life.

I was also additionally vulnerable at this time because I was in the middle of a relationship with a comrade, Barbara Creecy. The longer I was inside, the more difficult it became to continue this relationship. Were we to break it off, because release was so far away? Were we to hold on, assuming I would be out soon? In the end, we decided to end the relationship and it was very hard.

The period of detention threw up very important moral and psychological questions for me. I had seen how some people were not able to deal with detention. Some of these people, even those in leadership positions, on finding themselves alone in a detention cell, discovered that their level of commitment faltered. They had often been very brave when taking part in mass political activities. They were very knowledgeable about the ideas and theories of our movement. But they did not seem to have internalized this as a commitment that could carry them through unexpected hardships and loneliness in jail. These hardships were unexpected for all of us. We did not expect to be in jail for as long as we were, separated from loved ones for so long, with no idea when we would be released.

In my own case, I was adequately equipped because I had made an earlier commitment that I drew on, that gave me strength. I found my previous experiences were no longer of immediate, practical assistance in dealing with new levels of privation as the months of solitary continued.

I found, equally, that I could not plead for my release or make concessions in order to get out. I had already made choices that made it impossible to do certain things in order to obtain my release. There were opportunities. Every now and then, one was confronted with the possibility of release — if one applied to court and phrased your wording in such a way that implied a degree of distance from the liberation movement, or that you recanted on some beliefs. Small nuanced phrases may have been sufficient. And one could have found ways of "living with these phrases," as some detainees had done. I was very much affected by detention but I always managed to scrutinize documents carefully, to avoid any such hints or phrasing.

In 1987, I brought a fresh application for my release, and directly confronted choices and opportunities to dissociate myself from the liberation movement in order to secure it. However, I could not choose such a course of action, and lost the case. In fact, the judge referred to my being "resolute" as a reason for holding me.

This was very hard, but it was also a practical experience. I did not just lie there in my cell and suffer. I was interacting with prison officials and I tried to make those relationships beneficial. I did my best to form good relationships with the prison officials, so they would either make life better for me or not do anything to make it more difficult. I tried to reclaim some control over my environment and my own life. I used to give the warder who ran my section a list of things to do — what was called the "agenda." He would tick all these things off as he did them and then report back to me. For example, he checked the post or took me to fetch medicine from the hospital. In a sense, it was I who determined what happened to me, obviously within a very circumscribed framework. But I still reappropriated a degree of control over my own environment.

Strange as it may seem, and due to these efforts, I found myself in a supportive environment in the prison. Very few warders tried to give me a hard time. For the most part, they did their best to make life easier, given that I was on my own, they had to hold me there and I was not going anywhere soon.

CHAPTER 17

Letters from Detention, 1986–88

THE FOLLOWING letters were written from Johannesburg prison in Diepkloof, where I was detained from August 1986 to July 1988. Initially, I was with four other political prisoners — The Rev. Francois Bill, Maurice Smithers, Father Peter Hortop and Tom Waspe — whose company I shared for about eight months of the approximate 27 months I was detained under provisions of the 1986 South African state of emergency.

About 18 months of my detention were spent in solitary confinement, during which time my main human contact was with the warders who guarded me. I also had some semi-legal contact with convicted prisoners, to which prison officials sometimes turned a blind eye.

The smuggled letters, all sent to Barbara Creecy (see previous chapter), were written on very thin paper and glued between the covers of a cardboard file, which was used to convey study material in and out of jail. The prison officials were so intent on checking for subversive matter in the study material that they overlooked the letters concealed within the covers.

Letters, 1986

September 16
Dear Mom,

Thanks for the birthday greeting. It was one of those rather difficult periods… Luckily, I found it heavily depressing only once or twice. My objective circumstances have gradually improved, though I have misgivings, as this seems to indicate I might be here for some time…

In many ways, it is subjectively more difficult now. I can't settle down in the way that I did when I knew I was serving a fixed prison term… Three years outside have made prison seem a less "homely" environment than before. For the past 10 days or so, I have had one companion and, since yesterday, one more. It makes a difference. At first, I only had access to small exercise yards. We now run in a fairly big one every morning and do other exercises in the afternoon. I am very fit.

The surroundings are OK. I have some books so I can do some research. It is not possible to work systematically but, together with reading the magazines permitted, time passes.

My job still seems secure, though it is obviously a problem for the university, now and for the future. I have no idea when I can resume duties...

I suppose that you must have expected that I could be inside again. It has always been a possibility...

Please send everyone my love and tell them to write. I'm OK. I have to see myself in broader perspective. Things could be a lot worse... I know why I am here... There is no alternative but to handle it.

November 20
Dear Mom,

There seems little chance I will be released for Xmas (my ninth inside in 11 years). Nor is it certain that I will be released early in 1987. I am trying to come to terms with this. At the moment, my spirits are fairly high, compared with the others, who have either spent less time inside or have a better chance of release. Obviously, there is a vague chance of my getting out, so I can't help thinking of the outside...

Every now and again, I think of doing things, seeing people, etc.; thoughts that naturally enter your head when you have no fixed sentence...

For the past two weeks, I have been working fairly well. I think I am the only one who is quite reconciled to a 1987 release.

I don't know what will happen regarding visitors... They seem to refuse everyone now, including Cathi Albertyn, who had come on behalf of the law faculty, and many who play no political role. So, I'm not counting on anything...

Yes, I do have a place to go when I get out, though it is difficult to know precisely how things will turn out. The job remains secure. They pay me, but obviously have no idea when I will reappear.

In theory, I wouldn't say no to the idea of a holiday in Australia. From my cell, my mind wanders over all sorts of possibilities. But I know that, in the real world outside of "Sun City," it is not going to be easy to get away to Magaliesberg, let alone to Perth. But let's see...
["Sun City" was a nickname for Johannesburg Prison.]

I draw strength from the fact that I am quite clear as to the correctness of what I've done and the fact that most people know that.

December 1

Dear Mom and Sally,

It has been raining quite heavily for the last few days but has stopped now. Our main concern is for our exercise period outside, and that has not been affected. In fact, because we seem to get a controlled amount of exposure to sunlight everyday, I'm getting quite a tan. As usual, I probably look healthier in prison than outside.

I'm worried that I might be repeating what I've previously written. The range of things about which one can write is restricted, partly because of reasons of delicacy over certain questions, and problems in fathoming what is possible, but mainly I think because little is happening. The result is that one gets thrown into endless reflection on what it means to be here.

I am in good shape... Last year's emergency lasted eight months and there is no indication that this one will be briefer. Many take the view that I will be here till it ends.

I think I may be "over the hump" as far as handling it is concerned, because I have no illusions. Naturally, I'd like to be out this year. I'd even settle for January. But I count on nothing. Consequently, I think I'm starting to work better.

It may be that some of the others will be released soon. We are hoping for that, though it will obviously be more difficult for those who remain behind.

I was looking at photos of Lauren and Johanna, which I have just received from Alan *[my brother]*. They look very much how I imagine Australian kids to be. I get a lot of pleasure from them and from other pictures, especially ones of my new goddaughter *[Kim de la Harpe]*. Just looking at her cheers me up...

I see John *[my brother]* tomorrow and, hopefully, the following week. I doubt whether he has managed to alter the decision regarding visitors. In any case, I will probably see a lawyer during that period.

Sally *[my sister]*, I would like to thank you for bearing the brunt of the problems of the past six months. It has been important to me to feel there was one person on whom I could always rely. Everyone here at some point has felt incredibly frustrated by people failing to do seemingly unimportant things. Your help has been crucial. I am sorry that it has sometimes been tense...

December 7

Dear Mom,

Thanks for your air letter. I can't understand why you have only received one letter from me. I have sent five or six...

I was surprised when John told me that he was under the impression that we were getting newspapers. That is definitely not the case and remains a major problem.

I think that the prospects are looking very gloomy as far as detention is concerned and I still do not exclude a *very* long period...

I have to and will handle it, so no one should worry. I've known this would happen... I know why I'm here. Even with these spells inside, I feel I have still got more from my life than would even have been possible had I led a conventional, "successful" life. I feel that I am here precisely because it has meaning.

It would be good to see you. I doubt whether I could come over to Australia and I'm not sure how satisfactory it will be to meet up here, whether I'm in or out. But it would be good to speak without constraints...

December 22

Dear Mom,

It is the third week, at least, since I've heard from you — though I've no doubt that you and other members of the family have written. I started to write a week or so back, but anticipating an incoming letter, I decided to wait. When you write, I suggest that you and other family members head the letter and write on the envelope "Family letter: Mother/sister" or whatever...

We are into the Xmas period and it's not been so difficult, on the whole. For the past six to seven weeks, I've been in a good state of mind. I think this is because I'm working fairly well and I'm reconciled to the worst in regard to release, and that makes it easier to feel "settled."

It's not altogether natural to feel settled, I know, but I have to make some sort of accommodation with long-term detention.

I sometimes really have to struggle to keep on top of things. The ever-present, sounds of the radio [*Radio Highveld, a terrible local station, was played loudly all through the day and until mid-evening*] and other things are quite jarring, especially when my sleep has been interrupted. On these days, I am more aware than usual of what I'm blotting out.

But what's there to do about it? One just has to battle through because there will be no respite. The signs are that I'll be here "to switch off the lights," as one lawyer put it.

We have been hoping for release of one or two of the others. Since it has not eventuated, it has made people a bit anxious. However, we are getting on well and helping one another through.

We still run and play table tennis and do other exercises. I am now fairly tanned and very fit. Once, last week, I ran 14 km. in one go. How far I run depends on the time available and on the weather. It is easier when it's cool. I'm trying to build up stamina and speed. It may seem crazy but I could probably qualify for a half-marathon now. It works better than any drug, to put me back in control of the world if I wake up feeling rotten.

Although I still have problems getting the books I need, I have done some good work, "cracking" some philosophical writings. Getting through difficult books is the sort of thing I could only do in a place like prison.

So, things are as before here. Basically, I am in good health and spirits. I hope the same goes for you and rest of the family.

December 26
Dear Mom,

When you or other family members write, please mark it as a family letter, both on the inside and the outside — then it comes directly to me. *[At one point, the police said all family letters could pass directly through the prison censors, without first being shown to the Security Police. In practice, the prison officials were not sure what to do, and referred family letters to the police.]*

I am glad that you have heard from Pete *[Harris, my lawyer]* and John *[Suttner, my brother]* regarding official attitudes to my release. All evidence, sometimes via other people's lawyers, seems to confirm that I have to think of a very long time. It is quite alarming to visualize what it may be.

I think that we are all starting to understand this. When we went to exercise today, everyone was very quiet. I think that, at each phase, one starts to realize that this is going to be much worse and much longer than previous worst projections... The emergency has to be renewed in June, but, of all months, that's the worst from the point of view of release. *[June was the traditional month of resistance, coinciding with the anniversary of the Soweto uprising of June 1976. This resistance was often followed by repression.]*

So, the sky's now the limit in terms of length of stay...

Smuggled Letter
Date unknown, possibly 1986 or early 1987

It is now Saturday, around 5 p.m. I have my earplugs in, though I can still hear the cricket. I think I am in good shape. This is mainly because of my work, that I at last feel useful...

Re interrogation. My feeling is that it is unwise to refuse interrogation.

The other day they called Francois *[Rev. Francois Bill]* and me for *SB [Special Branch]* interrogation. It was actually not for questioning, but to take photos for Sandton *[police]*. I remember a heavy despondent feeling as I went up there. I could not joke with the others before I left (though I did joke with members of SB, once I arrived). I was preoccupied with the unknown — what they might do with me, whether they would charge me, how long I would be held and so on. Most of the time I suppress this anxiety. When I see it, it is almost as a detached outsider observing myself. Sometimes I feel quite weary. You feel they are never going to finish with you and I suppose that's it.

Letters, 1987

January 14
Dear Mom,

I'm afraid that your hopes for swift release in the new year seem unlikely to be realized. But it will be nice to see you. I'm sure you'll be given a lot more visits than normally, due to the distance and the length of time since we've seen one another.

Sally came with some magazines, including the *Far Eastern Economic Review* — which we found useful. Should you have the chance it would be useful to receive literature — via Sally — on places such as Vietnam and Philippines...

Who would have thought that I'd spend so much of my life in prison? Even accepting the first term, it's quite hard luck to land up in this emergency's haul instead of some brief spell.

I hesitate to say anything of my feelings because people tend to read too much into "feeling down," when in fact it is usually over after a day or so. I'm not feeling ecstatic today — but these things pass and, over the years, I've learned many ways of helping it to pass and of reigniting "joyful feelings."

When you're in this situation there is no alternative but to ensure you remain on top of things. I don't intend being some type of invalid, here or after release. Perhaps the way the powers-that-be appear to perceive me now reduces my alternatives. I've chosen a path that I know is right. I've also known that I will pay a price for it. Admittedly, I didn't expect it to have been so long — but I must have expected it subconsciously. I know that I have to handle it — so I will. Every time I readjust my expectations to a much later release date, it is surprising how much *easier* it becomes. In a sense, I've had to detach myself from it — to put things I'd like to do outside in cold storage and live here and now, forgetting about "normal," settled life for a while.

Sorry it's a bit gloomy, but that's something my family and I need to accept.

January 26
Dear Mom,

I think you are partly right and partly wrong, when you speak of my reaching an "accommodation" with a situation that is unacceptable. I explore what options are available. But most of the options available to some are not open to me. *[The UDF took the view that its leaders could not make personal appeals for release. I also took the view that, in any application for my release, there could be no suggestion that I recanted from my beliefs or dissociated myself from the liberation movement.]*

On the one hand, there are my own attitudes, and what I am willing or unwilling to do. And, on the other, there is the apparent determination to keep me here no matter what.

By the way, I do not regard my work as an "escape" from this situation. My object is to be a creative, active human being — and to determine my life as far as possible. This is not just to escape from unpleasant surroundings, but to better equip myself for the future.

I don't see prison as an unpleasant individual experience, but a social experience resulting from the relationship of certain categories of people with the authorities.

As I sit here, I am at once an individual but also part of a wider whole. The consciousness of that connection gives me strength and makes it difficult for me to indulge feelings of self-pity. I have to keep my feelings under control or experience them as not being solely an individual problem.

I am still fit, but less fanatically so — because I am reading a fair amount and don't need the exercises quite as badly, for morale purposes. I revert to intensive running whenever I start to feel down. I still run eight km. every morning.

January 28

Dear Mom,

I really feel very, very pessimistic about my chances of being released for some time. I have no idea what is intended. Certainly, release just hasn't arisen as an option yet. What is staggering, is to try and guess how long it could conceivably be.

I have to deal with it. But I've been taken a bit by surprise. I don't think that I expected so heavy a stint. But I suppose it is always hard to prepare...

Although I am glad to get these letters from Australia, it's a bit problematic that the local ones seem to be held up. Possibly these are of more "direct interest." For me, they are quite important in maintaining a link with the people I know.

In many ways, this period of detention has been a hundred times more disruptive of my personal life than spending nearly eight years in prison. I have been yanked out of ongoing activities and relationships, for no one knows how long, to return to who knows what? From 1975 to 1983, all was clear and relatively "secure," in that I knew what was happening. Now, I just grit my teeth...

Smuggled Letter,
Date uncertain, possibly January 1987

I've had a day that stirred me up a bit. I went to Lissoos *[the dentist]*. There were three SP *[Security Police]* with me. There are usually two. They were armed with pistols, with very long barrels, and led by Warrant Officer Steyn... First, they handcuffed me very tightly (I have previously had a run-in with the police about being handcuffed and led through the streets) and they were very hostile. I requested that my hands not be handcuffed behind my back — because it was very painful — but the police refused. They wouldn't unlock the cuffs till I sat in the dentist's chair...

Lissoos' waiting room was completely cleared and the door locked. They all came into the room when I was in the chair. I said to Lissoos: "Aren't I supposed to see you in private? I understand these guys may want to observe, but do they have the right to be on top of us?" He agreed (very softly to me) but the police refused to quit, saying they had "got their orders."

When we returned to the jail, I said to Steyn and the warders at the entrance that I wanted them to take note (as on previous occasions) of the marks from the handcuffs. Steyn got very heavy and suggested that I also complain about their presence at the dentist's — and I said I would do this.

I took issue, because, as I recall it, MASA *[the Medical Association of South Africa]* got Le Grange *[then minister of law and order]* to agree to private consultations. Although I did not need much privacy with the dentist, I thought I should not concede the principle.

What made me feel terrible was the attitude of these blokes. When Steyn first came here re interrogations, he was very courteous. This time, he was just a pig, like the others...

What is counterproductive for them is that, in these situations, I get very "the moer in" *[a vulgar expression, meaning to get angry]*. While I am scared, I stand much more on my rights than normally. If this *oke* [person] plans to interrogate me, he's fucked up whatever chances of a cordial meeting there may have been. In some ways, it helps to see who we're fighting — starkly, in human or inhuman form. It makes you realize why it's impossible to give in to these bastards.

What was interesting was the reaction of the prison *boere*! No one laughed when Steyn tried to mock me about my complaint. After Steyn left, they *urged* me to complain — through a number of different channels. (The *boere* had also witnessed the previous dispute regarding handcuffs.)

I found all of this quite upsetting and I had to take the orange gut pills for the first time for a while. I suppose we have a measure of peace here, and these guys represent a threat to it — a permanent threat.

In the past 10 days, I've used up masses of paper on requests and complaints. Basically, our negotiations have been very unsuccessful — for radios, open doors, watches, weights, papers — and we are now licking our wounds and deciding where to go from here.

This place is pretty bad... I gather that the black prisoners here, and at other prisons, are allowed out of their cells a lot more than we are. We spend a lot of time with nothing to do but read. My eyes are a problem, especially when they are tired. There is nothing to do when I can't read, and nothing to look at. In any case, it is claustrophobic.

February 19
Dear Mom,

Thank you for your letter of 11/2, received this morning. It's been quite a difficult week. Bit by bit, what hope each person has had of leaving seems to be receding. If, as Shakespeare says, the darkest hour is just before the dawn, I'm beginning to see that it's going to get a lot darker...

My eye has been a bit problematic... I've tried resting it, which has its own problems in this environment.

Smuggled Letter
Date uncertain, early 1987

Things are getting quite different from what our best and worst expectations might have been. If I am not released before March/April, I definitely won't be out in June...

Even if I am released, what about my job? I do not know whether people are able to consider things clearly yet, but I find it hard to visualize going back. It will be a matter of months before they *[the Special Police]* want me again. We will just have to think what people want me to do, given my various weaknesses and inclinations.

I am prepared (and the new state of emergency regulations tend to suggest this) for the possibility of a big PP *["people's power"]* trial. Or even to do years for refusing to be a state witness...

So, there are all sorts of gloomy possibilities. At the same time, we have been through these sorts of speculations before, only to find everyone released unscathed. I think that the possibility of a PP trial would be a very big thing to mount. On balance, I think it unlikely, at this stage.

All in all, we have a substantial degree of control over our lives here. We are nevertheless planning to push for better facilities. For example, to have more time outside our cells, to have radios and papers, etc.

I've tried to recapture the state of mind I cultivated at Pretoria, to get something out of this existence...

Smuggled Letter
Date uncertain, 1987

As mentioned, we do get access to *[smuggled]* news. We miss some days, but usually get only one or two papers. This could, of course, change suddenly.

There is no check on visiting days. Could get all sorts of letters in and out at the moment.

Our relations with the *bandiete* [ordinary criminals] are very good. Apart from some prisoners awaiting trial shouting *"ANC se moer"* ["ANC's cunt"], we seem very popular. They call me "Professor" and, as I walk along, I am greeted that way at one of the yards where we exercise. One of the *bandiete* introduces me as "the future minister of justice."

[Referring to Xmas/New Year period.] It has been very difficult lately. Our exercise and time outside has been ballsed-up and various things on which we depend have not worked out.

This is actually quite a bad place for a long stay. You never have peace. The cell is shared either with loud, terrible music, Charles Fortune [*a cricket commentator*] or some other sports commentator.

Sometimes, I am amazed when I think what this detention may mean. No one sees it as unrealistic for me to be in the whole of 1987 — that is, 19 months! I accept that estimate, or longer, as a possibility. There is no reason to expect an earlier release (apart from the election being preceded by a lifting of the state of emergency)...

The time seems to go fast. Right now, I just grit my teeth, stick in the earplugs, run like mad, play table tennis, read and write like crazy. Because of this, and my relations with the others, I am happy a lot of the time. (We clearly strike the *boere* as very happy. A lot of the young ones want to work with us. They find us very funny.)

I am much more "stabilized" than most of the others, precisely because I have so clear, though gloomy, a prospect. They have still not fully adjusted to the likelihood of a long sentence. This is not to say that there are problems. It is just that people are not so settled or working as well. In contrast, I have started to reacquire my Pretoria life-style.

Generally, I have a fair hold on things. Sometimes, however, I get glimpses of what I am repressing and the strain of it all. But I think we have to see this as part of a the broader struggle. None of us can have personal lives that are as happy as we would like them to be, inside or outside of jail...

Smuggled Letter
Date uncertain, 1987

I should tell you something of my state of mind... I have been here long enough to notice some things that I first experienced while in Pretoria jail.

I feel a sort of numbness and indifference to my fate... And, more and more, I find I cannot handle *normal stress*. This was very much the case inside...

I cannot cope with sudden questions/demands/requests.

The interrogators arrived today, and talked to some of the others. They did not get around to me. Their interrogation appears to have just been political discussion. I do not know when they will come for me and whether it will be the same for me. They referred to me as the *jakkals* [fox].

Smuggled Letter
Date uncertain, 1987

I feel I am seeing a number of "generations" of political detainees arrive — and none leaving, so far. There are still five of us here, and presumably will be for a couple of weeks. With these new arrests, and the likelihood of new arrivals being in jail for at least six months, I guess anything is possible.

Still, I know that my situation is, in a sense, stabilized — while yours is not. *[Barbara Creecy was then underground and being sought by the Security Police.]* And I know that you feel that you are building up more and more shit for yourself. In that sense, it *is* a sort of relief to be caught. And I wonder if some people do not subconsciously create the conditions for that to happen (as Freud says).

It is Wednesday and we have had a terrible day — all sorts of disappointments. I think I was feeling low, even without them. Some days, I just understand, with great clarity, what this means for me, and I feel quite down...

It is the next day. When it started, everyone was really feeling incredibly low. I have not felt like this for months. I think it is the hopelessness of our personal situations. I feel we have got to break out of this mood. Consequently, we have started to discuss the possibility of a hunger strike.

We are building a good community spirit... This is not to say there is no heaviness — but it is reserved for the authorities, when necessary! Overall, we have good relationships with them.

I dread some things. One is that my eyes are packing up. The bad one is constantly inflamed. It is caused by the lack of good sleep and, possibly, by the neon light. And the fact that there is nothing to do but read. If it fucks in, it will be difficult being compelled to absorb nothing but Radio Highveld. I was unable to read for weeks in Pretoria, but we had other music there. Medically, there is not much that can be done and I am just trying to nurse the eye. It is constantly surrounded by a red ring. But I am hoping to treat it with ointment.

(Sunday) I do not sleep well here. I start to feel down when it is especially bad. Yesterday, it was a bit like that, but now it's OK. This place is very noisy, even at 4 a.m., making it difficult to relax and to sleep.

This morning, I have that light, optimistic feeling (for which there is no basis). I have a vague feeling about being released some time...

We have a sort of inspection today, which means shoving all sorts of things under the bed, to give the illusion of tidiness. They do not say anything about my cell, which is now like my office. I think there is an agreement on both sides not to take issue over small things and there is a good vibe. Even on a personal level, some of the guards come and speak for long time — about all sorts of problems.

I intend resting for a while after I get out. I have suppressed a lot here...

I'm rather concerned re legal action about our access to newspapers. I/we had wanted all the lawyers to discuss this, with a view to mounting a case and to obtain finances. If it is important, *money can be got.* It is crucial for most black prisoners, who do not have access to anything like the number of books, etc., that we have. It is also crucial in terms of the politicization of these issues. Even if a case is lost, it can be a factor leading to the relaxation of prison rules...

I have just received a letter from the office of Divisional Commander Security Police: Johannesburg. It concerns: "Complaints: Raymond Suttner" — and is signed Brigadier G. N. Erasmus, who says:

"A standing instruction to all personnel from this office is that any person being transported whilst in custody, is to be handcuffed in a manner which most suitably prevents escape and/or personal injury to the person in custody.

"In addition, the personnel who transported you to the surgery on the date in question, were instructed to ensure you remained in their visual and audial (sic) presence at all times."

(Quite sensible, in fact.) But what I wonder is, what did the MASA get the minister to agree to — wasn't it privacy of consultation?

Interesting, that they are even engaging in correspondence. I had not expected any reply.

There are still only five of us here. It is eight months for me today. It must be nearly a record, for detention without trial for *whites*? I am in a constructive frame of mind now especially since becoming more "active" again. (Do you see now what my earlier anguish was about?) I want very much to become engaged...

On the running front, I am not as fanatical, though I usually do at least eight km., sometimes up and down stairs...

A *bandiet* here says he is going to write to Vlok *[the then minister of law and order]* about us. What happens is that, at a certain time of the evening, certain substances start taking effect on these people and they become very voluble. Anyway, he tells me his writing in English is not so good. "But in Afrikaans," he says, "jong, I am really dangerous!"

Jean got me this water bottle for running. After a week or so, I forgot to bring it back from downstairs. I thought that was it — that it would be used for some sort of illicit *bandiet* activity...

Anyway, one of the bou groep (building group) saw it and kept it for me. I had asked our sergeant to try and find it. On the weekend, one of the other *bandiete* said: "Professor, so this is your bottle. They were searching the whole prison for it. I thought maybe it's got whiskey. But it's just water. For this, they had all the generals searching. I don't want to hear no more about that bottle."

Nothing has been happening here, apart from visiting Lissoos again. A very heavy SB took me. He did not greet me, or say *one word* to me. I was handcuffed the same way again, then paraded through town while wearing cuffs. The SB sat right opposite the dental chair. It was the same *boere* as last time. Clearly, all this was a direct response to my complaint. You do not usually get the same people twice. The two dental nurses there were very sweet. They kept winking at me and were quite scathing to the *boere* — regarding the handcuffs and future appointments. I said, these people *[the SP]* want to know how many more appointments I will need. And the nurse said: "We're not clairvoyants — who knows? Let's keep them guessing." She told me they had received explicit instructions to clear the dentistry of other patients before I arrived....

Smuggled Letter
Date uncertain, 1987

It is now evening, 4.30 p.m. or so. Been feeling fragile this afternoon. It is always reflected in the level of my concentration on table tennis. It is amazing, if you think about it, how human beings can "psych" themselves into seeming to be happy for so many days during detention. Most of the time, it is just routine. We go out for exercise and run, or play table tennis in the afternoon — most of the time, fairly contentedly. I think what got me down was the volume of noise at lunchtime, and constant interruptions... Sometimes I can handle the noise. Some days, however, it just seems over the top...

Tom quotes Shakespeare back to me, about the darkest hour being just before the dawn, but we thought we had recognized the darkest hour many times. But this was premature, as there were many more, worse ones to come.

Our sergeant has injured himself and is away for a month or more. We have a very corrupt bloke in charge... His corruption is unfortunately of a type that hinders us a great deal and is very intrusive. He is a real lumpen shit who has been the cause of our films fucking out, and he shows everything to his captain... So, at moment, things are very bad.

Smuggled Letter
Date uncertain, 1987

This week has... been filled with the sort of fuck-ups that are peculiar to prisons. One night, as has happened in the past, a sort of alarm was broadcast through the loudspeakers in my cell for two hours. And, last night, there was a loud boxing broadcast.

April 7
Dear Mom,

We are OK here. Still a bit stunned by the swift dissolution of our community. *[The number of political prisoners had been reduced from five to two, after three of our number was released.]* I think Tom Waspe will also go in the next few weeks/months. I cherish some hope, but am not counting on things...

I am gearing up to suddenly finding myself alone again — and for a long time, possibly into the second half of the year. I don't think that will happen — it is a worst-case scenario...

Right now, I feel numbness... I just try to blot everything out and make what I can of this place.

April 18
Dear Mom,

I think we will soon know the best or worst in regard to my situation... *[I was bringing a court action at this time, and various people were making representations for my release.]*

I think I may be released... But even if the news is bad, it will be better to know the worst and prepare accordingly... The trouble is, as I have learned, prisoners tend to only grasp aspects of what is happening outside, drawing wrong conclusions when other people are released, etc. But from the little Pete has told me of his new approach, it does sound promising.

At any rate, this is the first time, since the early weeks of detention, that there has been the slightest glimmer of hope...

Smuggled Letter
April 20

I feel very together now — although maintaining my mood extracts a price. I still think I may be out soon. Simultaneously, I prepare for the worst. Most of the time, I throw myself into work and exercise. This place is my reality. I have to handle it. I do not intend to let it get the better of me. At the same time, the sort of work I do gives meaning to this period...

On Tuesday, the boer suddenly opens up my cell and says, *"veiligheidspolisie"* [Security Police]. It is Pitout and a sergeant, and Pitout starts with some friendly questions. "What do you want?" I ask. "Is this interrogation — what are the questions?" No, he tells me, it is not interrogation. "Then what are you here for?" I ask. "We are not friends." He answers: "Just to see if you have any complaints." I tell him that I have no complaints against the prison authorities or against individual police — just against detention.

He asks whether I still believe my detention is unjust. I say, not only unjust, but also illegitimate. And illegal, he asks? And I say, yes, it is also illegal — but for reasons that I am sure he does not want me to go into. He says he cannot do anything about my release. It is not in his power (which I accept) — but he says that if he were to recommend my release, it would not be without restrictions. So, I say: "That's their decision. I call for unconditional release. If they decide on restrictions, that's their business."

Anyway, I don't allow them to relax — and when they indicate that there is nothing more to discuss, I sort of get up. Then Pitout says that he admires my "arrogance." I was taken by surprise by this visit, but wanted them to know that a long period inside would not lessen my commitment...

But I think they have nothing to ask me, as I have been in for so long...

Smuggled Letter
April 29

I think in general we are starting to feel the effects of the lack of input consequent on there being only two of us here. In the black section, you are with so many people that it must be something like being outside, in a social sense. Whereas, in here, everything becomes much more of an individual psychological experience...

I do not allow myself to say too often, how much I hate this place and this experience. It comes out in all sorts of indirect ways — but I cannot dwell on the cacophony of terrible sounds, the terrible sights, smells, and so on — since I may have to live with it all for a long time to come...

I am really very weary of all this...

Smuggled Letter
May 1

One cannot help succumbing to hope every now and again. I just do not know what these guys have in mind for me. At a certain point, they will surely release me, but when? The thing is, what considerations do they take into account?

I can see no reason why they should let me out, if they see no advantage in it. And what advantage is there for them? They seem to be singling me out from the other whites — by subjecting me to this treatment, for so long. Surely, they do not want to make me into a heroic figure, which the continuation of this treatment may bring about?

May 29
Dear Mom,

We have finalized papers for the court application... It *[our case]* has a degree of novelty about it and is fairly strong — but I have never been to court with any real case before. I think that there is an outside chance of success here. The case is, basically, built around the reasons advanced for my detention last year. The question is, whether such reasons have an indefinite validity, whether they justify permanent detention and, in particular, my present or continued detention.

Along with the legal argument, there is emphasis on the impact that this is having on my professional career and on Wits's capacity to teach students without a full complement of staff, etc.

At this stage, this is the only show in town...

I am determined that the possibility of release will not "destabilize" me. It is, in fact, very unlikely...

It is getting colder, though still generally OK. We are running and playing table tennis and doing much the same things most days. I think it is more difficult for Tom, in that this is not so much a part of his past life as it is for me. In July, I will have spent nine years of my life inside.

I was thinking about how one can be very happy, at times, inside a prison. It's something Hikmet writes about — how, when you look at the sky sometimes, it's as if you are its discoverer — and you forget about much else. The same goes for a glimpse of green. I find that I can sometimes feel very happy.

June 10
Dear Mom,

Things have been fairly hectic and difficult in preparing for the court application, hearing what the apparent attitude is toward my release, etc., and having to adjust to the possibility of being here for a *very* long time. At the same time, this court case has not yet gone through all the motions and I am waiting for a visit from Pete to discuss the minister's reply.

In the meantime, we heard that Tom Waspe is to be released tomorrow. So, I must start preparing for what I have envisaged for some time — being on my own again. This is not necessarily to be for a long time, because there is another candidate, from another institution, who could join me at some stage.

I was very sorry to see the determination with which my release is being resisted. All of this indicates that if their intention is carried out I can almost definitely expect to be here till the end of the emergency, whenever that is...

I am trying to adapt to this prospect in a practical manner and have now tried to work more systematically on my thesis. I think that not having this "certainty" has prevented me from embarking on long-term work... Knowing the worst, I can at least prepare properly for what lies ahead.

June 23
Dear Mom,

I have been on my own for almost two weeks now and there does not seem any chance of anyone else joining me. I am likely to be in solitary for the foreseeable future and it is difficult to see how long that may be...

In the past couple of weeks, I have been very busy with preparation for the court application — papers that have been sent to you. I don't think that there is much chance of success, but it is an arguable case...

I saw Sally on Monday, but it appears they are only allowing fortnightly visits instead of weekly ones, so I won't see her again for another two weeks...

It has been very cold here. There is a lot of flu around, but I am hoping to avoid it because of my fitness. I am still running and doing the other things that have kept me going over this period.

I think that my last letter was written on the eve of Tom's departure. I was redetained under the new emergency at more or less the same time as he was released...

I know that it won't be so great, after a couple of weeks of this, with practically no one to talk to. But I've experienced this before and I know what can be done to mitigate the effects...

June 29

Dear Mom,

I wasn't devastated by my redetention. I don't say this out of bravado. It has always been a possibility.... My morale is fine — partly, I think because I haven't had a chance to experience solitary in its raw form, in this recent period. There have been a great deal of things on the go, surrounding the case — so I have actually been more preoccupied with things outside of the cell than I would otherwise have been...

My rearrest was conducted in my cell, at the same time as Tom's release.

In the middle of all this, there has been this court application and its result should be known quite soon. I didn't participate in the previous one, which was purely technical. For this one, I did quite a lot of work and it has occupied a lot of time in the last month or so. I was feeling optimistic and I believe that the lawyers are "cautiously optimistic." But, somehow, I don't think that it will work out — when I think of it rationally and how these things have tended to go through the courts in the past. But who knows?

On Friday, they introduced new regulations governing our conditions. I have been given these today and there is still some ambiguity as to their meaning — especially in regard to access to newspapers...

Yes — I'd also rather emerge immediately, in good shape, than come out more erudite. I don't think that I am going to be in bad shape, though I imagine that this is taking quite a toll at a subconscious level. Even at a conscious level, I am very aware that it has been very intense and difficult. Right now, I feel fine. I am fairly happy most of the time. But it is always a happiness which is artificial, born of successfully substituting some activity for one I would actually rather do, but cannot because of being confined. So, I appreciate the efforts made to secure my release and believe that they all help to make the "long run" a bit shorter.

July 7

Dear Mom,

This afternoon, there was a lawyer's letter informing me that the case has been lost. I am feeling fine, though I am starting to feel the effects of isolation. When I wrote to Ann on Sunday, I was quite down, but it passed. I think that's how it usually is — ups and downs. I am fairly determined about getting by and have tried to keep fairly strictly to my exercise and other routines. I have started some new exercises —

using weights and small dumb-bells — in the afternoon. I run in the mornings.

Work-wise, I have been getting back strongly into my thesis. I'm hoping to move much better now that "all is clear," in the sense that all is lost, in terms of official responses.

This is pretty terrible to contemplate — but, frankly, I am not contemplating it. I am living day-by-day...

I don't know what happens from here — whether I'm in for a few more months, another year or what. Having passed the one-year threshold, I think anything is possible...

July 14
Dear Mom,

I sleep very badly, wake up early and can be awake for hours. (At this time, I think I'm closest to my actual feelings about this place, and can't relax back to sleep). Not having slept, I can't always work well. You can't do much on your own and without music of your choice.

The solitary gets to me, off and on — mingled with a general feeling of "displeasure" about the situation, with all its awful potentialities, affecting all aspects of my life. I do not dwell on this. I just have to shut out these thoughts to get by, because getting by is difficult enough, without dwelling on what I am losing of my life. There seems little likelihood of anyone joining me for the foreseeable future. One person who was a candidate has just been released after a court application.

I am OK and the situation is under control...

July 20
Dear Mom,

It has been very difficult, off and on. I am just driving myself to keep at routines and all the various remedies against feeling down...

Being alone here means not only lack of company, but also lack of input...

I was feeling very bad a couple of hours ago and I just drove myself to do what I could do. I try to be active most of the time because activity and creativity makes this life more meaningful...

The time goes very fast. Although it feels terrible now to look forward to another week in this place, that week usually goes very fast and it will be next Monday before I realize it...

Otherwise, I am very tired. There is a lot of anxiety and pressure... Sorry I can't bring more "cheer" into this...

July 27

Dear Mom,

It is now more than six weeks that I have been on my own. And I have, at times, over the last couple of weeks, especially last week, found it rather heavy going. I understand from speaking to the doctor that this thing of sleeping a couple of hours and waking up and not sleeping for the rest of the night is one of the normal manifestations of depression.

This may seem obvious to you, but I have not thought of myself as being depressed most of the time. I have flashes of depression when I think of what this means, or rather pain at that thought, but I consciously avoid dwelling on it. Presumably, however, it continues to live in my subconscious and is one of the causes of this sleeplessness — of a type that I have never experienced before.

The situation also breeds great anxiety over the smallest matters. I am not consciously lonely, most of the time. I do sometimes feel that it would be nice to discuss X or Y with someone or other. But I feel it consciously when I go through hard times, or suffer disappointments. Then, I would like to have at least one person to communicate this with.

The situation remains under control. Last week was one of the worst experiences that I have had. But, even while it was at its worst, I consciously continued to pursue my routines and a certain degree of creativity. This week, things are OK so far and I don't feel so unhappy.

I have to assume that this may continue for a very long time, so I am trying to immerse myself very thoroughly in my thesis. There have been a lot of interruptions, but I have made substantial progress, though nothing has been written up yet. I must have read some 50 articles in the last two months. Once I have been through some key books, which I am still waiting for, I may be in a position to write up a chapter.

I am, frankly, very pessimistic about my situation, and am very concerned to build what life I can under these conditions. I am pleased that you are articulating your unwillingness to accept this and I hope that together with other factors it may have some effect. But I am preparing for the worst (though the goalposts are constantly shifting, and I no longer have any idea what the worst is)...

August 4

Dear Mom,

I will ask Pete to get you a copy of the judgment. I have not managed to read through it myself yet. I will need to do so, in order to discuss possibilities of appeal. It is very boring reading. The gist of it is this. The court has concluded that there are not grounds for it to question the minister's good faith in exercising his discretion. The regulations are framed in a manner that leaves it to the minister's subjective discretion. It is virtually impossible to prove that his discretion has not been exercised in good faith, since one has access only to objective data, which do not necessarily bear on his state of mind. There are also references to factors that might well have led the minister to conclude that I was "resolute" in pursuing my activities, but most of the judgment is very tortuous reasoning — a bit like a caricature, such as Dickens does in *Bleak House*.

I am wracking my brains for something to write about. I have been almost entirely preoccupied with my state of mind, my intellect, my body. I am not a fan of poets or artists who feel that contemplation of the self is essential for true art. Yet this situation forces me to be obsessed with my inner thoughts, emotions and what have you. Small things become magnified in importance and can be very upsetting.

There are also times I feel a great detachment from this environment — like an observer, rather than a participant. Though I have spent more than nine years of my life inside prisons, I still look at this place as somehow alien and shocking. I am still "together" and intend staying that way...

August 21
Dear Mom,

Yesterday, I saw Judge Goldstone, who comes around every now and again to see detainees about their conditions. He is going to raise the question of weekly instead of bi-weekly visits and the question of a radio. I must say that I did not feel particularly enthusiastic. Some months ago, such changes would have meant a great deal. Now, all that interests me is getting out.

It is now Saturday and I can hear the rugby commentaries.

[One of the more difficult aspects of detention at Diepkloof was simultaneous sensory deprivation and overload. The latter was in the form of loud radio programs, in particular the weekly rugby commentaries, which were very jarring to my nerves.]

August 22
Dear *[addressee not known]*,

I am feeling very "switched off" to my surroundings. I know that I am heading for 15 months and that is a respectable distance to have covered. A few weeks ago, I was feeling intensely about what this means, but now I am in a computer-like state of mind. I just do what I know needs to be done in order to keep going, and keep together. When I work, I am a bit like a machine. I just go through the books and photocopies, a bit like people consuming food in a competition. Being single-minded about that sort of thing means that I can exclude what is outside of my thesis a lot of the time, which is good in an immediate sense — though there is more to life than "handling" a situation like this. I am feeling very cut off from the world outside — substantially more so than a few months back. I think the length of time and my isolation is causing this. I go for the best part of two weeks without a proper conversation and very little in the way of correspondence. In order to handle this, I cultivate a sense of self-sufficiency. In some ways, this makes it more difficult for me to communicate when I need to. I almost forget how to do it when I have the opportunity.

August 25
Dear Jess [*Sherman, cousin*],

As I write, it is raining and has suddenly got cold again. This place is gloomy even on a summer day, when all is bright. When the weather is like this, it automatically limits an already limited "universe." But my mood was already fairly in tune with this weather. At this moment, I am feeling OK, but for the last couple of days, I have been feeling pretty terrible. I suppose it is mainly the isolation.

All sorts of emotions are bottled up inside me. And I want to share all sorts of observations with someone or other, about big and small matters. By the time I get out, I will have forgotten what they are. What worries me more is, what does this do to one's personality — not to express feelings, to have to just keep them locked away?

Previously, I did repress quite a lot, even when others were with me. That is a necessary fact of prison life, just as release is something to fantasize about. But I did not have to repress everything that was important to me. I had people with whom I could communicate some of these things.

I have been in solitary before. Because this was near the start of my period in prison, I was able to spend a lot of my time just reminiscing. I did so in John Vorster Square. It is amazing how many things happen, that you do not really get the chance to sort out in your head. I just lay on my mat at John Vorster, thinking how I should have done this or that and how I had messed this or that up, etc.

Now, the situation is different. If I think of things outside jail now — then those things are quite distant in time. My fresh memories are of things inside this place and they are generally not very rich and worthy of preservation.

I think my situation is generally treated with consideration by the prison authorities. And, in certain important respects, things have improved. But I am now a lot less enthusiastic about improvements than I would have been six months ago. Now, I think it is time for me to go home.

So, in one sense, I am much less reconciled to being here than I was a few months back. At the same time, I remain realistic. Even while feeling pretty bad today, I am carefully reading material relevant to my thesis.

August 31
Dear Jess,

I was very drunk this whole weekend. This was mainly due to the pleasant surprise of a huge influx of cards, which made me semi-drunk. One is used to nothing happening and then all of a sudden all these very nice sentiments descend from all sorts of people, from outside these walls. That is wearing off now... I alternate between being very orientated towards "coping" here, and needing contact with people outside very badly. I need to cope since I cannot rely on the contact most of the time. Often, how one copes can lead to an inability to communicate properly when one does get the chance to make contact with outsiders. I find that I talk myself into seeing my activities inside here as so crucial that I often begrudge time spent on communications with family and friends.

This experience, though much shorter, has been much, much worse than Pretoria. The intensity just never lets up and has been there from the very beginning until now — whether alone or with others.

I do not know whether I mentioned that I have injured my knee. A little thing like that is quite serious as regards my dealing with the situation. I cannot run for a week and am just praying that it is definitely cured after that, because running has been a life-saver inside...

September 6
Dear Al,

The isolation is affecting me quite a lot. I think that I have learned what depression is, because I cannot have ever really experienced it before now, and it suddenly descends on me for a couple of days and seems almost uncontrollable. So far, I have managed to remain in general control of the situation, with continued exercising and work. But the psychological dimension is something I do not really understand. For a couple of weeks, I have been seeing a therapist at the General Hospital, just to relieve the sensory deprivation — the fact that I basically have next to no conversations for almost all of the time. I go one day a week and, while it does not seem to get anywhere, it just allows me to speak to someone and feel more humanized.

[A number of black detainees also went to the hospital to see the therapist and the Security Police in charge were often fairly relaxed, allowing us to talk to one another. Here, I met my close friends and comrades, Mohamed Valli, who was then a UDF leader, Zwelakhe Sisulu, then editor of New Nation, *and Murphy Morobe, then a UDF leader.]*

I think this is another one of those critical periods, when my release may be considered. If I am not out in the next month or so, Wits will again have to find a replacement for next year. And if I am not out by December, it will be hard to have me in for lecturing until the second quarter. So, if I am not out by December, the sky's the limit.

As I sit here, I can hear loud rugby commentary in the background. This builds up from 2 p.m., starting with the history of previous encounters between the various teams, etc. I suppose you get the same thing with cricket in Australia. This aspect is the opposite of the sensory deprivation — "sensory overload," of unwanted sounds.

I am finding it hard quite a lot of the time, but things are under control...

September 8
Dear Jess,

In the past few weeks, I have become very depressed on Mondays and Tuesdays, possibly because they are at the beginning of the week... I consciously set about breaking the cycle this week and have succeeded, more or less. I do not know whether this means that I will feel very low in a few days, or what. I am just trying new ways of anticipating and mitigating these days of gloom. I have been told that occupational therapy is very good. Today, I was given the opportunity, in the sense of being asked to scrub the shower room — quite a big area, with a fairly dirty floor, from 15 months of non-scrubbing. I was pleased to do it, in the present situation. I tried to see it as a different experience and I am fit enough to not find it very tiring.

You see, every day I do more or less the same things: run, push weights, skip (now that I cannot really run with knee problems), various exercises and work. I think that this, in itself, has a demoralizing effect and I did find the scrubbing therapeutic. Maybe I will change my mind when I resume, since it is by no means over.

Turning to your letter — yes, I am very tuned into the seasons, since rain affects mobility, the gray sky seems an inducement to a gloomy mood. I used to like watching the rain in Pretoria, but here you can't see much from the cell, though you can hear it.

(Wednesday) Did more scrubbing and, in general, still managing to keep gloom at bay. I don't know whether this is scientific, but I hate feeling out of control, and I feel that by planning things I assert my active subjectivity in the situation.

September 15
Dear Kim and Jean *[de la Harpe],*

The thing about prison life is that it is very easy to become an object. In terms of regulations, you need not think of much. Many people eat, sleep, walk, etc., all at the routine times... To plan your own life, in this situation, is an assertion of one's character as a human being, a subject. Once you forget that, you either slip into an automaton-like state or deep depression, since you see no improvement in your situation other than that initiated by others.

I do not think that you have an altogether correct image of my handling of the situation. It is true that I do not feel I have any choice but to cope. But I do not always manage so well. Especially in recent times, I have not always felt that I have the resources to take on some things that I would have tackled some months back.

September 29
Dear Mom,

As you will have heard from Sally, I was at the Brenthurst last week for a minor operation on my knee... She will also fill you in more fully on the various aspects of the experience. The stitches come out tomorrow and it seems to be recovering very quickly. I am, however, wondering what to do in the future. If running on cement in a small space should have produced "surplus fat" behind the kneecap, requiring surgery once, can it not happen again? On the other hand, running is crucial to keeping a psychological balance. While skipping does get the heart pumping, it keeps me within a restricted space — in my own small yard, which is another factor making running more attractive (escaping from this very claustrophobic area). According to Dr. Read — who did the op — I should be able to start running again in the next few days.

I do not know whether there is any further prospect of court action... In general, I have very little idea of what, if anything, is happening in regard to my situation. There is nothing to indicate that anything other than my continued detention is being contemplated...

In the meantime, I have to prepare for remaining here. I have handled the "depression question" practically. I was very shocked at its first manifestation, as this is the first time I have ever experienced it. I am responding with a "total strategy." *[An allusion to the apartheid regime's use of the phrase "total strategy" to describe their battle against the liberation movement.]* I am planning my days and all situations where I expect the gloom to infiltrate. I consequently took careful steps to pick up the threads on my return. So far, it seems to have worked and it is more than four weeks since I last felt enveloped by gloom.

At the Brenthurst... the room cost 205 rand a day. The hospital facilities that I was permitted to use were comfortable. I nevertheless wanted to get back to a cell that I alone occupied and to return to my routines. *[I was watched in the hospital room by guards, who worked in shifts.]*

We have been experiencing very strange weather — very cold, with unprecedented floods in much of Natal. I am sitting here with a blanket over my legs. It seems as if spring is never going to arrive.

October 19

Dear Al,

The arrival of this excellent (gym) equipment was at once good and terrible. Terrible, because it is one of the things that I see as symptomatic of my being here for much longer.

About a week or 10 days ago, John got a negative reply to representations that he made. So, your hope that the time for my release is not far off, is just not on. I am still fairly together — I think. I was quite depressed about two months ago, but I have regained adequate control and work quite well and am trying to rebuild my exercise program — which will be easier with this home gym...

[The prison authorities presented me with a Gymtrim home gym, implying that they had bought it. I later found that this piece of exercise equipment had belonged to Klaas de Jonge, a Dutch citizen who had received sanctuary in the Netherlands embassy after escaping from detention.]

There also seems little chance of my having company for any length of time. I think there has been a decision to keep some people for "quite a long time."

October 28

Dear Mom,

(Thursday) A very difficult day. I cannot understand why it has suddenly become difficult again. I just find it hard to build up an interest in my daily activities — a state of mind that comes and goes. I had expected to get out to the physiotherapist and psychotherapist today and the police said they could not take me because of number of people having to go out on this particular day.

Although these outings are disruptive, they are useful as a safety valve.

For some reason, they have been bringing in various animals — hens, then a porcupine and a rabbit — in one of the yards. Very nice to see a bit of life here, especially the rabbit, which is very tame and relaxed — much like a kitten.

November 4

Dear Kim and Jean,

This cell has started to take on an appearance similar to my office and home outside, and the authorities have in fact offered the use of a second cell — but it doesn't seem to help. I just cannot work in a neat way.

November 9

Dear Mom,

I had a surprise visit from George Bizos. He is appearing for the defense in a trial that has gone on for some two and a half years or so. He came to see me because some of my things are exhibits, and with a view to a future discussion with one of the attorneys. I may also possibly be required as a defense witness (though that is unlikely)...

It is very hot here, in between brief storms. It is so hot, that I keep on thinking that the windows are closed, while they are in fact wide open. I think that I have become insulated against many of the sensory influences specific to this place, most days of the week, though on the day or two when I do not feel so wonderful, it is quite a bombardment.

I do not know whether I mentioned that there is a rabbit in the prison. Very beautiful, white and I try to see him most days. He has become very naughty, however, and was not to be found today. Sometimes, they find him at the reception or some such place. He is very tame and eats grass from my hands...

November 16

Dear Mom,

I do not have direct access to the yard where the rabbit is, but usually get down there for a while most days. But this guy is very naughty and tends to escape to other sections. It's very nice just to see such a thing in a place like this. When I stroke him between the ears, he just sits dead still and seems to almost fall asleep.

There are all sorts of birds around this place now, because some categories of prisoners are allowed pets. I was watching some budgies in cages and the way they paced up and down is much like many prisoners do, most or some of the time.

I may try to get a rabbit up here, though there is only cement. I gather, however, that the main thing is that rabbits should have shade, not necessarily grass. There are no rules for or against this, as far as I can recall — so I may have a try. Basically, I am OK, and hope you are.

November 18

Dear Ann, Eugene, Daniel and Gary,

I had a bad spell about three months ago, but since then I am feeling well, keeping fit and doing a fair amount of research. I have given up hope of release, so that when it comes it will take me by surprise. But coming to this realization, that there just is no cause for hope, has helped me to better adjust. It might seem strange to hear this, but having hopes produces anxieties and continual disappointments. Now that practically all causes for hope have been removed, I just have to make what I can out of this existence.

Being alone is quite difficult, but I think it helps to be the studious type, since study demands a degree of isolation. I try to convince myself — when I get upset — that this might really be "advantageous." I try to view this spell as a type of "study leave" or, because I exercise so regularly, some sort of "health cure."

The place is very bare and gray; but they have recently brought various animals into one of the yards, to which I have a degree of access. The animals include all types of birds, some chickens and a porcupine.

There was a rabbit till a few days ago, but he kept on escaping to other sections... I understand that he may have made a complete escape from the prison. I am sorry about that, because this guy was good to have around.

December 5

Dear Kim and Jean,

I had started a letter on Thursday night, but decided to wait. I was feeling very tired and irritable because of the heat and, I suppose, a general weariness about this situation. It is now a couple of days later, and much of that feeling is still with me, although I thought I detected a slight breeze as a prelude to a bit of rain.

The small things are very important in prison, where life is very basic and you often depend on others to provide what is so basic, or on natural forces, such as the weather. Because it's so hot, it is difficult to do most of the things that make creative survival possible. I have, for example, done very little skipping for the past week or so, because it is so hot in the afternoons. When you do less exercise, it has repercussions the next time you are locked up. There is no way that I can let up in this place. I was trying to think about ways of taking it easy, but all of them carry the danger that they make one more susceptible to gloom. I find that I just have to pre-plan all of the time. I am especially conscious of the potentialities of the "festive period" — so I am trying to build up a momentum with my work and what have you.

One of the ways that tension manifests itself is in an abnormal level of exhaustion. Still, I keep at it...

December 8

Dear Mom,

The three years that I spent outside of prison, before this spell, are starting to seem insignificant in terms of my almost continuous life inside. I genuinely can see no end to this.

I recently had a legal consultation with Gilbert Marcus and Zac Yacoob. It was in relation to a trial, about which George Bizos came to see me a month ago. Apparently, I am cited in the prosecution's further particulars. It involves quite a lot of things that I have written about. They need to consult as to the meaning of some things and what happened at various meetings and possibly also call me as a defense witness...

December 12

Dear Jess,

(Sunday) This weekend has ended up seeming very heavy — mainly, I think, because I have not seen grass or the rabbits. And that means just seeing concrete and steel, albeit sometimes out of doors. In this situation, one sometimes feels unhappy and it is hard to work out why. If one is "normally" feeling OK, why the sudden change? Or why should one normally feel OK? Perhaps that is more of a question. I think, however, one can usually anticipate the sort of situations that are going to have a negative effect and take various measures to overcome them. Right now, for example, I am sitting with earplugs in my ears, creating a measure of quiet. When feeling OK, I can handle the sounds — but if not, these sounds are very jarring. I am already starting to feel a lot better, having blotted out or lowered the volume of some of the sounds.

December 28

Dear Mom,

It is some time since I last received a letter from you. One, I know, was sent down to the police for censoring. There has also been a prohibition on Xmas cards coming in or going out, since December 18, so that mail has dried up completely. This time of the year, as you know, is difficult. I had prepared for that being the case, and phase one — the Xmas weekend — is now over…

The pace of work has slowed a bit. While I do try and maintain a steady amount of research, exercise, etc., at these times — during the "festive season" — I try to be more flexible. Now, for example, I am reading a novel. One of the symptoms of my suppressed feelings, I find, is the way I react very emotionally to films and novels and even to reports of poignant events. Without human beings to communicate with, all my emotions are expressed in reaction to these media.

The rabbits are still around. Because of the heat, they spend most of the time, when I get down to their yard, hiding in the stairs — to which I do not have access. I wish that I had a camera to capture some of their gestures — washing, scratching or stretching.

I am still exercising regularly and the knee seems OK now. It makes clicking sounds, but does not hurt at all. This home gym is still very good and I probably will get one when I get out.

That is the situation here…

Letters, 1988

January 4

Dear Jess,

The festive season has passed more or less OK. I had expected it to be difficult but, possibly because of the precautions I took, it has passed without sending me into any serious dip. The heat has been very bad, making it quite difficult at times to find the energy to do much besides sit on the bed. During the day, it has made the yard so hot that time inside has been preferable to time out.

January 5
Dear Mom,

There is a third rabbit — a white female, still a baby... It really is very enjoyable to have such a thing around. She is completely tame — very inquisitive about everything and just wants to be picked up and stroked, which is just what I want to do.

The festive season is over and I must have been preparing for it, because it was not as difficult as I had anticipated... We are experiencing a terrible heat wave here... There is very little relief. For the last two nights, there have been a few drops of rain for about 30 seconds and that is all. The weather bureau says it will lift on Thursday — but it will probably return, which seems to be the pattern this summer.

I am feeling very drained and wake up weary. I gather that if depression is not manifested in outward gloom (which is not the case with me) then it finds expression in one's sleep, level of irritability, etc. Still, I need to be able to control things at a conscious level and that seems OK.

January 14
Dear Kim and Jean,

The rabbit story is not so simple any more. The original two keep out of sight, so I do not see much of them. The female must be expecting babies any day. There is a third baby one, which was actually staying up here, in the yard... Anyway, she has thus far not been able to come back here. I spoke to the psychiatrist and he is going to recommend that this rabbit be kept up here as a pet. It makes a *huge* difference to me. This little one is very tame and just loves to be picked up and comes onto my chest and sticks its mouth against my chin. So, I hope she is allowed to be here as long as I remain. When I do not feel like reading and have exercised, there are times when there's little to see besides cement. Then it is nice to just watch this little thing scratching her head or washing herself, or dozing, or to scratch her head and watch how the eyes close with pleasure or in relaxation.

I feel that the longer I am here, the more difficult it will be to readjust when I get out. I also find the existing situation very hard. Most of the time, at a conscious level, I do handle it. But I find that I wake up weary and it takes most of the day before my neck and shoulders untense.

The solitary is definitely getting to me. I imagine the sleep problems, weariness, physical tension, are a result of suppressing the need to communicate...

You say that some people hoped I would get out for Xmas. The way I feel now, whenever I get out, it will take me by surprise. Right now, there is just no cause for hope, as far as I can see.

February 8
Dear Mom,

I am sorry to hear that you have not been well and that you are experiencing some of the symptoms that I have. I suppose this thing has just been going on for so long that a sense of powerlessness breeds frustration, which cannot really be resolved. It is not as if a 'remedy' can be found through self-analysis. It is a recurrent problem and one can only ameliorate it. I think the exercises you mention can be quite useful. On some days, my neck and shoulder muscles are tense throughout the day and I have to do exercises repeatedly, until the tension breaks for a while.

It has been very difficult for some weeks... I more or less get things under control, and then some external event precipitates another spell of gloom. I hope that I now am on the way up again.

I think the weather is also a very important factor... It is quite stifling in these ovens.

I am not making much progress on my thesis, but continue to work at it... I have been given permission to get an exercise bike, which John had offered to buy me. The home gym does not really provide for aerobic exercises, equivalent to running, but these are important for combating depression. I think that the bike will have a speedometer, which will enable me to set targets and keep at a particular pace.

I believe Sally mentioned that I have not been happy with certain things in letters. I am not in a position to be more explicit. The best I can do is ask you to please be guided by the content and tone of my letters. I would like you, please, *to deal mainly with family matters*. I cannot, at this point, afford to be upset by things that can be avoided. I appreciate that this has not been your intention — but it has been the case that your reactions to things here have not been based on a proper understanding of what is happening and what needs to be said and what needs to be left unsaid. I realize that you are not to blame for not knowing such things. But, in the meantime, I think that restraint as to tone and great care as to content is required. You may feel that you do not have much to write about, in which case you must not feel that it is essential to write as often as you have been doing, or at any length.

I have managed to draw some birds into my yard lately with crumbs — mainly small ones, such as *mossies* [sparrows] and turtledoves and one finch. I think that these ones get edged out of the way when they try to get crumbs in the bigger yard, which has also got grass and a tree. This sort of thing has not been a great interest in the past, but it now goes to make life a little richer...

The recent refusal to release me did not surprise me. What I found interesting is that my name came up for consideration — which I think is a positive thing, attributable to international factors, for which I am grateful. I have spoken to Pete with a view to contesting some of the reasons for my being here.

March 1
Dear Mom,

This whole year has been incredibly difficult. I am doing very little research and have slept very badly. I am hoping that all this is the past tense, but every time I think I have put things right, I encounter an objective problem, which sets me back. I think that, in a sparse environment such as this, the very basic, simple things are what you depend on, and if something goes wrong with them, it is very hard to keep your balance.

I appreciate how you felt about the rejection of the Strauss "representations"... *[Franz-Josef Strauss, Chancellor of Bavaria, made representations to the then minister of foreign affairs, Pik Botha, for the release of myself and some others.]* The fact that my name was raised at all, is a reflection of international interest in my case.

The weather has improved a bit... but it has not rained much and remains muggy. The exercise bike is convenient. It can be carried outside or inside, depending on the weather and whether I am out of my cell for a sufficiently long time. It is very useful for aerobic exercise, which seems to have a substantial effect on my state of mind.

Two rabbits remain in a yard below, to which I have some access. The female has recently had babies, two of which have died. They are born without hair and blind, but now, after about 10 days, are starting to look like actual rabbits. They are very beautiful. I saw them feeding and it was quite funny. At this stage, they can't yet see. And there was much jostling and falling and lying on their backs — all very out of place here...

March 8
Dear Mom,

I am physically well but very exhausted from the length of my stay and contemplating an uncertain period ahead. I am more or less OK, but the first two months of this year were terrible. I have started to work again, but it is very hard to maintain enthusiasm under these conditions. The exercise and some studies are undertaken not really for their own sake, but to contrive a "positive state of mind." Obviously, this trick cannot work as well after 21 months as it did in the beginning.

The impact of solitary is starting to be quite apparent. For example, there is something called "the startle reaction," which I read about only after having experienced it for some time. You get a huge fright when someone speaking to you interrupts your "solitary." Even the radio announcer suddenly speaking after a piece of music can give me a fright.

In addition, my present period of incarceration has started to merge in my mind with the years 1975 to 1983. I often react as if I am in Pretoria jail, or expect one of my former companions to say something. I sometimes even put my hand under the bed, looking for the wooden dustbins we used to have in our cells at Pretoria. Perhaps I did not really understand the extent of the trauma I experienced then. Perhaps I am now experiencing it, and the two periods as one and continuous.

Nothing out of the ordinary is happening here. I think that all of the baby rabbits, possibly bar one, have been taken away, though I have not been in that part of the prison for a few days. They really make very nice pets...

March 16
Dear Mom,

There has been little input into my life since I last wrote. I have not seen much besides cement and steel. I hope I have regained adequate control over the situation. I am still not sleeping well, but am managing to do some work again and generally starting to feel more "positive"...

This period on my own has not always been as difficult as it is now. I think that, in any period of imprisonment, you can draw most sustenance from within the prison walls. That was feasible in Pretoria. But, in this situation, it means drawing more and more out of myself, or from sports equipment and books. And these resources are really becoming quite depleted now. There is no way of "replenishing myself" for most of the week, apart from anything I can come up with myself.

The seriousness of the situation is shown by how difficult it has been to work. I had more or less given up on my thesis for the first two months of the year. Even now that I have resumed work, it is not with great confidence in what I am producing. I have never found it difficult to produce and find it quite interesting that I should be feeling the work is not up to standard...

I think that I am starting to get back into shape, though I am not so sure that one can expect to regain the resources that one had at the beginning. Still, I am working and exercising well and not feeling consciously depressed now.

March 28
Dear Mom,

The general response to things, like requests for new visitors, seems to indicate an unchanged atmosphere. I am used to things being as they are, and it is not really an unmanageable burden to find that new possibilities do not eventuate. I am starting to feel better, but am still trying to consolidate...

It is only when I start to feel better that I can use the limited amount of time in which I am feeling alert as effectively as possible. Some people look towards June 10, expecting this day to toll the bell for their release. But, as I see it, there is probably a lot more of this ahead... *[Friday June 10, 1988, was the day when the state of emergency had to be renewed and all detainees had either to be released or else "released" under the expired regulations and redetained under the new regulations.]*

It is now much more difficult to carry out the practical tasks of survival... But there are no alternatives.

April 18
Dear Mom,

Ja — the Easter period was not too good, but I am still living partly off the food parcel, which was very nice. *[The Jewish community had provided a food parcel for Passover.]*

Though, to be honest, things like this are no longer very exciting.

May 16
Dear Mom,

I think you are misinterpreting my reaction when you say: "It is no use for us all to give way at this point, having got through so much already." I do not intend to give way. What I have tried to convey, which may not be what you have interpreted, is that I need a break. I am much more in need of getting out now than was the case this time last year.

All the same, I remain prepared to handle the likelihood of spending some time here. My intention now is to return to a situation where I am productive and relatively creative. This may in fact be an unattainable goal, given that I have not managed this for some four months or more.

In the immediate future, I face almost certain redetention on June 10, and have to get into a state of mind where I do not look at that date with optimism — a state of mind that assists me to act resolutely.

I am better than I was a couple of weeks back, though I am finding it very difficult to sustain my "recovery." Many things operate independently of my willpower and consciousness. I am constantly overwhelmed by exhaustion and it is not always possible to focus on my thesis. It is important to remember that, if I write anything that sounds unhappy, it is always within the context of being absolutely committed to getting by in the correct way. I do not intend to seek any form of surrender or capitulation. Insofar as I am "down," I always intend to get "up" again. I have never stayed down, though my up periods are not nearly as creative as they were a year ago.

I know that is how you would want it to be...

May 26
Dear Mom,

It will not be long before you know the outcome of the June 10 business... I am able to put it out of my mind because I have to be prepared for staying...

I am still getting what pleasure I can from the birds, and from the rabbit (when he makes an appearance). It is interesting to note how much more aware I have become of colors. There are some things that I would not normally have noticed, and did not even bother to look at, when I first came here.

I may have mentioned that I have started "relaxation therapy." *[When I saw the therapist at the hospital, another member of the hospital staff would instruct all detainees in relaxation exercises.]* This week was the second time, and the exercises are very useful in reducing anxiety. I have done some relaxation exercises before, but have not previously undertaken a series relating to the whole body...

May 26

Dear Kim, Jean,

I have just got this typewriter back... I really felt quite lost without it... Without this machine, I have spent a lot of this week "tidying" and throwing away things that I no longer need.

I am doing a lot of things, but do not seem sufficiently organized to be able to work on the thesis. I think my lack of contact with others has led me to go round and round in circles. I keep thinking that I have no solution to various problems and keep on reading and rereading.

Some days, I just cannot work. I think it is easier to do something that involves typing than, say, reading. It sometimes takes two hours before I stop feeling exhausted and can concentrate. Sometimes I need to write letters, to express my emotions, rather than do research. I normally have no problem with motivation for research. But, here, I really have to work on myself, to keep to the thesis.

You wonder how I cope with various things that upset me when already feeling depressed. It varies. I find that the more I plan my life here, the easier it is to cope with upsets. Most of the things that go wrong are predictable and I try to prepare myself for them. Sometimes, when I have slept badly and have been upset, I tend to get abnormally anxious about small things and it is quite hard to break out of the cycle. I think that many things would be less upsetting if I could discuss them with others. On my own, they sometimes assume a huge importance.

I have continued with my normal activities here and planned for work that will continue later this year. So, if I stay, it is not likely to destabilize me.

I cannot afford to go into year III feeling perpetually exhausted and uncreative.

Yes — the rabbit makes me very happy. On Sunday, he was up in this part of the jail for more or less the whole day. Perhaps he fled up here when they were cleaning "his" stairs. He was very relaxed and sat on my bed most of the time. I have not seen him since. I am well aware of why I feel so much for this animal and other animals nearby — because of my isolation and the fact that there is no real outlet for my feelings.

Smuggled Letter
Date uncertain, pre-June, 1988

The Security Police took me out yesterday — supposedly to the general hospital for an appointment that I had never heard of. When I queried this, I got a very rude response and was handcuffed and put in the back of the car with an African comrade. I was taken to Sandton *[police station]*. I did not ask any questions. After waiting an hour or so, one of the SP said that Captain Pretorius had wanted to speak to me, but was apparently not sure when he would be back. After waiting another two hours or so, they said it did not seem that Pretorius was coming back in time, and they returned me to prison. I was quite surprised to find myself in this situation... I was planning to say I would not cooperate, since I had nothing further to say that could contribute to the goals of the state of emergency...

I played it fairly cool, though it really destabilized me. It happened early in the morning, I had not finished exercising, had not eaten anything, and when I came back, it was as if the normal morning rituals had not been completed. At 2 p.m., I had not yet done a lot of what I usually do at 9 a.m.

I found it very consoling and sedating to have the baby rabbit around, just wanting to be picked up and stroked and giving me an outlet for some of my feelings...

I think it is quite urgent to get more things done, in a more coordinated way, about my situation. Right now, we are looking at the certainty of my being detained until June. That is, one year straight (15 months total) in solitary. We are looking at the strong likelihood of this continuing into 1989. I think it is important for people to grasp what this means — that I have been in for this shockingly long time, but that there is the near certainty of spending the whole of my second year in solitary. This is a unique situation. There is no other detainee in this situation, as far as I am aware. Precisely because I will get through it, I am storing up worsening psychological problems, which will arise in readjusting after release. In some ways, if you crack up, you are "normalizing," in the sense that you are allowing your normal needs to predominate over your sense of what it is necessary for you to force yourself to do. So, while I will not have the hang-ups of someone like X *[a prisoner who broke down]*, I may have a lot suppressed that will take time to come out, and there will be a whole pattern of behavior to unlearn...

Smuggled Letter
Date uncertain, pre-June, 1988

Today, I have been here for 18 months... I thought of it for a few seconds, possibly because I have worked for about five hours today, which is a near record. I just think that one cannot afford to get emotional about dates like this, because the trend is so obviously against my release even being considered. ...

I was walking in the yard a while ago, thinking of what Gramsci said about prison library books — that political prisoners must be able to draw blood out of stones. I find that I have to depend on myself, especially on these weekends when my guard is off *[duty]*, to draw all sorts of emotions out of these stones, or out of myself.

The rabbits are so important, because they provide the only situation in which I can give vent to normal emotions. They provoke emotions that are dormant most of the time here, without my even realizing it. Not seeing grass since Friday also has a definite effect — because being "out" is (at the same time) like not being out, and, at a certain moment, tends to have a negative effect — when I am in this little yard.

June 6
Dear Mom,

I have been "tranquil" and intend to stay that way. I suspect that I will still be here after Friday. I hope I am wrong, but you will know soon. Luckily, I have managed to get myself into much better shape — so I feel confident that I can deal with whatever arises.

I console myself with the thought that all the work that you and others have been doing, while it may not succeed this week, definitely brings closer the day when I can leave this place...

There are snooker tables in the prison — quarter size, or smaller. I can use them some weekday mornings and it's quite a nice change and suits my present mood. I do not know whether it's a fluke but I have beaten the sport organizer and two warders...

One of the forms my tension is taking, is that I can hardly keep my eyes open. Just now, I had to pause and close them for a while. There is so much going on in my subconscious these days, and what happens at a conscious level is probably much tamer fare. I have regimented my conscious life into continuing along the same tried and tested lines and somehow or other the strategy is still working. I have not tried to come to terms with what another detention will mean, after June 10. I will adjust more fully if and when it becomes necessary. In the meantime, I am very happy that it is only a few days before I know whether the worst has happened again.

If I am redetained, I know that you will be very upset. I think, nevertheless, that you need to know that I have made myself ready for that possibility and having your support over this period makes it easier to handle...

June 13

Dear Mom,

As you know, I was redetained on Friday. I seem to have been prepared for it, in the sense that I was and still am able to handle it calmly. While I intend that to remain the case, I do not think that I have had time to digest precisely what it may mean and it is usually something that gradually sinks in and saps away at one's morale after a couple of months.

I have been in fairly good shape for about a month and I am trying to get back into my thesis and create some momentum that will enable me to feel creative and less prey to depression.

I am very tired, because this is the day that I go out to the therapist and for relaxation therapy and miss my usual lunchtime lie-down. I am not used to talking to anyone for very long and the intensity of normal conversation is very draining...

June 16

Dear Mom,

I have been in redetention for about a week now... I do not think I have had time to digest or understand precisely what it may mean. I have no idea whether it may mean release in a few months' time, or whether my detention is semi-permanent... No doubt, if this uncertainty continues for the next few months, it will again become difficult to handle.

I was taken to town today, to see two district surgeons, Drs. Jacobson and Krausey. Jacobson had hoped their director could also be there, but this was not possible. We discussed my situation and the various psychological and physical symptoms resulting from the stress involved. They are recommending that I see a physician, which I gather was going to happen anyway, because of my being sent for an ECG. And, although we did not have time to discuss it fully, I think they will be making recommendations relating to the isolation.

In general, I am OK. There are always "ups" and "downs" over here and the downs are difficult to deal with, irrespective of redetention. But my main concern is to be in adequate shape to deal with the situation, and that is the case...

June 26

Dear Mom,

I do not think that detention after June 10 was inevitable, though I prepared for it as the most likely outcome. I think there remains a possibility that I will be released in the next few months, though I am not counting on it. I remain adapted to this place and am doing what I can to make things as easy as possible.

I have recently received permission to have a kettle in my cell. I have also been given a pet bird — a lovebird/parakeet.

This seems part of a vague indication that my situation is coming under consideration.

This bird is great. In the first few hours, he resisted my attempts to hold him and bit me very painfully. After a while, he got used to me and liked resting under one of my tracksuits (and excreting very regularly on the other). He is a lot like a baby and even smells like one. He is lying right now, with his beak against my chest. I let him fly around the cell (his wings have been partially plucked) but feel anxious about him hurting himself, upsetting my things or falling into the milk. He is now very relaxed with me and I take him with me when I go down to the bottom yard or to the prison hospital and it is easy to get him back when I let him run around.

My relationship with him is a bit like a warder with a prisoner. He hates being in his cage/cell. He paces up and down and climbs up the sides until I take him out. I have to check out the places that I take him, in case he flies out of a window.

Most of the time, he just sits on me. For example, he sits on my back while I ride the exercise bike. He is very naughty — if I try to get a pen from my tracksuit pocket, he'll take a very quick nip at my finger. I also irritate him if I pull him out to stroke or kiss him. He sometimes marches straight back inside.

There is little happening on the thesis front. It is a question of organizing time, rather than it being difficult to work. I was planning to really move on it now, but the past week or two have been full of new things — such as the bird. I have also been out to doctors and so on...

My general state of mind is OK. This is artificial, in the sense that it is not OK. But one goes through "up" and "down" phases — and I have spent a lot of time preparing for the present up phase, because I knew this period could be very hard...

June 28
Dear Helen *[Bradford]*,

The pre-June 10 mood has remained, in the sense that I prepared both for the possibility of leaving and the likelihood of remaining...

In prison, you are always waiting for *something*. I think John Berger refers to this in one of his works... Anyway, I do not feel in a hurry to get out. Release has never been the focus of my life here. Once it becomes that, it is impossible to draw anything out of life inside. And I still try to use my time as productively as possible.

I remember that, in Pretoria, one person's way of handling things could really upset others. If you are upset about the food or some such thing, it doesn't help to throw a tantrum. That just upsets you more. You learn to control a lot of these things. Quite a few things upset me here but I seldom show it, seldom get very angry in front of others. I generally manage to keep my behavior along lines that are fruitful, given the limitations of diplomacy inside.

While this present term is, as I say, more difficult than my previous experience, without that experience it would have been much, much harder. I just have a basic way of handling these things...

With regard to what you say about nurturing hope in the longer term... I actually try not to dwell too much on hope, since I find it immobilizing. It will possibly make things harder to adapt when I get out, but it is hard enough getting by right now. I do not want to take on anything else...

I do not think the porcupine was someone's pet, though I do not know how it got here. I think there were cats here when I first arrived, and that you are correct in guessing that they were removed because of the birds.

I now have permission to keep a pet — lovebird/parakeet, which has been with me since Thursday. Right now, he is under my tracksuit, parked on my chest. When I first got him, he resisted all attempts to hold him and bit like mad. I held him tightly for a while and he began nestling up to me, under the tracksuit. I suppose it is the warmest place around here. If I walk around this place — down to the prison hospital or to the yard downstairs, where there is some grass — he sits on my shoulder.

I went to "the gen" [*Johannesburg General Hospital*] today to see the therapist and took this guy along and he was quite a hit there. He smells just like a baby and I feel a bit like a mother/father towards him, being quite careful to ensure that he does not harm himself in some way. I am also his jailer, in the sense that there is a cage. When he is locked in it, he paces up and down like a prisoner and sometimes climbs the walls. I only put him there when we are both going to sleep. I show him when it is time to sleep by putting a towel round his "cell."

I do not know how tame he actually is, though he seems to relate to me fairly well. He sometimes gets very impatient and bites me. Yesterday, a couple of extra wings were clipped and this made him furious and every time I tried to stroke him, he would bite me and march past my hands and into the tracksuit. This evening, he is also a bit irritable. (I just performed a test — and tried to take him out. But he clung to my shirt with his beak and would accept nothing less than total capitulation from me. Now he is back, resting face downwards. If I so much as look at him under the tracksuit, he tries to bite my fingers.)

The fact of my rearrest was anti-climactic in some ways, but it was also a bit stunning — in that it did not have a clear meaning. I am still interpreting and reinterpreting things... But I am very wary of becoming obsessed by this. Initially, I thought I would be out in July 1986. It is a long time since I have had any hope... While I do see possibilities ahead, I am leaving them for others to speculate about... while I cajole this bird out of my sleeve, speak to the rabbits and get what I can from this environment.

July 11
Dear Mom,

It is quite cold, but they say it's going to get warmer. It seems characteristic of this winter that you get a few days of freezing cold, then it warms up again. I do not actually find the winter as bad here as people outside seem to imagine. There are inconveniences, such as the unpredictability of the water supply, but otherwise I am used to it.

I am still unable to get back into my thesis. Not that I sit idly, doing nothing. I do use my time, but it is clear that I cannot do sustained research anymore. It is not a question of motivation, or some such thing. My capacity to do some things is no longer there and I have started to feel that continually failing in attempts to recover lost ground is demoralizing. I retreat to a lower level of defense and carry on with things that are within my capacity.

I have not played snooker lately — for about four weeks — but am planning to do so again. I am wondering whether having a "thorough break" from pressure on the thesis could provide the basis for resuming.

The bird remains great. During this cold weather, he just spends most of the day against my chest under the tracksuit. He is fairly tame, but still bites me. I am trying to prevent this but I think he knows that he has me beat if he gets in a very savage bite.

I have seen Drs. Jacobson and Krausey, the district surgeons, and a physician — Dr. S. Hurwitz. All three have sent reports regarding the impact of my isolation on my state of mind and my consequent need for medication. The ECG and chest X-ray showed no problem.

Otherwise, it remains the same place and the same routines, just that the actor in this set is getting very weary. But I still seem to be firmly rooted in the mindset which sees no alternative to just keeping going and keeping sufficiently fit to be able to do this.

That is the situation here...

Smuggled Letter
Early 1988, date uncertain

I am feeling very elated after spending hours with Valli and others [*at the hospital*]. I came back with some of them, and had time for long discussions... There seem to be many ways that I can help the younger ones with their studies and study methods... What is nice, is that we have now got into some broad discussions. I find, also, that I am able to play a much more useful role than I used to, that people have saved questions for these discussions and that when we are not rushed, as was the case today, we get a lot done.

I have been thinking that something dramatic has to be done [*regarding my case*]. I am not going to give in and that reinforces their will to keep me. At the same time, this is taking a toll...

One of the symptoms of "my state" is that, for the past five days or so, I have been reading a novel — in tears most of the time. It had started earlier when I read a photographic essay by Lesley Lawson in *Leadership* magazine. The essay was about Thursday being the traditional "afternoon off" for domestic workers in South Africa, and I just broke into tears. I don't know if this is significant, beyond it indicating my suppressed feelings. But I have started to worry about what this experience is storing up for me in the future, when I get out. How long it will take to be put back together again? Right now, in fact, I do not feel it is a huge problem. But what is happening over time?

Smuggled letter,
Date uncertain, 1988?

Despite exhaustion... I just cannot sleep... The noise in this place, you just cannot imagine! Early in the morning, around 4.30 a.m., some *bandiete* start making a noise. Sometimes, at around 4 a.m., a fucking rooster starts cock-a-doodle-doing in the passageways of the prison. This place is totally *befokked* [crazy]. I stick my mirror out and find — on the second or third floor in the passage — that there are these fucking roosters and chickens and they do not listen when I shout, "fuck off!" In the evenings, there is also a lot of shouting between the *bandiete*, from one to another. But once I identify who is doing it, I can usually speak to them privately. And, just as now, I periodically hear: "*Praat sagter man, die politieke man is besig om te studeer.*" ["Talk softer man the political man is busy studying."]

I appreciated what you said re people's response to what I have been doing... These things are also rather worrying, in the sense that my being viewed in that way may also harden their hearts and possibly instill fresh determination to fuck-me-in at some stage. I know it will not be this round, because I definitely will get through, no matter how long it takes. I know I have the will to never crack — but I am not sure what that means (running out of space)...

I think one can be forced while under torture to do some things against one's will, but I do not think I will ever do anything voluntarily — witness, statement, most obvious examples... But I do not think it is correct to condemn some of the martyrs who did give information under very heavy torture (to be continued).

Smuggled Letter
Date uncertain, 1988?

Things continue to be very bad in a low-intensity way. I am not very down, but the gloom is always there and I am very tense in my shoulders and neck a lot of the time... You learn to count on a few things to make things easier. But suddenly you cannot count on them and have to fight over big and small things. Your emotional resources for dealing with such things are, however, depleted.

I do not see the total institution as defined by active interference, vindictiveness. I think its characteristic feature is that it plans the life for every individual as a unit [*eenheid*]. The normal prisoner is not supposed to think for himself/herself. It is when we try to plan our own lives that we pit ourselves against this. We generally succeed in defining our own conception and pattern of life in these places — but, inevitably, that conception/pattern is mediated by their overall goals, which they try to retain as the overarching authority, within which you can do your own thing to a limited extent only.

I also do not think that this is a situation where we are deprived of power. Rather, we are at an overwhelming disadvantage in relation to the power that they wield. However, although they are in a stronger position, I think the people here [*the prison authorities*] generally prefer not to get into battle and for our relations with them to be peaceful.

Smuggled Letter
Date uncertain, 1988

By the way, re the effects of solitary — now that I am conscious of it — this thing of getting frights is quite important. Some of the *boere*

think it's a big joke. When I am reading and they suddenly say "hullo!"
I just jump.

Regarding what people say when I tell them I'm feeling like shit,
my reservations are confirmed by experience with Y, who interprets it
as an "internal conflict," and says I must not judge myself harshly and
what have you. No doubt, her view is influenced by the way a relative
of hers experienced solitary. But negative self-evaluations are just not
part of the picture for me. It is not an existential crisis for me.

Most people's experience of these things is so limited; they have to
rely on what they know of others. The case of Y's relative is not the
same as mine...

CHAPTER 18

House Arrest

IT WAS around August of 1988 that I sensed — some weeks before it actually happened — that I would soon be released from detention. Prior to this, there had been a buildup of concern about the condition of my health. The district surgeon, Dr. Jacobson, asked to see me and sent me for various tests and examinations. At one point, I was taken for tests to Weskoppies, near Pretoria, a notorious mental institution, where ordinary prisoners were sent — or were threatened to be sent, with phrases like "you will land up in a straitjacket in Weskoppies." The psychiatrist asked questions that did not have much bearing on my situation. For example, had I ever been concussed? He completed various diagrams and filled in endless forms. Then I was returned to my cell.

I heard from my brother that the police were prepared to release me, but wanted to know where I would live after I was freed. They wanted to monitor me.

On September 5, 1988, 27 months after my arrest, my lawyer, Peter Harris, fetched me from prison and took me to John Vorster Square, where I received a restriction order, signed by the then minister of law and order, Adriaan Vlok. The order, which seemed very stringent, specified that I was to remain under house arrest every night, from 6 p.m. till 6 a.m. In addition, I had to report to the police twice a day, between 10 a.m. and 11 a.m., and again between 3 p.m. and 4 p.m. I was not allowed to enter an educational institution, nor could I leave the Johannesburg magisterial district without permission. I was not allowed to meet with more than three people at any one time. I was not to engage in any political activities. I could not prepare anything for publication nor take part in the activities of various organizations, including the UDF and National Education Union of South Africa.

Peter took me to a house in Parktown in Johannesburg, where I was to stay. A number of press people were there. But I could not speak to them because of the restrictions. My lovebird, "JB," was in my hand or perched on my shoulder as I greeted well-wishers.

The police did not hesitate to harass me. On the first night, only hours after I had come out of jail, they raided the Parktown house and indicated they were not entirely happy with my release. Gesturing with his hands, one of them said: "You know, your release was a little bit of this and a little bit of that." The slightest infringement of my banning order, he said, and I would find myself back inside. Periodically, the police returned to monitor me.

This time, I found I was in far worse condition than I had been after my previous term of imprisonment. I was very tense and anxious and had to find time every few hours to do relaxation exercises. I found it difficult to engage in intense discussions. At first, I found it hard to do practical things, such as cooking my own meals or driving my car. The pace of life was too fast for me and I had to lie down three or four times a day.

A week or two after my release, I relaxed for a moment and forgot to report to the police in the afternoon. That evening, there was a vicious raid by a group of Security Police, who just burst in, turning the place upside down in order to "teach me a lesson."

Reporting to the police dominated my daily life. It made it impractical to go too far from the police station, in between reporting to them and returning home for house arrest.

It was hard to relax when there was always this time constraint. Whenever I did relax, I was liable to forget to report. I was free from prison but the conditions of my release were always with me. The state constantly intruded into my life.

Being under house arrest was a continuation of surveillance. The difference was that, instead of being guarded by police, I now had to practice surveillance on myself — ensuring that I complied with regulations, reported on time, and was in my residence at night and so on.

I came out of detention with an immediate sense of insecurity, a feeling that the police still viewed me as their prisoner and possibly in transition between one detention and another. The restrictions resulted in a form of surveillance of my life, which had a similar effect to that of detention. Every time I wanted a variation on the restriction order, or to go somewhere outside the magisterial district to which I was confined, I needed permission, in writing, from the police. They usually answered at the very last moment. At the end of the first month, when I was supposed to move out of the place to which I had been released, they did not answer my request until the last day, when they refused. This created great inconvenience and anxiety.

Through Professor Mervyn Shear, who showed a lot of concern during this period, Wits University offered me accommodation. The police examined the new house and said they would only allow me to reside there if the university sealed off the back door. This they did, by cementing up the door, and I stayed there for some months.

On May 1, 1989, after it was inspected and approved by the police, I moved into a house in Bezuidenhout Valley. That day, David Webster, a Wits academic and leading human rights campaigner, was gunned down in front of his house by an apartheid hit man. We always knew that assassination was a possibility, though we did not then specifically expect Dave to be a victim.

People began to worry more about my situation and we developed a system whereby friends would phone to check whether I was all right. But my phone would periodically go dead for a few days a week. This may have been a technical matter, but I never experienced a similar difficulty at other periods. At the time, I certainly interpreted it as further harassment.

I took various practical steps to protect my security. The South African Council of Churches gave me funds to build a wall in front of my house. I learned to regularly check under my car before driving. Some people had been killed on the way to report to the police, so I started to vary the route I took to get there.

Warrant Officer Robert Whitecross monitored me while I was under house arrest. In the mid 1980s, while acting as a police spy, Whitecross had sent ANC activists Carl Niehaus and Jansie Lourens to jail. He gave me various security tips — for example, not to stand in front of the door if the doorbell rang, not to sleep opposite a window, to have a fire extinguisher in the house and so on. I do not know whether this was intended for my safety or a matter of the police covering their backs in case something happened to me. It may also have been that they were trying to scare me into packing up and leaving the country.

House arrest had a broad impact on my social life. I could not spontaneously visit people. Most arrangements had to be made in advance. Any appointments made for the evening had to be at my house. Certainly, my home was larger than that of the average African person, but I still felt claustrophobic and would have liked to have left it more often. It was very inconvenient for people, especially those with children, to have to see me in this way. The terms on which we met were dictated by the state.

My state of mind was very fragile. Some nights, I might begin feeling all right. But later, this would not be the case. I still felt very depressed. To deal with the isolation, I hired videos very regularly, as a safety measure, just in case I did not feel well later in the evening.

At an objective level, there were very substantial differences between detention and restrictions. An impersonal official did not lock me up behind a grille at night. I could switch off my own light whenever I chose. I had the food I wanted. I could drive a car. I was surrounded by colors I had not seen in prison. I saw women and children. There were substantial differences... I was, nevertheless, dealing with a continuation of trauma and stress, in a different form. House arrest was a lot better than prison but, at that particular point in my life, it was very difficult. On the surface, I might have seemed in reasonable shape, but I paid a price to appear this way. I survived through means similar to my period in detention. I required medication for depression and insomnia. I still experienced the tension I had felt inside prison, and had to prepare myself to deal with my responsibilities. If I had to meet someone, I would try to plan the day in such a way that I could also fit in relaxation exercises, just in case the meeting imposed stress. I still did extensive physical exercise and continued using many of the coping mechanisms that I had employed during my prison period.

The decision whether or not to go to David Webster's funeral, which involved breaking my restriction order, caused me a certain amount of consternation. Many of those who were restricted in the townships ignored aspects of their restriction orders. But I was more exposed, being the only restricted person in a white area. I feared reprisals. I did go to the funeral, accompanied by my lawyer, Peter Harris, and there was little fall-out.

My state of mind was that of a prisoner, who, when confronted by something new or risky, fears that the gains or luxuries of the present may be endangered. However bad your life in prison may be, it is a life you have built. The authorities design part of your life, but as a political prisoner, as a conscious human being, you struggle to reconstruct that life in your own image. Your life is a combination of their intentions and your own – and any change to this elaborately constructed existence is a bit fearsome.

I was a free citizen but, at the same time, fell under the administrative authority of the police. I was a lawyer but I could not deal with the police on a similar basis to other lawyers. I did not grovel, but I could not relate to the police purely as a professional lawyer. I did not abide by all my restrictions, however, and did engage in political work. I wrote anonymous articles for publications of the Mass Democratic Movement (MDM), a term referring to a wide range of anti-apartheid forces, in particular, Cosatu (Congress of South African Trade Unions), the UDF and the churches. These articles were on pressing issues of the time, such as political negotiations. I feared, however, that the police might arrive while I was writing and before I could hide the computer floppy disk.

Engaging in political activities was important to me, not only politically, but to my mental well-being and recovery. It was reempowering. House arrest had an isolating effect, similar to solitary confinement. It was very hard for black comrades to visit me without attracting attention, so I found it hard to be politically involved. This, in itself, was dehumanizing and depressing — in that a crucial aspect of my identity was being denied. In solitary confinement and house arrest, one concentrates on personal survival and getting by. And, insofar as one becomes increasingly inward looking, it is a depoliticizing process.

In August 1989, I decided on a more serious act of defiance. A meeting of the Organization of African Unity (OAU) was to take place in Harare in Zimbabwe — in order to adopt what was to become the ANC-sponsored Harare Declaration on a negotiated settlement of the apartheid conflict. A delegation from the MDM would attend, to show the support of the internal leadership. It was suggested I be part of that delegation. I consulted with Cyril Ramaphosa — then general secretary of the National Union of Mineworkers — and others, who all felt I should go. This meant breaking my banning orders and leaving the country. My close friend and comrade, Neil Coleman, drove me to the airport and watched to see that I got through safely. Surprisingly, the police had left me with my passport — which had been returned in 1985 — and I simply went in, trying to look slightly different from my normal appearance. The airport computers did not react when I presented my passport and bought my ticket. While waiting to board, I noticed one person whom I knew, but he did not recognize me. Soon, I was on the flight and on my way to Harare.

Sydney Mufamadi — then deputy general secretary of Cosatu and later South Africa's minister of provincial affairs and local government — had been in contact with the ANC and said someone would meet me at the airport. When we landed, I told the person at immigration that I had left South Africa illegally. He asked me to wait on one side and, after letting others go, also let me through. But there was no one to meet me. What was I to do now? I tried phoning Professor Reg Austen, whom I knew slightly, but he was not around. I wandered about the airport for hours. It was now in the early hours of the morning. One of the airport staff offered to put me up at his flat, but I was a bit suspicious. Eventually, I tried phoning Hugh Lewin, whom I had never met, but knew of as a former political prisoner and the author of *Bandiet*. Hugh was not too happy about fetching someone at the airport at that time of night. He nevertheless took me into town, to a hotel. The next day, I connected with the ANC and MDM delegations.

I stayed a few days in Zimbabwe and then went to Zambia, where I reconnected with Jeremy Cronin, who was then out of the country for a year or two after being sought by the police. I also met up with Sue Rabkin, wife of the late David Rabkin — my prison comrade who died in Angola — and their kids Joby and Franny. After discussions with various comrades, it was decided that I should not simply go back to South Africa, but do some traveling, including a visit to the Soviet Union for medical treatment. I spent some five months outside the country, visiting Australia, the UK, USA and USSR. I also gave talks in these countries, including a speech to the United Nations (see following chapter).

I spent a month in the Soviet Union, a large part of this, at the end of 1989, in a health resort in Sochi near the Black Sea. At this time, I listened to BBC radio describing the collapse of the Eastern European socialist states. My only chance to visit the Soviet Union was when the system of socialist states was collapsing! I found strange contrasts: on the one hand, some of the party officials who had taken charge of me in Moscow seemed somewhat cynical. On the other, I went to a celebration of the October Revolution in Sochi and watched old veterans marching proudly to commemorate the revolution. I remember meeting an engineer and I talked with him, somewhat guardedly, about my own situation. I was still professing to follow a purely legal course within South Africa. This man looked at me and said he understood my situation. As a youth, he had helped the partisans in their fight against the Nazis. He understood.

In Moscow, I met for the first time Harry Gwala, the ANC/SACP leader and Robben Island veteran. He told me how his guide was messing him around financially. I remember raising this with party officials and they seemed unperturbed and indicated no desire to investigate.

On the other hand, I met a comrade like Vladimir Shubin — who was responsible for liaison between the Communist Party of the Soviet Union and the liberation movement and was totally devoted to our struggle.

The country seemed filled with paradoxes. I was struck by the hospitality of people in all walks of life. In Kiev, I met with academics in the law faculty and they interrupted their meeting to offer me some brandy. I explained that I did not drink brandy but they insisted that it was a Ukrainian custom. And, if I respected their culture (a Leninist principle), I would have to drink with them. I traveled one evening on the train from Kiev to Moscow and people took out their tablecloths and unpacked hampers of food, which they offered to me and to everyone else in the cabin. I noticed how a Ghanaian, who was there, seemed completely at home. On the other hand, I heard from South

African students that they were experiencing a lot of racism in the Soviet Union.

While I was out of the country, various people urged me to remain in exile, but that was never my intention. My family and various pressure groups requested assurances that I would not be prosecuted on my return to South Africa. The authorities were noncommittal, although the longer I stayed out, the less likely prosecution seemed. I finally returned to South Africa without having received any firm assurances.

Quite a few people met me at the airport, holding banners and singing. Although my lawyer Peter Harris was not able to attend, his law firm sent Norman Manoim, one of their partners, to ensure that nothing happened on my arrival. The police kept a low profile and I was left alone. When asked by the press about my restrictions, I replied that I regarded myself as no longer being banned. The police were later reported as saying they were investigating the infringement of the restriction order.

I went to my house. My lovebird, "JB," still appeared to recognize me, sitting calmly on my hand — despite having been left in South Africa for this period, when a friend, Robyn Solomon, looked after him.

Two or three days later, all speculation about the infringement of my banning order became academic when it was announced that the ANC and SACP were no longer banned organizations. I remember being in Braamfontein, in Johannesburg, below the offices of my lawyers, Cheadle, Thompson and Haysom, when pandemonium broke out as people shrieked their approval.

A new phase had opened. Quite different challenges would arise in rebuilding the ANC back home in South Africa, now that it had become a legal organization.

CHAPTER 19

Speech to the United Nations

Raymond Suttner delivered this statement to the United Nations in New York on the Day of Solidarity with South African Political Prisoners, October 11, 1989.

IT IS an honor to have this opportunity to speak at the United Nations, an organization that has done so much to further the struggle against apartheid and for peace and justice in South Africa, an organization that has played so important a role in highlighting the plight of prisoners of apartheid.

The prestige of the United Nations is high in South Africa. While it is detested by the racists, the organization is cherished by the people. While the forces of liberation have sought to weaken and isolate the government within South Africa, the United Nations has played a crucial role in mobilizing the international community towards the same goal.

In periods when the struggle has been at a low ebb internally, the United Nations has sometimes taken new initiatives. A very significant case that comes to mind, is the removal of the South African government's delegation from the General Assembly in 1974. The reason given was that the delegation did not represent the people of South Africa. Coming as it did at a time when resistance at home was relatively weak, this was an important contribution towards the de-legitimization of the minority regime.

Today, we meet to express solidarity with political prisoners in South Africa. I speak with experience of 10 years in prison — most recently, 27 months detention without trial, 18 of these in solitary confinement. I remain a prisoner, in the sense that I was released under restrictions, including house arrest.

I have come here without permission and may well face victimization under the emergency regulations on my return — victimization for exercising my basic human right to freedom of movement, expression and association.

But I speak as a white South African democrat who returns to the country with full confidence in the future of South Africa, the new South Africa that the popular forces are striving to build. I do not fear majority rule because I know that the African National Congress and the Mass Democratic Movement are committed to values that are universally respected — values such as democracy, nonracialism and peace.

I am a proud newcomer to this event. I imagine that many of those present may wonder whether this occasion is worthwhile and fear that it may have merely ritualistic significance. I want to assure you that for those in the cells, the support of the United Nations on occasions like this boosts our morale and spurs us on to continue the struggle. It makes you realize, in your prison cell, that you not only have the support of the oppressed people and democratic forces amongst the whites in South Africa, but that the majority of humankind stands behind you.

This support helps us maintain our dignity and our determination. The prisoners of apartheid are not merely victims — whether under restriction, detention without trial, on trial, sentenced to terms of imprisonment or on death row. All continue their struggle.

In the past year, we have seen the heroic and historic fight from within the detention cells, where hundreds of detainees secured their release through hunger strikes.

This was a great victory, but it needs to be consolidated. Detentions continue, just as the resistance of prisoners, through hunger strikes and other methods, persists.

This struggle continues because the present minority government regards our struggle for liberation as *criminal*. Even acts which do not fall within the very broad category of political activities, and which they have defined as offences, may invite punishment.

Thirty thousand of us have faced long terms of detention without any charge or trial. Some 700 have been released under heavy restrictions. This generally means self-surveillance, through reporting to the police once or twice daily, and self-imprisonment through house arrest.

These restrictions also bring to the fore the danger of assassination. Two people have already been assassinated on their return from reporting to the police, while house arrest makes one an easy target.

The government, in its repression, makes little distinction between peaceful and violent, lawful and unlawful, resistance. In general, it has sought to suppress all effective resistance. It has stood in the way of any constructive peace process.

We, as part of the broad forces for liberation, seek a long-term settlement of the apartheid conflict. Our struggle is for national liberation and self-determination: to realize rights considered vital in contemporary international human rights law. I refer, for example, to the Universal Declaration of Human Rights of 1948; the 1960 Declaration on the Granting of Independence to Colonial Countries and Peoples; and the 1966 International Covenants on Human Rights. In addition, there is the 1970 Declaration on Principles of International Law concerning Friendly Relations and Cooperation among States in Accordance with the Charter of the United Nations, and many other international instruments.

Our struggle for liberation is a struggle for peace. Just as the United Nations Charter in Articles 1(2) and 55 connects peace with human rights, we see the eradication of apartheid, and securing basic human rights in South Africa, as part of the peace process.

But what is the road to peace? It is necessary to ask this afresh, because there is much speculation about the possibility of Pretoria itself taking this road.

But the route to peace I want to suggest is different — it demands conditions that the South African government has by no means undertaken to fulfill.

The Organization of African Unity and the Nonaligned Movement have adopted a negotiation package, the preparation of which involved both the African National Congress and Mass Democratic Movement.

What is essential to this negotiating process is, firstly, an agreement about our objectives; in short, the elimination of apartheid and the establishment of a nonracial, democratic, united South Africa.

This process cannot even begin without various parties, including the South African government, accepting this ultimate goal.

In order to start this process, certain conditions have also to exist, including the release of *all* political prisoners. Regarding this, I am delighted to hear of the imminent release of Walter Sisulu and other leaders. This joy is tempered by the recognition that these people should never have been in jail in the first place and that they leave many others behind them, still in jail.

Their release is due to struggle inside and outside the country. Without such pressure, their release would not have been contemplated. Further pressure is necessary to secure the release of those who remain imprisoned.

The negotiation process, which we support, demands:

A common objective, which Pretoria definitely does not share.

Realization of certain minimum conditions, in order to create a climate for negotiation; conditions that have not yet been realized and which cannot be achieved through individual releases — despite the great significance of having such people as Sisulu, Kathrada, Mlangeni and others rejoin our communities.

We have to assess the recent moves of the new South African leadership against this background.

It is not correct to say that nothing has changed in South Africa following the accession of Mr. De Klerk to the Presidency and leadership of the Nationalist Party. Despite the fact that the overall objective of Mr. De Klerk and his government remains the retention of white overlordship, mass struggle within the country and international mobilization against apartheid has *forced the government to make some concessions* – for example, peaceful marches are now allowed. Further pressure may ensure that this victory is consolidated and extended.

The limitation of any of the manifold powers of the apartheid regime cannot primarily be attributed to a change of heart or mind on their part. The timing of the release of Sisulu and others (for the Commonwealth summit) has clearly been intended to take some heat off the government. They do not represent elements of a coherent process towards democracy.

The government itself has not itself put forward any program to dismantle apartheid.

Only the combined pressure of the South African people and the international community has made De Klerk modify the methods of domination. We cannot be sure that this modification will be permanent and do not know how far this "new approach" will be extended. The conditions within which we struggle against apartheid may have changed, but continuance of apartheid remains the objective of the De Klerk regime. There is no sign of a commitment to end minority rule.

In these circumstances, it is our belief that it is vital for the international community to continue and increase its pressure. To further isolate the regime is crucial. "Encouraging signs" do not mean apartheid has been dismantled.

We in the movement for national liberation are ourselves planning to rid our country of apartheid. We ask you to continue to assist us. We ask for your help in securing peace in our country and the Southern African region. We need intensified action to rid the world of the apartheid crime and to allow the people of South Africa to enjoy their basic rights to self-determination, peace and justice.

CHAPTER 20

Conclusion

MY LIFE changed after February 2, 1990, when the ban on the ANC and SACP was lifted. A few months later, I started to work full time for the ANC, heading the organization's political education section, until I was elected to South Africa's national parliament in 1994.

I learned a lot during this period, particularly from watching the conduct of people such as Walter Sisulu and Nelson Mandela, who, through everything they did, built and maintained unity and avoided sectarianism. I also saw their generosity towards all who played a role, however small, in liberating South Africa. I watched how they tried to build a nation from all the people; how they and people such as ANC/SACP leader Chris Hani (who was assassinated in 1993) reached out even to those who had been wrongdoers under apartheid.

In 1990 and 1991, I served on the ANC Interim Leadership Core, which generally sat together with the National Executive Committee (NEC) after its return from exile. In rebuilding the ANC at home, we were combining a number of traditions. We were bringing together former inmates of Robben Island and of other prisons, plus people returning from exile and those who had remained inside the country. This was a difficult task, which continues to this day. It required appreciation by each group of the contribution made by the others, humility in recognizing what we can learn from one another.

At its 1991 national conference, I was elected to the ANC's National Executive Committee and later that year to the Central Committee of the South African Communist Party. I served in both of these roles until I became South Africa's ambassador to Sweden in 1997.

At the time of writing, I was based in Sweden, where I will be posted until August 2001.

THIS BOOK describes my choices and journey as a white South African activist who joined the liberation struggle. At the time, few could have foreseen that, in the 1990s, we would be enjoying liberty from apartheid, under a government led by the ANC. I did what I believed was right. I had no idea when our struggle would succeed.

At times, I have felt a certain embarrassment about writing this story. Sometimes I have felt apologetic, as if I had no right to speak about my experiences. I have sometimes feared that I might be seen as immodest or attention-seeking or as claiming that I went through ordeals far worse than those suffered by others. But I have come to believe that I do have a story to tell, and I hope the telling of it will help to heal me, (for I know I have been damaged). I hope my story will interest others, many of whom have perhaps grown up in a different South Africa — in which ANC and SACP members can now wear T-shirts that legally, proudly and publicly proclaim their allegiances.

This book is also my own way of making sense of what happened, of looking back and interpreting the past and the present. It is not clear that what I did was a major factor in bringing about any decisive victory. But I like to think that I was there when the going was hard and it was difficult to be in the liberation movement, and that I helped further our cause in the dark years between the Rivonia trial and the Soweto uprising.

As I write this difficult book, I am mindful of the need to help other South Africans find ways of telling their stories and of validating their experiences. In a sense, the telling of a story of imprisonment — even in post-apartheid South Africa — cannot escape the history of privilege, availability of skills and material circumstances to write and find a publisher. I am conscious of the challenge to take steps to avoid reproducing patterns in which the lives and experiences of black people are invalidated.

Apartheid could only be preserved — or brought to an end — through our individual and collective action. In telling our individual stories as white and blacks, the larger South African story can be appreciated and our history as a whole understood.

I am proud to have made a contribution to the collapse of apartheid. My decision to be part of the struggle, however, had consequences for my family and affected their lives in many ways. Nevertheless, they all supported me and made unremitting efforts to improve my conditions while I was in prison. For this, I am very grateful.

When I was underground and under arrest, I saw myself as a revolutionary, and tried to model my conduct accordingly. Looking back on these hard experiences, I know that I was sustained by a commitment that many may now view cynically or see as old-fashioned. Yet, without this set of beliefs, this moral conviction, it would have been impossible for me to survive. Some of the things that I did may now seem a little extreme and mechanistic, but my revolutionary consciousness gave me the moral strength to get through.

In the course of my underground work, and during periods of detention, I learned various survival techniques. Some of these necessitated the suppression and repression of many of my deepest feelings and wishes. I considered this suppression necessary, in that it allowed me to survive with integrity. Time has passed, but many of these habits remain, and continue to affect my social behavior, interpersonal relations and sleep patterns.

But my experience was not solely one of never-ending privation. It is true that being imprisoned for so long meant I missed some things. I do regret not having fulfilled my potential in various careers. My choice also brought me gains as a human being. The ANC and SACP gave me an opening, gave me a way of escaping from acquiescence in apartheid South Africa. In a sense, I got a fresh start in life. I felt I could not celebrate my own humanity unless I threw my weight in with the people. I was given the opportunity to realize my humanity, to be truly "humanized." This is something very important and irreplaceable that I gained from the struggle.

In much of the period covered by this book, I was engaged with others in efforts to overthrow the South African state. In recent writings, it has been suggested there was something both naive and irresponsible in our efforts to create an insurrectionary climate. It is said by writers such as Hein Marais, in his book *South Africa: Limits to Change* (1998), that we were not adequately exploiting opportunities to achieve significant reforms, and were captives of an "all or nothing," "revolution or reform" mindset.

I do not agree. We risked our lives to bring down the apartheid state because, in the 1960s, 1970s and 1980s, there were only limited opportunities for reform. These opportunities were, indeed, fully exploited — by the liberation movement, by the labor movement, the UDF and its affiliates. But the political space was limited and constrained by apartheid violence. That is why we took the insurrectionary path.

It was only after attempts at insurrection brought the regime to the negotiating table, and only then, that the possibility of more peaceful transformation arose. What reforms were available in this period were primarily there to widen the base of the apartheid ruling bloc. We exploited all reforms that could be used to advance democratization. In general, however, an insurrectionary perspective was the result of the conditions of repression imposed by the regime.

Furthermore, I believe that many of the insights of the insurrectionary period — in particular, the attempts to build grassroots democracy — remain valuable and are necessary if we are to ground the transformation of South Africa in popular consciousness and involvement. People may have had illusions as to how far we had progressed with the establishment of elementary organs of people's power, but this was an important period, and its gains, especially the creativity that it unleashed amongst ordinary people, must not be lost. The insights of that period need to be deployed in building popular involvement in our new democracy.

It is now 30 years since I chose a political path that led me to jail, torture, redetention and house arrest. These past three decades have been eventful ones in our country's history and the world at large. I do not think that everything I believed then remains valid today. But what was central to my involvement was not an attachment to any particular social model. My involvement was primarily in order to find a way of bettering the lives of the majority of South Africans. I like to believe that a sense of justice and commitment to this process of transformation still motivates very many people in our liberation movement.

I have undergone some changes in my perspective since those early days, as the transition has unfolded. But the basic commitment that drove me throughout this period remains. That is why I want to remain part of the building of a democratic South Africa.

APPENDIX

Release Document, 1988

[This document was provided by Dr. Rupert Taylor of the University of the Witwatersrand. The original, which is written in Afrikaans, is held in the William Cullen Library of the University of the Witwatersrand under Police Documents (1980-1996); Captain Vermeulen's Office]

CONFIDENTIAL

S7/4/4(WWR 2/88)

Enquiries: Lt. J van Heerden

Tel No: 310-1228

RELEASE IN TERMS OF REGULATION 3(8) OF THE STATE OF EMERGENCY SECURITY REGULATIONS 1988: DETAINEE RAYMOND SORREL SUTTNER: DETENTION NUMBER WWR 2/88 (42 YEARS OF AGE). APPENDIX ATTACHED.

1. SUTTNER has been detained since 12 June 1986 in terms of the state of emergency Security Regulations. SUTTNER was the education officer of the Transvaal region of the United Democratic Front (UDF) and he served on the executive of the Johannesburg Democratic Action Committee (JODAC). His detention is a result of his involvement in the propagation and promotion of the "People's Power" concept, which was aimed at establishing alternative structures in the RSA with the aim of overthrowing state power and of making South Africa ungovernable. During 1986 SUTTNER held meetings with members of the African National Congress (ANC) in Sweden regarding the establishment

of so-called alternative structures as a manifestation of "People's Power." He is a self-confessed communist and a seasoned ("geharde") activist who made very knowledgeable attempts through speeches, statements and publications, to persuade individuals in the RSA to overthrow state power. His activities threatened public safety, the maintenance of public order and undermined and endangered the goals of the state of emergency.

2.   SUTTNER was sentenced to seven and a half years in prison on 13 November 1975 as a result of his participation in the activities of the ANC and advancement of the objectives of communism. He maintained his convictions throughout his period of imprisonment, and openly declared that he is a communist. After his release SUTTNER continued with his activities and concentrated, inter alia, on advancing and propagating the "Freedom Charter".   SUTTNER tries especially to create an environment in the academic world, which would advance the goals of the ANC. It is in this regard and the state of emergency Security Regulations that SUTTNER should be prohibited from participating in the activities of organisations and/or institutions which endeavour to propagate and implement alternative structures on the educational terrain. The specific organisations to which this document refers are the National Education Crisis Committee (NECC), the National Education Union of South Africa (NEUSA) and the Education Policy Unit of the University of the Witwatersrand. A copy of the complete memorandum regarding SUTTNER's activities is attached. (Appendix A)

3.   At present it is a known strategy of radical persons and organisations to meet at night in a clandestine manner, in order to plan how to carry out their activities. In order to prevent these attempts by such persons, it is necessary to restrict them to their homes. Such a restriction has the added advantage that SUTTNER's activities can be adequately monitored by the Security branch of the South African Police.

4.   Confirmed information has already come to light that a well-planned campaign has been launched, and that this campaign will be intensified in order to disrupt the elections, which are to take place in October 1988. It is expected that the organisations in which SUTTNER previously participated will make all efforts to involve him, inter alia, in the achievement of this goal.

5. He has been detained for more than two years. His psychological health has deteriorated significantly, and as a result he is suffering from depression and period lapses of memory. Currently no criminal charges are being investigated against him.

6. Considered in the light of SUTTNER's mental condition it is advisable that he be conditionally released. His conditional release is recommended by the NGBS release committee.

7. The restrictions were submitted to the Legal Unit, who are of the opinion that they are completely valid.

Lt. Gen

Commissioner
JV van der Merwe

APPROVED/NOT APPROVED

MINISTER OF LAW AND ORDER

MEMORANDUM WRITTEN BY: Lt J van Heerden
Tel No (012) 310 1228

MEMORANDUM CHECKED AND AGREED TO: Brig. H P Noppe

0618/mus

CONFIDENTIAL

I WAS NEVER ALONE
A Prison Diary from El Salvador
By Nidia Díaz
Nidia Díaz (born María Marta Valladares) gives a dramatic and inspiring personal account of her experience as a guerrilla commander during El Salvador's civil war. Seriously wounded, she was captured in combat by Cuban-exile CIA agent Félix Rodríguez. Nidia Díaz was the FMLN's Vice-Presidential candidate in 1999.
ISBN 1-876175-17-6

PRIEST AND PARTISAN
A South African Journey of Father Michael Lapsley
By Michael Worsnip
The story of Father Michael Lapsley, an anti-apartheid priest, and how he survived a South African letter bomb attack in 1990 in which he lost both hands and an eye.
ISBN 1-875284-96-6

SLOVO
The Unfinished Autobiography of ANC Leader Joe Slovo
A revealing and highly entertaining autobiography of one of the key figures of South Africa's African National Congress. As an immigrant, a Jew, a communist, a guerrilla fighter and political strategist — and white—few public figures in South Africa were as demonized by the apartheid government as Joe Slovo.
ISBN 1-875284-95-8

MY EARLY YEARS
By Fidel Castro
Introductory essay by Gabriel García Márquez
In the twilight of his life, Fidel Castro reflects on his childhood, youth and student days. In an unprecedented and remarkably candid manner, Fidel describes his family background and the religious and moral influences that led to his early involvement in politics.
ISBN 1-876175-07-9

CHE: A MEMOIR BY FIDEL CASTRO
Preface by Jesús Montané
Edited by David Deutschmann
For the first time Fidel Castro writes with candor and affection of his relationship with Ernesto Che Guevara, documenting his extraordinary bond with Cuba from the revolution's early days to the final guerrilla expeditions to Africa and Bolivia.
ISBN 1-875284-15-X